**W9-AFT-821**

# JANE AUSTEN'S ANGLICANISM

In her re-examination of Jane Austen's Anglicanism, Laura Mooneyham White suggests that engaging with Austen's world in all its strangeness and remoteness reveals the novelist's intensely different presumptions about the cosmos and human nature. While Austen's readers often project postmodern and secular perspectives onto an Austen who reflects their own times and values, White argues that viewing Austen's Anglicanism through the lens of primary sources of the period, including the complex history of the Georgian church to which Austen was intimately connected all her life, provides a context for understanding the central conflict between Austen's malicious wit and her family's testimony to her Christian piety and kindness. White draws connections between Austen's experiences with the clergy, liturgy, doctrine, and religious readings and their fictional parallels in the novels; shows how orthodox Anglican concepts such as natural law and the Great Chain of Being resonate in Austen's work; and explores Austen's awareness of the moral problems of authorship relative to God as Creator. She concludes by surveying the ontological and moral gulf between the worldview of Emma and Oscar Wilde's *The Importance of Being Earnest*, arguing that the evangelical earnestness of Austen's day has become a figure of mockery by the late nineteenth century.

*To my husband, Tyler Goodrich White, and*
*to the memory of the late Reverend Jane Heenan*

# Jane Austen's Anglicanism

LAURA MOONEYHAM WHITE
*University of Nebraska – Lincoln, USA*

**ASHGATE**

Published by
Ashgate Publishing Limited
Wey Court East
Union Road
Farnham
Surrey, GU9 7PT
England

Ashgate Publishing Company
Suite 420
101 Cherry Street
Burlington
VT 05401-4405
USA

www.ashgate.com

**British Library Cataloguing in Publication Data**
White, Laura Mooneyham.
    Jane Austen's Anglicanism.
    1. Austen, Jane, 1775–1817 – Criticism and interpretation. 2. Austen, Jane, 1775–1817 –
    Religion. 3. Christianity in literature. 4. Christianity and literature – England – History –
    18th century. 5. Christianity and literature – England – History – 19th century.
    I. Title
    823.7–dc22

**Library of Congress Cataloging-in-Publication Data**
White, Laura Mooneyham.
    Jane Austen's Anglicanism / by Laura Mooneyham White.
        p. cm.
    Includes bibliographical references and index.
    ISBN 978-1-4094-1863-4 (hardback : alk. paper) — ISBN 978-1-4094-1864-1 (ebook)
    1. Austen, Jane, 1775–1817—Criticism and interpretation. 2. Austen, Jane, 1775–1817—
    Religion. 3. Christianity in literature. 4. Christianity and literature—England—History—
    18th century. 5. Christianity and literature—England—History—19th century. I. Title.
    PR4038.R4W55 2011
    823'.7—dc22

                                                                              2010036570

ISBN: 9781409418634 (hbk)
ISBN: 9781409418641 (ebk)

Reprinted 2011

Printed and bound in Great Britain by the MPG Books Group, UK

# Contents

# List of Illustrations

# Acknowledgments

Many thanks to various colleagues at the University of Nebraska-Lincoln who helped me shape this book, including Susan Belasco, Robert Stock, and Steve Behrendt. I thank past English Department chairs at the University of Nebraska-Lincoln, Linda Pratt and Joy Ritchie, for fostering my research. I am also grateful to Mary Poovey and Patricia Spacks for beginning my life-long scholarly interest in Austen, and to friends such as Kay Young, Deborah Kaplan, Antje Anderson, and Devoney Looser who have helped shape my thinking about Austen through the years. Thank you also to Susan Ford for her notes on Sheridan from the Chawton House Library and many other thoughtful suggestions, and to the Special Collections of the F. W. Olin Library, Mills College, Oakland, California, for the facsimile image of the prayer attributed to Jane Austen. Most of all, thank you to my dear and loving family.

Part of Chapter 3, in a different form, was published in *Persuasions On-line* 27.1 (Winter 2006), http://www.jasna.org/persuasions/on-line/vol27no1/white. htm; my thanks to the editor for allowing me this material to be reprinted here.

# List of Abbreviations

E      Austen, Jane. *Emma*. Eds Richard Cronin and Dorothy McMillan. *The Cambridge Edition of the Works of Jane Austen*. Cambridge: CUP, 2005.

J      ———. *Juvenilia*. Ed. Peter Sabor. *The Cambridge Edition of the Works of Jane Austen*. Cambridge: CUP, 2006.

L      ———. *Jane Austen's Letters*. Ed. Deirdre Le Faye. Third edition. Oxford: OUP, 1995.

LM      ———. *Later Manuscripts*. Eds Janet Todd and Linda Bree. *The Cambridge Edition of the Works of Jane Austen*. Cambridge: CUP, 2008.

MP      ———. *Mansfield Park*. Ed. John Wiltshire. *The Cambridge Edition of the Works of Jane Austen*. Cambridge: CUP, 2005.

NA      ———. *Northanger Abbey*. Eds Barbara M. Benedict and Deirdre Le Faye. *The Cambridge Edition of the Works of Jane Austen*. Cambridge: CUP, 2006.

P      ———. *Persuasion*. Eds Janet Todd and Antje Blank. *The Cambridge Edition of the Works of Jane Austen*. Cambridge: CUP, 2006.

PP      ———. *Pride and Prejudice*. Ed. Pat Rogers. *The Cambridge Edition of the Works of Jane Austen*. Cambridge: CUP, 2006.

SS      ———. *Sense and Sensibility*. Ed. Edward Copeland. *The Cambridge Edition of the Works of Jane Austen*. Cambridge: CUP, 2006.

# PART 1
## Jane Austen and Anglicanism

# Introduction

I am ashamed to remember for how many years, as a boy and a young man, I read nineteenth-century fiction without noticing how often its language differed from ours. I believe it was work on far earlier English that first opened my eyes: for there a man is not so easily deceived into thinking he understands when he does not.

—C. S. Lewis, *Studies in Words*, 311–12

Late in her too-brief life, Austen wrote three different texts in which she imagined figures from the past arising to vent their surprised displeasure at how modern life has turned out. First, in her last completed novel, *Persuasion*, she pictures the reaction of the Musgrove ancestors to the newfangled parlor at the Great House, decorated by the young women of the household, Louisa and Henrietta: "Oh! Could the originals of the portraits against the wainscot, could the gentlemen in brown velvet and the ladies in blue satin have seen what was going on, have been conscious of such an overthrow of all order and neatness! The portraits themselves seemed to be staring in astonishment." These eighteenth-century ancestors look in dismay upon the little tables, grand piano-forte, harp, and flower-stands that create the "proper air of confusion" desired by young ladies' "modern minds and manners" (*P* 43). Second, in the very last words of fiction Austen wrote, at the very end of the fragment of *Sanditon* (signed March 18, 1817, with a finality that bespeaks her recognition that the manuscript would extend no further), Austen invokes a similarly discomfited portrait figure. Lady Denham's first husband is represented in her sitting room only by a miniature, set on a desk among many others, while a large portrait over the mantelpiece honors her second husband, who brought Lady Denham her title: "Poor Mr. Hollis! –It was impossible not to feel him hardly used; to be obliged to stand back in his own House & see the best place by the fire constantly occupied by Sir Harry Denham" (*LM* 209). In this case, the old has been displaced by the new, even though the new is itself deceased. My third example is the very last thing Austen wrote of any sort at all, just three days before her death on July 18th, 1817: a comic poem, a burlesque curse brought down on the heads of those attending that summer's Winchester Races. She imagines St. Swithin, Winchester Cathedral's founding bishop, rising from his tomb to castigate the revelers for forgetting him and ignoring Winchester's Christian heritage: "Oh, subjects rebellious, Oh Venta depraved /When once we are buried you think we are dead / But behold me Immortal. –By vice you're enslaved / You have sinn'd & must suffer." The saint goes on to thunder, "You shall meet with your curse with your pleasures / Set off for your course, I'll pursue with my rain" (Selwyn 18). In all three cases, the past re-arises to communicate its displeasure with the present; Austen implies that the past is right to be so displeased, because modern life has become confused, disordered, and irreligious.

Austen is now in the position of the Musgrove ancestors, Mr. Hollis, and St. Swithin; she can arise before us to protest our modern errors only in the imaginations of the living. It is worth noting, however, that Austen herself believed she would be "Immortal" like the saint, not because she would leap from her tomb to speak to the present but because she would be gathered to "an eternity of happiness . . . in thy heavenly kingdom" (this phrase comes from her last written prayer). This book has been written to speak from the dead, as it were, about Austen's religious beliefs and presumptions, ideas that formed her worldview and shaped her fiction. It aims to reconstruct her deeply held Georgian Anglicanism, and to show the traces of its presence in the novels, especially in those places where our secular contemporary gaze can no longer easily track it. Unlike St. Swithin, I hold no intention of rebuke for modern revelers (or readers); after all, the particulars of Austen's religious inheritance are long gone, even in much of modern Christianity. Rather, my hope is that readers will have a much fuller and more accurate sense of Austen's work if they know the values she held and on what foundational religious ideas those values are based. I aim to recapture that world of Anglican belief in all its strangeness and remoteness to modern readers. Understanding this world can help the reader today avoid mistakes of back-projection, assigning to Austen's fiction values Austen would herself have found incoherent, immoral, or irreligious. In particular, the school of criticism that celebrates Austen's subversive wickedness and independence might benefit from a submersion into a sub-culture within the historical past (English Anglican gentry) that seems alien to us today. A late-eighteenth-century Christian view of Austen's wit, ironies, and moments of rebelliousness yields a different picture. The challenge is to place Austen's malice, irony, and worldly knowingness (all demonstrably real and vigorous elements of her art) within the context of her religious inheritance and preoccupations.

Without this understanding, readers may well not see the vestiges of her most central commitment. Austen was rarely explicit in her fiction about her religious values, though they are evident everywhere for those with eyes to see. As I explain in Chapter 2, her religious decorum was occasioned primarily by a belief that "serious," that is, religious subjects should not be treated at length within popular fiction. This idea was bolstered by her evident sense that readers would be less likely to read her novels were they more explicitly didactic (we know she herself disliked heavily evangelical fiction, such as Hannah More's *Coelebs in Search of a Wife*).

Contemporary Christian readers may feel that they have an advantage over their more secular counterparts in terms of an enhanced awareness of Austen's worldview (as a cradle Episcopalian, I long nourished this fond misconception), but they are likely to be mistaken, at least in part. This is because, though the central doctrines of the Church remain unchanged, much of the foundational worldview of the Georgian Anglican Church and that of contemporary Christians differs considerably, and the presumptions each hold about the social and cultural role of the church are even farther apart. For instance, it cannot but surprise and dismay contemporary believers to learn that not only did eighteenth-century Anglicanism *not* embrace democratic and egalitarian forces but further that it considered the democratic impulse specifically un-Christian, because democracy disorders the "natural" hierarchies set by God.

The Georgian Church's expectations for its clergy and its membership in terms of practice are likewise barely recognizable today. Anglicanism was (and is) a liturgical denomination, which means worship follows strictly laid out scripts of prayers and scripture. What modern Christians cannot comprehend is the effect of liturgical repetition on the committed Anglican of Austen's day, who would have had family prayers for both Morning and Evening Prayer every day, two services of two to three hours each on Sunday, daily private prayers on awakening and on going to bed, and grace before each meal, with thanksgiving after. By my conservative estimate, Austen would have said the Lord's Prayer over 30,000 times in her life. All that repetition must have made a signal mark on her consciousness. Further, the world of Anglican clergy in which Austen was entirely at home presented behavior and values that have little to do with modern practice. It is hard to imagine, for instance, the spectacle of the parish priest collecting each tenth egg from his farmer neighbor on a weekly basis, but this comical procedure was one primary way in which tithes were collected.[1]

One of the most longstanding debates among Austen critics is over the question of whether Austen's Christianity "counts," that is, whether it truly shaped and affected her fiction. Since D. W. Harding's highly influential reading of Austen as a subversive and malicious author in "Regulated Hatred: An Aspect of the Work of Jane Austen" in 1940, many critics have claimed that Austen could not have been more than a nominal Christian. F. R. Leavis felt that her Christianity was not present in her novels (10), a position also taken by Laurence Lerner, who, after noting her depiction of faulty clerics and her lack of Biblical quotations, argued that "Austen the novelist did not believe in God because a belief or a value matters only if it is artistically present . . . . She did not arrange, control, or interpret her deepest experience in the light of [her piety]" (20, 23). Avrom Fleishman, writing on Austen's most palpably religious book, *Mansfield Park*, said that Austen's vision was humanistic, not marked by piety: "At every level—psychological, mythic, and social—the vision of *Mansfield Park* is humanistic. It squarely acknowledges the imperfection of its historical situation while maintaining the secular hope that was to animate the nineteenth century" (77). Gilbert Ryle maintained that her moral vision came from Aristotle via Shaftesbury: "she draws the curtain between her Sunday thoughts, whatever they were, and her creative imagination. Her heroines face their moral difficulties and solve their moral problems without recourse to religious faith or theological doctrines" (117). Joseph Duffy acknowledged her Anglicanism, but argues that her religiosity is the "barren artificial thing of rationalist Anglicanism," lacking "caritas" (86–7).

---

[1]    Mary Lascelles, one of Austen's best early critics, noted in her celebration of Austen's capacity to create "this extraordinary illusion of actuality" that one consequence of that reality-effect is that modern readers tend to collapse what they know of religious experience with Austen's, to consequent befuddlement: "I have failed to satisfy an enquirer who wished to know why Henry Tilney bore so little resemblance to her Lutheran pastor; but perhaps she expected too much" ("Jane Austen and the Novel" 241).

Other critics go farther, positing in Austen a wide-ranging irony that, like acid, destroys every moral certainty it touches.[2] These authors in particular prefer a fully subversive Austen, an Austen who was not finally subject to religious or cultural limits on individual freedom. Biographers and critics such as John Halperin, David Nokes, Clara Tuite, and to some degree Claire Tomalin are figures who hold this position. A common approach is to cite any of the Austen family's many statements about Austen's piety, including the famous ledger stone at her grave in Winchester Cathedral, and to claim that members of the family misrepresented her true nature out of a desire to protect Austen's reputation and their own; as Nokes noted, "I prefer to present her not in the modest pose which her family determined for her, but rather, as she most frequently presented herself, as rebellious, satirical and wild" (7). Other of the best Austen critics ally themselves with this view, including Claudia Johnson ("I cast my lot with the queer Austen" [27]), D. A. Miller, William Galperin, and Jill Heydt-Stevenson.

Against this school is opposed another strong set of critics who acknowledge the importance and centrality of Austen's Anglican beliefs to her work. Irene Collins argues that "Jane Austen was a deeply religious woman. It is unlikely that she ever thought of the morality which she advocated in her novels as anything other than an essential part of Christianity" (*Jane Austen and the Clergy* 182). Alastair Duckworth has noted Austen's two moral imperatives: "The first is that it is to religion that the individual owes his duty; the second and connected answer is that it is to society. Ultimately, I believe Jane Austen's morality is based in religious principle, and religious responses are not uncommon in her fiction" (*Improvement* 26). Oliver Macdonagh concurs, finding that "Jane Austen's Christianity was Christocentric in the orthodox pious-Protestant sense" (7), while Gene Koppel, responding to Wayne Booth's 1998 re-estimation of *Emma*, finds a Christian narrator: "'Jane Austen' wants us to ask ourselves where we look for our standards of perfection. I believe that Jane Austen would be surprised if her readers do not realize that 'Jane Austen' draws *her* standards from a strong Christian faith, and that the presence of that faith and its wisdom can always be distinguished on the horizon of her novel" (57). Michael Giffin has perhaps argued the case

---

[2]   Anne Richards, for instance, is speaking of Wayne Booth's amended (as of 1988) reading of *Emma*: "Some have ascribed to Austen's novels an overarching irony under which no ideology should be taken seriously" (144). The *reductio ad absurdum* of this approach is posited by that well-known academic trickster, Stanley Fish, who points out that if one presumes Austen's irony to be endemic, one could just as well discover in her work a non-ironic position in which nothing is satirized, not even Mr. Collins's proposal to Elizabeth Bennet in *Pride and Prejudice* (347–8). Booth himself, however, in *A Rhetoric of Irony*, notes that irony can be deployed in the service of a sincere message (3–6). After all, to give the extreme example, even Jesus deploys irony, as in *Luke* 12:6–7, when he instructs his disciples: "Are not five sparrows sold for two farthings, and not one of them is forgotten before God? / But even the very hairs of your head are all numbered. Fear not therefore: ye are of more value than many sparrows." One does not argue from the fact of Jesus's ironies that he did not endorse specific moral values.

most strongly: "She is an Anglican author who writes Christian stories. If we—her readers, her biographers, and her literary critics—fail to grasp the centrality of that fact, and do not rise to the challenge that it presents to reading and biography and criticism, then we will misunderstand her life and misread her novels at their most profound level of interpretation" (27).

That the issue is so undecided follows, I believe, from modern ideas about religion that are anachronistically applied to Austen. For instance, we tend to assume that religious faith is hard won and the result of a serious existential debate. Religious writers, we expect, should represent a soul's wrestling with God, as do Graham Greene or Flannery O'Connor. Those who live in post-modernity cannot avoid religious doubt, but, as I argue in detail in both Chapter one and two, Anglicans in Austen's day were not much affected by the claims of German higher criticism or by the possible disruptions of religious explanations of nature by scientific discoveries. Most Anglicans felt they had every reason to trust in the truth claims of Christianity; their dilemmas were not doctrinal but rather social and cultural: how to reinvigorate a lax church. Thus, Austen's religious commitments can be, as Bruce Stovel has said, "powerful in her life and not difficult to trace in her novels, but quiet, untheoretical, and rarely openly expressed" (201).

The book furthers the pioneering work done by Irene Collins (a biography, *Jane Austen: A Parson's Daughter* [1998], and a work of criticism, *Jane Austen and the Clergy* [1994]), both foundational to the work at hand; Michael Giffin (*Jane Austen and Religion: Salvation and Society in Georgian England* [2002]); Gene Koppel, *The Religious Dimension of Jane Austen's Novels* [1988]; and William Jarvis (*Jane Austen and Religion* [1996]). Collins's approach is largely biographical, offering a comprehensive view of the religious elements in Austen's own experience, while both Koppel's and Giffin's projects work to reveal the Christian didacticism and quasi-allegorical nature of Austen's fiction. Jarvis, an Anglican priest (now deceased) set out a straightforward account of the ways Austen's novels and life show Anglican practice. My approach builds on all these excellent works and aims to be both foundational and heuristic: I provide the relevant eighteenth- and nineteenth-century history (of ideas, of church practice, of culture), primarily through the lens of primary sources of the period, and place Austen's work and life firmly within the contexts of Anglicanism thus established, focusing particularly on the ways her Anglican worldview, informed by that particular historical moment, affected her fiction. I intend this book to help a range of readers come to a fuller understanding of Austen: Austen scholars, graduate and undergraduate students of Austen, and the many lay readers (i.e., admirers) of Austen such as the tens of thousands of members of the Jane Austen Society worldwide. Students and scholars of the eighteenth- and nineteenth-century church and, more broadly, of Anglican culture, history, and ideas, may also find this volume useful.

Part 1, "Jane Austen and Anglicanism," explains the history, ideology, and social system of the Georgian Church and Austen's relation to them all. The first chapter gives the complex history of the Georgian church, an institution with which Austen was intimately connected all her life, through her family, her culture, and her individual religious commitments. It explores the Anglican dread of "enthusiasm," the church's quiescence and latitudinarianism, its structural deformities (e.g., nepotism, absenteeism, pluralism), and its strong ties to the state and to the upper classes. The chapter also traces the Church's slow response to the forces of revolution and reform, including the Evangelical movement, and its relative insulation from the challenges posed by German higher criticism. I discuss the *Book of Common Prayer* and liturgical worship—and their effects on orthodox practitioners—as well as the basic elements of Anglican orthodoxy, including its reliance on natural law. Throughout, I note the relevance of all these considerations to Austen's own experience with the church and with her society.

In the second chapter, the central conflict between Austen's malicious wit and her family's testimony to her Christian piety and kindness is put into context through an examination in detail of Austen's personal practice of liturgical Anglicanism. It describes her experiences with the clergy, worship, liturgy, doctrine, sacraments, and sermons and other religious reading, and draws connections between these experiences and their fictional parallels in the novels, and it explores the three prayers she wrote that were saved by the Austen family. The third chapter goes on to describe the intellectual and religious worldview Austen inherited, especially the concepts of natural law, the Great Chain of Being, Providence, probability, and typology; I then examine the resonances, echoes, and partial reconfigurations of these elements of orthodox Anglicanism in Austen's treatment of language, social hierarchies, history, and nature.

In the final section, "Sins of the Author," I turn to the two key moral issues that Austen's religious commitments brought to the fore as she wrote her fiction, that is, possible sins of speech and possible sins in writing fiction at all. I argue in the fourth chapter that Austen's propensity for malice and subversive wordplay is leavened throughout her fiction by her awareness of this inclination as a moral and spiritual failing, and her growing appreciation of the virtue of "candor" (in her day, "candor" meant generous sympathy, not honest criticism—the shift in the word's usage is but a part of contemporary mis-interpretations of Austen's meanings). The fifth chapter examines Austen's awareness of the moral problems of authorship (that is, creating fictions) relative to God as Creator. It explores the sub-creators of her fiction, "imaginists" of shapes and degrees whose workings reveal the moral problems of imagination and creation, as well as Austen herself as creator of that almost god-like being, the narrator "Jane Austen."

The coda surveys the ontological and moral gulf between the worldview of *Emma* and that of Oscar Wilde's in *The Importance of Being Earnest,* first produced 80 years after *Emma's* publication—a comparison invited by the casual resemblances between their comic plots, wordplay, and wit. In it I argue that the evangelical earnestness that was first becoming a cultural force in Austen's day has not only become a figure of mockery by the late nineteenth century, but that the wider religious inheritance of Anglican orthodoxy is figured as bankrupt in Wilde's wildly popular play.

My hope is that this volume will help quiet the immortal shade of Jane Austen, by bringing her readers a more comprehensive sense of how her faith informed her fiction and life.

# Chapter 1
# Jane Austen's Religious Inheritance:
# The Georgian Church

Since the High Church movement commenced [in the 1830s] . . . the theology of
the 18th century has become a byword. The genuine Anglican omits that period
from the history of the Church altogether.

—Mark Pattison, "Tendencies of Religious
Thought in England, 1688–1750," 1889

It is one thing to know that Jane Austen was a committed Anglican Christian. But
it is another altogether to know what it meant to be an Anglican Christian in her
day. By all accounts, the Georgian Church that fostered Austen was a low-water
mark in the annals of the Church of England—it was rife with structural and moral
problems, and under increasing assault by outside forces. And yet for the most
part, members of the Church, including Austen, presumed that the Church and
its ways were immune to significant change. Readers of Austen may well find
valuable an enhanced understanding of the concerns of the Anglican Church in the
late eighteenth and early nineteenth century, exactly because these were Austen's
concerns as well. What were the Church's theological precepts, and what were
the threats to its worldview? What social conditions threatened its dominance?
To understand Jane Austen's fiction and the premises of her thought, it helps to
understand her religious inheritance in terms of both its beauties and its warts.

## The Eighteenth-Century Anglican Church

The Established Church of the eighteenth century was notable chiefly for its
contrast with its predecessor in the seventeenth, a church riven by religious and
state conflict. The English Civil War, or, as Marxists would term it, the English
Revolution (1642–1651), and the Interregnum under Cromwell (1649–1660) were
accompanied by a wave of religious zeal or "enthusiasm." With the restoration of
the monarchy through the coronation of Charles II in 1661, and the restoration of
the Anglican Church as the established state church, the dominant English feeling
was that dangerous politics and dangerous religion had both been vanquished,
at least temporarily. The eighteenth-century dread of visionary, mystic rhetoric
followed from this defeat of the forces of "enthusiasm," though the visionary
strain in religious rhetoric continued underground in the work of such writers as
Christopher Smart and, later, William Blake.[1]

---

[1]    As Jon Mee notes in his review of Romantic views of enthusiasm, "the primary
meaning of the word enthusiasm for about two centuries or more in English defined a specific

Enthusiasm privileged emotion over reason, individual urgings of the spirit over orthodoxy, and an intensely figurative rhetoric over commonplace speech (Irlam 22). The eighteenth-century mainstream verdict against enthusiasm was harsh indeed; the Anglican priest Robert South gave a representative judgment when he called enthusiasm "that pestilent and vile thing, which, wheresoever it has had its full course, has thrown both church and state into confusion" (IV.41). In Johnson's *Dictionary*, enthusiasm is defined as "a vain belief of private imagination" and connected to passionate violence.[2] Viewed as particularly dangerous and incendiary was the predilection of enthusiastic preachers to employ deeply metaphorical language; as South put it, "You have the shallow, brutish, unthinking multitude worded out of their religion by the worst and most detested appellations fasted upon the best of things and the best and most plausible names applied to the very worst sort" (IV.206).[3] As we will see in Chapter 3, Austen's use of metaphors—in general, employing only the deadest and most conventional ones—owes much to her cultural inheritance of the reactionary eighteenth-century mandate that figuration should be contained and controlled lest there be dire socio-political consequences.

Key to the defeat of "enthusiasm" was its cultural re-branding as an individual pathology rather than a social, religious, or political movement. As Michael MacDonald has argued, advocates for the Anglican status quo published numerous pamphlets employing a famous passage in Burton's *Anatomy of Melancholy* (1621), in which Burton had characterized English Puritans as carriers of mental disease: "Wee may say of these peculiar sects, their Religion takes away not spirits only, but wit and judgement, and deprives them of all understanding: for some of them are so farre gone with their private Enthusiasmes, and revelations, that they

---

religious error," that of confusing human imagination with God's purpose (2). See Clement Hawes for a survey of the subterranean survival of the "manic" mode in religious and literary thought in the eighteenth century. Despite the "obvious political failure," he argues, "the manic mode persists . . . much longer and more impressively than its fringe-group origins or brief heyday in the Interregnum might suggest" (4). See also Irlam, who charts the "idioms of Enthusiasm and a rhetoric of Heaven" through the "black hole of English poetry between neoclassicism and romanticism" (1). The last chapter of Ronald Knox's *Enthusiasm* also deals with the later stages and reception of enthusiastic rhetoric, including the literature of enthusiasm, while Susie Tucker's work traces the semantic changes in the term over centuries. There was a telling revival of the "idioms of Enthusiasm" toward the end of the century, as millennial hopes were re-awakened, particularly in light of the seeming end-times heralded by the French Revolution. Coleridge, for instance, was a millennialist and one can trace his hopes in his 1794 "Religious Musings"; after the disappointment of 1800 when the end did not in fact appear, his prophetic "Blake-like voice" diminished (Korshin 388).

[2]    Here is the full definition as given by Dr. Johnson: "a vain belief of private revelation, a vain confidence of divine favour, heat of imagination, violence of passion."

[3]    This passage is cited in Irlam, who also notes the denunciation of enthusiasm in Swift's *Tale of a Tub*, in Shaftesbury's "A Letter on Enthusiasm," and in *The Spectator*, no. 201 (42).

are quite madde, out of their wits" (Burton III, 387). The successful pathologizing of enthusiasm served to undercut it and ultimately to silence most of its adherents (Hawes 5).

The legacy of its squelching is clearly read much later in Austen's own ambiguous views on enthusiasm and her association of linguistic excess with selfishness, imposture, or mental instability. The most wildly excessive passages in Austen can be found in the speeches of Sir Edward Denham in her last work, *Sanditon*, and in these we can read not only Austen's condemnation of the cant of sensibility but also the Anglican condemnation of rhetorical excess. Sir Edward speaks of "the coruscations of Talent" and "indomptible decision" and "a literary Alembic" and "anti-puerile Man"—our heroine can hardly understand his meaning but does infer that he has lost his moral compass (*LM* 176, 182). The passages in Austen that yoke enthusiasm with authorial approval are all notable for their restrained figuration as well as their orthodoxy of substance and style. For instance, Fanny Price's encomium in *Mansfield Park* on the beauties of nature is rendered with apostrophes, certainly, but apostrophes set in Johnsonian parallels and marked by asyndeton: "'Here's harmony!' said she, 'Here's repose! Here's what may leave all painting and all music behind and what poetry only can attempt to describe. Here's what may tranquillize every care, and lift the heart to rapture!'" (132).

English exhaustion with political and religious fervor was a major cause of the relative quiescence of the body politic and of the Anglican Church throughout the eighteenth century. As Christopher Hill has argued, "Milton's nation of prophets . . . became a nation of shopkeepers" (15). Students of the Anglican Church have generally considered its eighteenth-century history as something of a backwater. Caught between the religious turmoil begat by bourgeois fever for political and religious freedom of the 1640s on the one hand, and the fervor for religious reform begun in the 1830s with the Tractarians and the Oxford Movement on the other, the eighteenth century has been seen as a period in which, relatively speaking, nothing happened: "The eighteenth century church has suffered from the accident of falling between the intensities of the seventeenth century and the widespread and varied revivals of the century that followed it" (Neil 191). As Perry Butler notes, "After the religious upheavals of the preceding century the prevailing desire was for stability. The Church stood for moderation. Morality was exalted above dogma, [while] a sober practical piety [was valued] over mysticism or emotion" (30). Further, because Anglican churchmen of the eighteenth century were generally quiet and regular—not a noisy crew—they have left less of a trail to interpret, unlike the robust Methodists of the 1780s or the inflamed dons at Oxford in the 1830s.[4] There were very few Church reforms during this period, and no serious liturgical changes, even

---

[4]    As G. J. Cuming notes, the Tractarian enthusiasms had a literary substrate in ways parallel to the poetry of enthusiasm, which underwrote the Puritan Revolution, in that the desires of the Oxford Movement to connect with the most authentic "primitive" Church were partly propelled by the "the romantic enthusiasm for the Middle Ages kindled by the novels of Sir Walter Scott" (193).

though many serious structural concerns needing addressing, as I discuss below. The predominance of Whig power throughout the century ensured the Church was undisturbed by reform: Whigs saw no need to provoke the predominantly Tory bishops on these fronts, and Tory bishops were not eager themselves for reform, and were in any case in no position to press for it.[5]

Until the Evangelical challenge of the late eighteenth century, the spiritual health of the Church was hard to discern, but was certainly open to charges of "pastoral neglect and worldliness" (P. Butler 30). The received view of the Church during this period is of a church known for its political expediency and "comfortable [and] prudential morality" (Roston 98).[6] In fact, as the headnote to this chapter shows, the pre-eminent nineteenth-century historian of Anglicanism, Mark Pattison, went so far as to declare that "Since the High Church movement commenced . . . the theology of the 18th century has become a byword. The genuine Anglican omits that period from the history of the Church altogether" ("Tendencies" 254; qtd. in Legg 1). Rational approaches to religion dominated, chiefly guided by probabilistic arguments (such as those engaged by Thomas Sherlock, one of Austen's favorite writers of sermons), and arguments for submission and acceptance of the social order were equally widespread. The ecclesiastical tone was lukewarm as well. When Bishop Lowth, author of the highly influential 1762 *A Short Introduction to English Grammar*, asked the actor David Garrick how he could rouse his audience so with his speeches onstage, even though he knew the speeches were a fiction, while preachers, believing what they preached, had so little effect comparatively on their listeners, Garrick replied that actors deliver their lines with the "warmth of truth," while preachers "pronounce the most solemn truths with as much coldness and languor as if they were the most trivial fictions" (Hall 40). Furthermore, the Church was allied with forces of social quietude, in part because of its basic theology of the Great Chain of Being and of natural law. Murray Roston notes in this regard the hymn by Isaac Watts that urges the poor to keep to their place: "What though I be low and mean, / I'll engage the rich to love me, / While I'm modest, neat and clean, / And submit when they reprove me" (99; Watts 343). Acceptance of the social status quo is praised as a form of religious decorum. As we shall see, Austen's own dedication to religious decorum is inextricably linked to the moral value set on social stability.

---

[5]    As A. S. Gilbert reports, "The organizational and human resources of Anglicanism changed scarcely at all between 1740 and 1812" (7).

[6]    As we shall see in Chapter 3, this cultural preference for the safety of conformity had its consequences for the literary taste of figures like Johnson, Goldsmith, and Cowper, three of Austen's favorite authors. Shunning peculiarity and the unexpected led Dr. Johnson to lodge this famous complaint against Donne: "Who but Donne would have thought a good man is a telescope?" (*Lives* I.26).

## Absenteeism, Pluralism, and Non-residence

The general placidity of the Anglican establishment masked some very serious problems. Among them, absenteeism was a key concern.[7] The rate of church attendance was low, and, worse, many rural communities had grown accustomed to indifference. Dissenters had been urging a sense of crisis about waning faith since the beginning of the century, but Anglican Evangelicals had little effect in their arguments about the erosion of religious practice in the nation: "When in 1789 Hannah More noted that there were whole village populations in England no less estranged from the services of the Church than heathens were, she was simply recognizing for the first time a fact which men like Whitefield and Wesley had been proclaiming for decades" (Gilbert 7). More and other reformers were bent on reinvigorating a church that had become in some cases almost entirely inert. The facts of attendance, for example, were so disappointing that one bishop, John Butler, who commissioned a survey of the number of communicants in 1789 to update an earlier survey in 1747, felt he could not publish his results: "Communicants in the year 1747 appear to have been many more, so many more, than those reported in the year 1789, that I am unwilling to recite the numbers" (Virgin 5). Again, Whig dominance, in place up to 1740, played a role, for Whig politicians had no strong motives for enforcing laws against irreligious behavior; after all, doing so would only strengthen the hand of the Tory religious establishment. In consequence, state sanctions, such as fines for citizens who did not attend church, were relaxed. There were laws on the books—the Uniformity Laws—that held, for instance, that one could be assessed 12 shillings for missing a month of services, but they were rarely enforced.[8] Absenteeism was also rife in the new urban centers. The Church was remiss in reacting to the changes in demography following from the movement of rural workers to industrial and urban centers or the changes in transportation (such as the growth of the canal system or the Macadam-led improvements in roads), which moved populations away from the established country parishes. Peter Virgin points out that "[m]ost of the inhabitants of the new industrial towns did not show any great enthusiasm for the services of the Church of England. This, in the circumstances, was just as well; had they all decided to attend, there would have been nowhere to put them" (5).

Absenteeism was to some degree influenced by two practices that suggested that the clergy were not particularly concerned about whether their parishioners showed up or not—pluralism and non-residency—both of which meant that the clergy sometimes did not show up for church services either. Pluralism was the

---

[7]     Among the many surveys of eighteenth-century Anglicanism and its problems, of particular note are the early views of Abbey and Overton (1878), Legg (1914), and, later, of Sykes (1954). More contemporary scholars include Virgin, P. Butler, Neil, Snell and Ell, Gilbert, Walsh and Taylor, and Soloway. Virgin's title—*The Church in an Age of Negligence*—tells much of the tale common to these works.

[8]     Gilbert argues, "For the dominant political party, tacit acceptance of religious apathy had become part of a policy of increasing the subordination of the religious Establishment to the secular" (11).

common practice of allowing Anglican clergymen to hold more than one living while non-residency, the inevitable consequence of pluralism, allowed them to live outside at least one of their parishes. By the late eighteenth century, approximately one-third of all Anglican clergy held more than one living (Collins, "Displeasing Pictures" 116–7). George Austen, Jane Austen's father, was himself a pluralist, in that he held two livings (Steventon and Deane) and lived only at Steventon, leaving the affairs of the parish at Deane for most of the year to a curate (for whose services he himself paid, the usual practice). Austen's brother James was also initially a pluralist, with four small parishes to attend to; one can gauge the growing distaste for pluralism in the early nineteenth century by the fact that James later, as the rector of Steventon, turned down a second living, "apparently as a matter of principle" (M. Butler, "History" 204). But in the late eighteenth century, even voices for reform, such as Richard Watson, Bishop of Llandaff, were culpable—his 1783 public letter to the Archbishop of Canterbury urging a fairer distribution of ecclesiastical revenue and reductions in pluralism and non-residency was undercut by the fact that he himself held *sixteen* livings (Soloway 3).

While Bishop Watson was rich, and made rich in part by his many livings, most clergymen held multiple livings because it was the only way they could get by economically. Livings often paid poorly, and in thousands of cases, very poorly indeed (Soloway 48). Steventon's annual income was £100, Deane's £110; with tithes, income from farming glebe land (i.e., land owned by the parish for the use of the clergyman), and, in George Austen's case, tuition from boarding students, the burgeoning Austen family with its seven children at home made do with no more than £600 a year (M. Butler, "History" 197). This clerical family was relatively well-off. At the bottom of the clerical scale of incomes was the lowly curate, who was usually paid between £20 and £75 a year; by statute, the former amount had been set as a required minimum in 1714, the latter as a maximum (!) in 1796 (N. Sykes 208).

Furthermore, as a clergyman it was not always particularly easy to gain all the income to which one was putatively entitled. The expectation that all parishioners were to tithe—to give the clergy 10% of their income—made clergymen unpopular with their communicants, especially in times of agricultural depression. And, as Virgin details, tithing was in practice extremely complicated. In general, rectories were to be given both 10% both of animal produce (great tithes) and of agricultural produce (small tithes); vicarages were due only the small tithes, and curates received no tithes at all, only cash payment from the clergy who had hired them. Increasingly throughout the end of the eighteenth century and the beginning of the nineteenth, enclosure and the appeal of greater convenience led to "commutation"—a practice in which parishioners gave a piece of land in exchange for the freedom from further tithing. Tithes were payable in some cases through "moduses," a system whereby a clergyman would take his payment in eggs rather than chickens, for example, or milk rather than cows. The expectation that members of the clergy would gather their own tithes sometimes led to the low comedy of their scooping up every tenth stack of hay or searching through henhouses for the tenth egg. It also meant that clergy in many cases had to operate as farmers and accountants to get the income they were due—and they would need to market the goods they themselves could not use (Virgin 36–8). Virgin tartly notes that "All of this, naturally enough, could provoke resistance. The parson would be told curtly to collect his milk every day rather than every tenth day, and to do so early in the morning. . . . The collection of hay and cereals was made difficult, and the breeding habits of the farmyard were kept as secret as possible" (38). A survey of 12 English counties in the 1790s reveals that Hampshire, Austen's home county, was among those shires in which these forms of "tithing in kind" were commonly practiced (Virgin 38), and so Jane Austen was well-used to the idea of the clergyman as often-unwelcome collector of agricultural goods (though her own father depended instead on the agricultural productions of his glebe land). In fact, when in *Pride and Prejudice* Mr. Collins visits Longbourn and admires its furniture, plate, draperies, and so on in the spirit of one who is to possess it all in the fullness of time, one might wonder if Austen has captured in Mrs. Bennet's answering pique something of the annoyance Georgian farmers felt when members of the clergy admired their crops or their animal husbandry.

The pressing need for greater ecclesiastical income created pluralism; pluralism created non-residence. There was no particular law that forced clergymen to live in their parishes, and it was not just bishops, living in the West End and in the universities, who saw their parishes only once a year (usually before Christmas, to confirm new clergy in what were called Ember Days—this is when Edmund Bertram is ordained in *Mansfield Park*). In fact, some clergymen never saw some of their parishes during a given year at all (Collins, "The Rev. Henry Tilney" 159). A parliamentary inquiry in 1812 confirmed that a little over 1,000 parishes were without a minister of any sort (Gilbert 7). This finding was determined by the fact that though there were 4,813 members of the clergy who were non-resident, only 3,694 curates served their parishes in their stead (Snell and Ell 84). One important reason was the crudity of parish housing; in some parishes there was no rectory at all while in others it was ramshackle and/or too small. While a parliamentary act to make "provision for the more speedy and effectual building of [clerical] houses" was passed in 1777, and while there is some evidence of improved living conditions for clergy during this period, non-residence remained a problem (Snell and Ell 84). The records of one bishop from the late eighteenth century record a cornucopia of reasons for granting clergy requests for non-residence: successful petitions noted such factors as lack of housing, the ill-health or advanced age of the clergyman or his wife, the small value of the living, or, as a bishop noted in one particularly "sad case," "'on account of your being utterly incapacitated from performing any clerical duty whatever'" (Snell and Ell 85).

Reforms followed, but their utility was, at best, mixed. Virgin summarizes the state of affairs by the end of the eighteenth century:

> There was no shortage of plans for reform . . . ; the difficulty was to implement them. Reformers said more or less the same things, proposed more or less the same remedies, and achieved more or less the same result: almost nothing. . . . [C]umbersome diocesan geography remained the same; . . . cathedral establishments remained the same; and the tithe system remained the same. The laws regarding pluralism and non-residence were not altered. (191)

The revival of Queen Anne's Bounty in the 1780s remedied some inequities (the Bounty was a government fund, established in 1706, overseen by a panel of bishops empowered to make financial dispensations for the needs of the Church) (Best 59–60). Moreover, Soloway notes that legislation in 1803–1804 made some impact on pluralism and non-residence by creating better pay for rectors as well as for the even poorer curates paid by absentee incumbents (bishops had defeated an effort to make similar reforms in the 1780s) (46). But even with the more substantial reforms of the coming decades, as late as 1850 well over 1,000 clergy were non-resident at one of their livings (Snell and Ell 85).

## Patronage and the "Squarson" Alliance

Another condition of the Georgian Church was its troubling reliance on patronage and nepotism. The House of Bishops held the power to appoint approximately 2,500 of the kingdom's 11,600 livings, while the rest, excluding the roughly 600 livings controlled by Oxford and Cambridge, were in the hands of individual landowners, either as a direct property right or in consequence of their being Members of Parliament (Collins, *Jane Austen and the Clergy* 24–5). In most cases, both the bishops and the landowners reserved these livings for family members, near or distant, or for others with personal ties or claims on their patronage. When the familial bonds were weak or non-existent between the patron and the holder of the living, as between Lady Catherine de Bourgh and Mr. Collins in *Pride and Prejudice*, there were also distortions, as gratitude for such an unexpected favor on behalf of the clergyman sometimes led to the clergyman's servility (Mr. Collins presents an extreme case, one hopes). For the most part, the system of patronage and the nepotism it entailed was considered a necessary element of clerical structure. It provided social cohesion: "patronage was accepted as axiomatic . . . [and] the forms taken by patronage [were seen] as a wholly appropriate exercise of influence" (Virgin 171). When in 1808 Maria Edgeworth published a novel called *Patronage*, which argued implicitly against the practice and for a distribution of livings based on merit, she was at best an early promoter of a sentiment that strengthened much later in the century (M. Butler "History," 98). The many clergymen related to Jane Austen by blood or marriage all benefited in one form or another from patronage, and she plainly did not deplore the practice, even though she could mock its excesses or be sorry when a worthy young cleric seemed to be held back (as often happened) by lack of a patron. In fact, Austen seems to have agreed with Dr. Johnson, who felt that inequalities in clerical income followed from the unassailable rights of private property. As Johnson explained to Boswell, "You must consider, that the revenues of the clergy are not at the disposal of the state, like the pay of the army. Different men have founded different churches; and some are better endowed, some worse. The State cannot interfere and make an equal division of what has been particularly appropriated" (Boswell 340). Private property is explicitly confirmed in the Articles of Religion, found within the 1662 *Book of Common Prayer*: "The riches and goods of Christians are not common, as touching the right, title, and possession of the same, as certain Anabaptists do falsely boast; notwithstanding every man ought of such things as he possesseth liberally to give alms to the poor, according to his ability."[9] Austen's orthodox respect for private property thus informed her support of patronage, which in turn takes its place as one of many elements that formed her sense of the deep interconnections between the Church and the social world, a primary foundation for much else in her worldview.

Perhaps the deepest interconnection between the Church and the world in Austen's day was its status as the Established Church, in a country whose monarch holds the title "Defender of the Faith" (and "Faith" here means the faith of the Anglican Church, not Christian faith more generally). The heads of the Church, the bishops, and the Archbishop of Canterbury, were political figures who, then as now, served in the House of Lords. All changes to church practice or government had to be done through parliamentary law; the Church had very little independence of action. Despite some calls for disestablishment, that is, severing the connection between church and state, the alliance held (and holds).[10] As Stephen Neil points out, there was much to be criticized about this arrangement, including the "far from edifying" spectacle of bishops jostling for position, services, and appointments (193). Bishops remained throughout the year in London, as practicing politicians, usually returning to their home dioceses once a year to confirm and ordain their flock (Soloway 3). Neil adds, in the bishops' favor, "yet few of them were really bad men" (198).[11]

The interdependence between patron and living-holder and between Church and State was matched by the interdependence more generally between the clergy and

---

9  A particularly robust celebration of private property came from Ambrose Phillips, the English poet and rival of Pope's, who in 1714 wrote in a patriotic epistle, "But who advances next, with cheerful grace, / Joy in her eyes, and plenty in her face? / A wheaten garland does her head adorn; / O Property! O goddess, English-born!" (93).

10  See Norman Sykes, *Church and State in England in the Eighteenth Century*, on the eighteenth-century development and strengthening of these ties, especially in chapter 7, "The Alliance of Church and State in England." Coleridge, incidentally, before 1802, was adamant that such a severing of church and state was necessary but came to argue for the virtues of a National Church. Coleridge gives as epigram to his *On the Constitution of the Church and State*, written in 1830 as his last prose work, a passage from his earlier *Literary Remains*: "O that our Clergy did but know and see that their tithes and glebes belong to them as officers and functionaries of the Nationality,—as clerks, and not exclusively as theologians, and not at all as ministers of the Gospel . . . . [confusing] the claims of the Christian pastor and preacher with the legal and constitutional rights and revenues of the officers of the National Clerisy. Our Clergymen, in thinking of their legal rights, forget those rights of theirs which depend on no human law at all" (v). However, though Coleridge saw the problems this confusion created, and also the problem caused by the Church's reliance on State money (what it gives can be taken away), he staunchly defended the National Church in arguments close to those made by Tory county interests (see Morrow, esp. 648–52).

11  In the same exculpatory light, we have Legg arguing that "malice has not been wanting in attempts to exhibit the English clergy [of this day] in the worst light" (105).

the gentry; as A. D. Gilbert claims, by 1800, Anglicanism and gentry society were "virtually co-terminous" (12). Earlier in the eighteenth century, the clergy had not been so closely tied to the landowner class, partly because, before the final Jacobite defeat in 1746, the aristocracy and gentry would have feared having too close a tie to clerics who might inconveniently turn out to be closet Catholics (Collins, *Jane Austen and the Clergy*, 57). However, when this fear was allayed, and, perhaps of more importance, when improvements in agricultural technology and science made glebe holdings and tithings more profitable, gentry patrons began to place their own sons and relations into parishes and to improve their rectories (Collins, "The Rev. Henry Tilney" 161). Thus by the late eighteenth century, the social status of parsons had risen considerably. Sixty percent of Oxford and Cambridge graduates became clergymen (Collins, "Displeasing Pictures" 118). Further, not only did landowners allow their sons to become clergymen but they also allowed their daughters to marry them, creating dense ties of interrelationship such as those that linked the clergy household of Austen's childhood with numerous county and aristocratic households.[12] In fact, the increasingly respectable option to send sons into the clergy helped solve a persistent problem of primogeniture-bound society: what to do with the second, third, or fourth son who will not inherit the family estate. In an 1812 letter to Sir Walter Scott, the poet George Crabbe admitted that he was bringing up two of his sons to be clergymen "because I did not know what else to do with them" (58, qtd. in Virgin 134).

The relation between gentry families and the clergy was strengthened by the parish system, in which all inhabitants of a given geographical district were assigned into the care of a given church and its rector, with the living commonly in the hand of the greatest landowner or squire. These divisions, incidentally, had remained essentially unchanged since the creation of the National Church under Henry VIII (Snell and Ell 78). The "squarson" (i.e., squire/parson) alliance was central to rural administration, and the health of rural agriculture affected the squire and parson both, the former through rents and the latter through tithes. Poor farmers were not slow to notice that they owed money to both; the radical William Cobbett testified to hearing grumbling on this account in his country researches (Collins, "Displeasing Pictures" 115). Good or bad harvests thus affected how welcome the Anglican clergyman was in his parish; unfortunately, between 1793 and 1812, there were 14 bad harvests (Virgin 45), with other bad harvests to come in 1814 and 1815.[13]

---

[12]    Irene Collins's *Jane Austen and the Clergy* is invaluable for tracing the intricacies of these ties, particularly chapter 1, "Jane Austen's Clerical Connections" and chapter 7, "The Clergy and the Neighborhood." See also Deborah Kaplan's *Jane Austen Among Women*, which explains the distaff side of these interconnections with great clarity.

[13]    1815 was popularly known in England as the "year without summer," because Mount Tambora's massive volcanic explosion obliterated the Indonesian island on which it stood and propelled pulverized rock into the atmosphere, creating 150 times the ash generated by Mount St. Helens' explosion in 1980. Crops failed all over Europe that year.

As Walsh and Taylor note, the parish church engaged not only loyalty to Anglicanism but also "localism and atavism" (28). In fact, in one-sixth of English parishes, the parson also functioned as magistrate, settling disputes and arraigning wrongdoers (Virgin 8). The localization of power had substantial effects upon religious practice, for "when a resident clergyman in a manageable parish enjoyed the wholehearted support of the local landowners . . ., he could guarantee high rates of religious practice and make religious Dissent virtually untenable" (Gilbert 11). If the power of the magistrate and the landowner strengthened the hand of the clergyman, the clergyman strengthened the hand of the secular authorities. Clerical authority was viewed as supporting the "vested interest of a propertied governing class" (Walsh and Taylor 29). G. F. A. Best notes that by the late eighteenth century, the establishment promulgated with vigor "the social affinities of clergy and laity, tending to glorify their interconnexions and mutual dependence"—an interdependence most richly sponsored and developed in the rural parishes of southern England, such as Austen's natal Hampshire (61).

Admittedly, Austen's own novels do not reliably depict this alliance. The relationship between landowner, priest, and village is clearest in *Emma*, where it is plain that Mr. Woodhouse has given Mr. Elton the living (in part, because he has no sons or other relatives who need it), and we see the village of the parish in detail (Mr. Knightley is not Mr. Elton's patron, because his estate, Donwell Abbey, is in an adjoining parish). Marilyn Butler notes that in *Mansfield Park*, the novel in which the great estate and the rectory are shown in most detail, the village and parish are entirely undepicted ("History"). One interesting moment in *Pride and Prejudice* reminds us of this void, of the fact that we never meet the clergyman who serves the parish in which the Bennets live. Writing with a signal lack of Christian charity to Mr. Bennet late in the novel, Mr. Collins avers that Lydia should not have been received at Longbourn: "It was an encouragement of vice; and had I been the rector of Longbourn, I should very strenuously have opposed it. You ought certainly to forgive them as a christian, but never to admit them in your sight, or allow their names to be mentioned in your hearing" (*PP* 403). We meet neither this unnamed "rector of Longbourn" nor any members of the family who hold the living, as they must be the absent gentry who lease Netherfield to Mr. Bingley. Further, Austen's own early life lacked this example of the "squarson alliance," as the living for the parish of Steventon was given by Thomas Knight II, an immensely rich landowner who lived in Kent; his large house in Steventon was let to tenants, the Digweeds (as Kellynch Hall in *Persuasion* is let to the Crofts). Butler notes, "This meant that the rector's family was of consequence around Steventon, as representatives of the landowner, but it also confined their circle to the clergy of adjoining parishes and the owners or tenants of half a dozen substantial houses within reach" ("History" 198–9). This system seemed stable enough to its practitioners and those related to them, despite the fact that the early nineteenth century was to provide substantial pressure from alternative economic and political forces. As Gilbert argues, the squire/parson alliance joined the "two parties with vested interest in preserving as much as possible of the pre-industrial status quo" (12). And from the establishment gentry position, particularly "[i]n nucleated village settlements, such as those predominating in the English rural south, the organizational structure of the Church was adapted to local needs, and . . . substantial agrarian and demographic changes had still not harmed the inherited parochial patchwork" (Snell and Ell 79).[14]

All these connections between clergy and gentry inevitably brought the social practices of clergymen and their families more in accord with their lay relatives and benefactors. Increasingly, members of the clergy lived in houses aspiring to elegance, had at least one servant, kept horses and carriages, and held at least some land of their own. Virgin notes, "They were gentlemen, fulfilling the demands made upon gentlemen" (94). By not expecting supernatural virtue from clergymen, or even what Victorian Anglicans would later require, a sense of "vocation" or special calling from God, Austen was in keeping with her beloved Dr. Johnson: "A man who is good enough to go to heaven, is good enough to be a clergyman" (Boswell 339). The demands upon clerical time were limited to two services each Sunday, the occasional baptism, wedding, or funeral, and general visitation of the flock; some clergy, of course, were far more involved in the life of their parish, especially in the life of the poor, than others. One has no sense that Dr. Grant, for instance, is over-sedulous about his obligation to visit the sick and poor. Mr. Elton provides something of a contrast—he almost visits a poor family, does indeed find charity for the village ostler, and meets regularly with Mr. Knightley, Mr. Weston, and other property-holders on parish business. Nonetheless, Harriet's early view of Mr. Elton—"'. . . so excellent in the Church! Miss Nash has put down all the texts he has ever preached from since he came to Highbury'"—seems naïve, and seems to give credit to Mr. Elton simply for preaching, one of his key duties (*E* 80).

Priests of her day did not have any distinctive clerical dress for everyday (though they wore clerical robes, usually a white surplice, during services), for the "dog collar" had not yet been invented, and so most of the time they were indistinguishable in garb from other gentlemen (Collins, "The Rev. Henry Tilney" 159). They kept substantial libraries if they could afford them, as did George Austen, or small ones if they could not. In general, Jane Austen seems to have had no qualms about the dual character of the gentleman who was also a man of the cloth. As Irene Collins points out, William Wilberforce's attack on the clergyman of his day as "a sensible, well-informed and educated, polished, nobleman's and

---

[14]    The bishops, though they spent almost all their time in London, were equally vested in promoting the gentry/clergy alliance. They expected the Church would remain rural and pastoral. This presumption follows from their backgrounds; as Soloway notes, "No more than seventeen of the 104 bishops who led the Church between 1793 and 1852, when England was largely transformed from a rural to an urban country, ever held an urban living" (5). Further, the bishops shared the "education, values, and family connections" of the "landed governing classes" (5), especially as half of all the prelates in this period came from the peerage or the gentry, and many of the remaining came from clergy families with connections to the aristocracy and the landowners (9).

gentleman's house-frequenting, literary and chess-playing divine" would have described several of the clergymen in her family and many of the clergymen within her extended kinship bonds ("Displeasing Pictures" 114).[15] In *Mansfield Park*, admittedly, Dr. Grant is rebuked for being a gourmand, but part of Austen's point seems to be that his selfish absorption in what is laid on his table keeps him from being a better priest, not that good food is itself suspect. Further, when in *Pride and Prejudice* Mr. Collins makes a risible defense of the acceptability of a clergyman dancing, Austen's satiric target is his scrupulousness and defensiveness, as well as his poor footwork, not the fact of the dancing itself.[16] After all, *Northanger Abbey*'s hero Henry Tilney is a clergyman, too, and his dancing at Bath is praised. We also have no sign in particular of her disapproving of what Wilberforce called "the race of buck parsons," that is, clergymen who hunted, especially clergymen who participated in the county habit of fox-hunting. In letters she wrote while she still lived at Steventon, she makes plain that she sometimes tired of her brothers' hunting exploits (too often carcasses were left about the house); however, there is no sign that she thought clergymen such as her father or her brother James (who continued to hunt once he took orders) were violating decorum by being "mighty Nimrods of the cloth," a term used by Evangelicals to deplore hunting parsons.[17]

## Threats to the Church and the Role of Evangelical Reform

The coziness of this Anglican world, with its undemanding spirituality and worldly offices, came under direct threat during Austen's lifetime, first through the French

---

[15]    Collins provides a useful catalogue of the ways in which clergy seem to have far too much time on their hands in the novels, from Mr. Collins's gardening to Mr. Tilney's month at Bath ("Displeasing Pictures" 113).

[16]    Frank Bradbrook notes that Austen may be remembering a bit of pretentiousness by William Gilpin when she allows Mr. Collins to make a defense of his dancing: "'I consider music as a very innocent diversion and perfectly compatible with the profession of a clergyman'" (*PP* 113), for Gilpin wrote in his preface to *The Observations on Cumberland and Westmorland*: "The author . . . hopes he should not greatly err, if he allowed . . . the amusements furnished by the three sister-arts, to be all very consistent with the strictest rules of the clerical profession" (xxiii; qtd. in Bradbrook 57). Irene Collins surveys the codes governing clergymen dancing and Austen's experience with the same in *Jane Austen and the Clergy*, pp. 112–3.

[17]    While still at Oxford waiting to take orders, James Austen conceived the idea of a satiric literary journal modeled on *The Spectator* and *The Tatler, The Loiterer. The Loiterer* did not last long, but in its February, 1789 issue, he entered a fictitious advertisement for a "Curacy in good sporting country, near a pack of fox-hounds, and in a sociable neighborhood; it must have a good house and stables. . . . Whoever has such a one to dispose of, may suit themselves by sending a line, directed A. B. to be left at the Turf Coffee House, or the gentleman may be spoken with, any Tuesday morning at Tattersall's Betting Room" (qtd. in Collins, *Jane Austen and the Clergy* 23). James Austen cannot have been too serious in his critique of the hunting parson, as he himself continued to hunt after he was ordained.

Revolution and the Napoleonic Wars that followed; second, through Evangelical reform; and third, through the multitudinous shifts in social and economic organization occasioned by the Industrial Revolution. The latter is not much felt in Austen's narrative universe; no early trains run through her landscapes, no Luddites attack agricultural machinery, and the only worrisome itinerants are the gypsies we see in *Emma* (these gypsies are *not* a sign of cultural change because gypsies had been roaming England since the early 1500s). The clearest sign of the demographic changes effected by the Industrial Revolution comes in the relative depopulation of *Emma*'s Highbury and in the capitalistic schemes of *Sanditon*. But in general, her rural parishes are untouched by industrial forces. Nonetheless, the forces of Revolution and reform leave clear marks.

As many biographers and critics have noted, Austen, while not the "war novelist" Kingsley Amis mischievously called her (440), still had every reason to attend closely to the cataclysmic events across the Channel—two of her brothers were serving in the Royal Navy, and one was in the militia, while her cousin and later sister-in-law Eliza de Feuillide lost a husband to the guillotine. It is not accidental that in *Persuasion*, we learn in a early small detail from the *Baronetage* that Sir Walter's son, who, had he lived, would have saved his sisters from disinheritance, was stillborn in 1789—a year Austen chose no doubt for its historical resonance as a year of revolution and of undoing old orders. Austen also paid close attention to the Revolution and its aftermath because she was a highly patriotic daughter of Albion. Importantly, she would have understood the French Revolution in terms of its direct effects on the Church and its interests. The Anglican Church understood the French Revolution as a serious threat to its existence, given the new French government's hostility to and persecution of established religion, including the execution of hundreds of priests, monks, and nuns. The conservative apologist Robert Southey, writing under the *nom de plume* of "Richard Yates," voiced the common view: "We, who live in the present age, have had the most awful and instructive lessons presented to our experience, written in blood and heightened by every human misery. We have seen that Law, Science, and Civilization,—Liberty, Wealth, and Order, may all sink under the want of Religious and Moral Principle" (Yates 88; qtd. in Clark 268). As Marilyn Butler shows in detail, the 1790s saw a host of Anglican apologists defending the war with France as a "defense of religion, the family, and the gentry way of life" (196). The War was understood as a Christian mission, to defeat dangerous forces of secularism and irreligion.[18] This broadly held confidence built on the sense of religious exceptionalism that had

---

[18]    Butler notes that in so doing, "the upper and middle orders were given a coherent if idealized self-image which has been the basis of British Toryism ever since: a personal ideal compounded of independence, honor, decency, patriotism, public service, chivalry to women, and civility to inferiors" (196). She also points out that modern readers, assuming religious experience to be essentially private, often miss "the national significance and the public aims of the wartime religious reform movement" ("History" 207) and thus also often are not in a position to see how thoroughly for Austen the nation and the Church were indivisibly yoked.

been present in eighteenth-century English society even before the disturbances in France, the conviction that since the Glorious Revolution of 1688, the English nation had been peculiarly blessed by God with religious moderation that held off the "superstition of popery" associated with Roman Catholicism on the one hand and the "mindless enthusiasm" of Lutherans, Calvinists, Quakers, Baptists, and all their Dissenting ilk on the other (Gregory 70). Austen held this view with vigor; her Anglicanism and her nationalism were, as Oliver Macdonagh argues, "mutually supportive and interpenetrating" (7). A letter of 1814 speaks to her national faith (the subject is the threat of reawakened hostilities with the United States): "If we *are* to be ruined, it cannot be helped—but I place my hope of better things on a claim to the protection of Heaven, as a Religious Nation, a Nation in spite of much Evil improving in Religion, which I cannot believe the Americans to possess" (*L* 273–4).

Anglican propaganda for the Church as a bulwark against all the evils of revolution in the 1790s and the first two decades of the nineteenth century suffered from a major disability. How was the Church to provide all this national and spiritual protection if its own house was so poorly in order, so rife with the problems of absenteeism, pluralism, non-residence, worldliness, and nepotism?[19] Voices for reform were raised from within the Church, starting with William Law early in the century and continuing with a rising crescendo from figures such as William Wilberforce, John Bowles, Charles Simeon, Zachary Macauley, and Richard Watson.[20] The Church was slow to respond, however; in fact, as Soloway notes, "since the opening years of the new century, prelates had been . . . congratulating themselves and their clergy for surviving" the backwash of the French Revolution (46).[21]

Austen herself was entirely aware of the range of critique directed at the Anglican Church, and, by implication, directed against her own father and brother as well as against every one of the hundred or more clergymen she knew at one point or another in her life. She seems to have felt that the Church's existence was not direly threatened. The heart of her position seems to have been defensive

---

[19]    Soloway describes the state of affairs circa 1790–1820: "The Established Church was so weighed down with internal physical and spiritual abuses that it might soon prove completely inadequate for its special secular role as a stabilizing agency of the State and its religious role as a guide to eternal salvation" (47).

[20]    For details about the early stages of such calls for reform, esp. regarding William Law, see Roston, pp. 101ff.

[21]    Gilbert makes a related point: "Contemporary churchmen . . . could not know that England stood on the brink of profound industrial, demographic, and social changes which would threaten the Establishment with redundancy" (12). The bishops were nonetheless alarmed by the larger social and religious unquiet they were forced to confront. The early nineteenth-century explosion of newspapers meant that the diocesan comfort of the breakfast table must have been often shattered by what a given bishop was sure to read in his morning paper: "a volume, and a range, of censure, which [could well] induce severe alarm and acute despondency" (Virgin 14).

without being apologetic. She was not troubled by the linkage between gentry society and the clerisy; in fact, she celebrated that link and would have had every personal interest in reinforcing it, and she strongly believed in the establishment of the Church. The letters show she disapproved of the moral failings of particular clergymen, but in her novels, the worst of them—Mr. Collins, Mr. Elton, Mr. Grant—are depicted as doing their jobs capably, if without ardor, and she makes three of her heroes clergymen (Henry Tilney, Edward Ferrars, and Edmund Bertram). She was troubled by non-residence and pluralism, and uses *Mansfield Park* to voice her criticisms of these practices. In this novel, the Church's newest priest—Edmund—is determined to live at his rectory (with the approval of his father, who holds his living), a narrative feature that implicitly argues that the Church will reform itself, given time.

The novels testify to her willingness to criticize individual members of the clergy, though she found herself criticized for doing so, on the grounds that depicting faulty clergymen could paint all of the cloth with the same brush.[22] Collins notes that Austen seems to have altered her perspective about the propriety of showing faulty clergymen, for in *Pride and Prejudice*, Austen betrays no awareness that Mr. Collins might make all clergymen look bad, while in the later *Mansfield Park*, the discussion between Edmund and Mary about Dr. Grant's faults shows that Mary has not illogically drawn conclusions about clergymen from this one bad example (110). Fanny defends Dr. Grant on the grounds that "'a sensible man like Dr. Grant, cannot be in the habit of teaching others their duty every week, cannot go to church twice every Sunday and preach such very good sermons in so good a manner as he does, without being the better for it himself'" (*MP* 131).

Austen's clearest statement on the Church and its clergy comes in Edmund's defense of the cloth in *Mansfield Park*. Importantly, his speech is rendered in terms as hyperbolic as that other more famous defense Austen makes of novel-writing in *Northanger Abbey*. In that earlier apology, the superlative is central. The novel, Austen's narrator claims, is "work in which the *greatest* powers of the mind are displayed, in which the *most thorough* knowledge of human nature, the *happiest* delineation of its varieties, the *liveliest* effusions of wit and humour are conveyed to the world in the *best chosen* language" (*NA* 31; my italics). But in *Mansfield Park*, Edmund's defense of the clergy demolishes Mary Crawford's estimation that "'a clergyman is nothing'" not merely with superlatives, but with superlatives that cannot be overreached: "'I cannot call that situation nothing, which has the charge of *all that is of the first importance to mankind, individually or collectively considered, temporally and eternally*--which has the guardianship of religion and morals, and consequently of the manners which result from their influence'" (*MP* 107–8; my italics). When Edmund a few moments later insists that the clergy oversee manners and conduct because manners and conduct are the "'effect . . .

---

[22] See Collins, "Displeasing Pictures," 110, regarding the 1816 incident of Mrs. Wroughton's displeasure.

of those doctrines which it is [the clergy's] duty to teach and recommend,'" he is forwarding a religious justification for the centrality of the Church in society (109). And when he argues that to the degree that the clergy fulfill their duties, the nation will thrive, he is promoting an idea common to Anglican Tories: "'it will . . . be every where found, that as the clergy are, or are not what they ought to be so are the rest of the nation'" (109). That Edmund speaks for Austen herself is made plain by the fact that Edmund's speech is followed by a gesture rare in Austen's novels, in which one character is allowed to give an implicit "hear, hear" after another's speech for no other reason than to proffer further endorsement of the first speech's substance. In this case the virtuous heroine makes the author's perspective clear: "'Certainly,' said Fanny with gentle earnestness" (109). For Austen, the Church was rightly a national church, and, as we will see in Chapter 3, she also believed that beyond its national boundaries lay an authority and a foundation immune to the reproach of contemporary circumstance.[23]

To the degree that Austen countenanced reform related to the key issues besetting Anglicanism, she was allied with the goals of Anglican Evangelicalism, the heart of these calls for reform. It is important to distinguish the Anglican Evangelicals from Lutheran, Methodist, or Calvinist Evangelicals, who were all religious dissenters.[24] Neil notes, "Evangelicals in the Church of England have never been a party" (190). Rather, Anglican Evangelicals were distinguished from their fellows by mood, tone, and level of commitment, not by special doctrines.[25]

---

[23] As A. M. Allchin argues, the *Book of Common Prayer*, the basis of Anglican worship, promotes this worldview: "Here in the *Book of Common Prayer* was a vision of the Church as a corporate reality at once of time and eternity, the context in which the individual finds his way to God, presented in pages of memorable prose, straightforward yet solemn" (315).

[24] Even the important growth of Anglican Evangelicals in this period of (roughly) 1790–1820 could not begin to compete with the spectacular growth of dissenting Evangelicals. Anglican Evangelicalism was in part a response to the then unmistakable success of non-conforming church movements. For the relevant statistics, see Virgin, p. 18. At heart, Evangelicalism was an international movement, drawing on German pietism, the American "Great Awakening," and at least three discernible English strands: "Arminian Methodists following John Wesley, Calvinistic Methodists following George Whitefield, and those still in Church of England" (P. Butler 32).

[25] In Thomas Sheridan's *Lectures on the Art of Reading* (the fourth edition of 1790, which was owned by Austen and now resides in the Chawton House Library), Sheridan tried to create more evangelical zeal among Anglican clergy by helping them transmit the emotional content of the liturgy more fully to their parishioners. For instance, Sheridan offers advice about how to read the General Confession, a part of every service: "'We have followed too muc'h the devices and desires of our own hearts.' Here, by laying the stress on the word, *much*, there is no more implied, but that we have given way to our inclinations more than we should do; and that may admit of being interpreted, but in a small degree. But when it is repeated thus—'We have followed tòo much' the devices and desires of our own hearts' it implies, in a great degree, there are no boundaries fixed to our wanderings; and not only so, but the tone of voice accompanying that emphasis, includes at the same time self

As Sir James Stephens described the distinction in 1850, "an orthodox clergyman [was] one who held in dull and barren formality the very same doctrines which the Evangelical clergyman held in cordial and prolific vitality; . . . they differed from each other as solemn triflers differ from the profoundly serious" (II.155; qtd. in Neil 193). Anglican Evangelicals felt they had rediscovered the urgency of the Gospels, without losing the connection to state or national purpose.

It is partly for this reason that one of the key quarrels between Anglican and dissenting Evangelicals was the Anglican commitment to parishes in opposition to Wesleyan itinerism. In England, John and Charles Wesley were this idea's first ardent proponents. Itinerism holds that one walks the face of the earth seeking new souls to save (by traveling to Oglethorpe's colony in Georgia in 1735, both men performed their adherence to this commitment, baptizing Native Americans and colonists alike). Anglicans strongly resisted this movement, insisting that the parish must be the center of religious life. The Anglican Church is at heart, after all, episcopalian—that is, it is run by bishops within whose dioceses (or "episcopates") parishes function. Thus undermining the system of parishes was understood as "an unwarranted attack on clerical authority" (P. Butler 33).

Itinerism would have been one of the least attractive features of dissenting Evangelism for Austen, though she would not have been attracted much either by the movement's noisiness and reputation for fanaticism.[26] In fact, this issue of tone set Anglican Evangelicalism apart from other Evangelical strains; unlike the Methodists, for example, Evangelicals within the Church of England in general discouraged believers from focusing on emotion and feeling. The Anglican Evangelical John Newton, the reformed slave-ship captain and author of the hymn "Amazing Grace," is reputed once to have said, "'Don't tell me of your feelings. A traveler would be glad of fine weather, but, if he be a man of business, he will go on'" (Neil 194). Austen's novels and her prayers testify to her endorsement of duty over feeling, as well as her deep commitment to the ideal of stringent moral self-examination.

Anglican Evangelicalism was propelled to the fore of the Church through the urgency of the problem posed by the French Revolution. In 1789, Wilberforce's rallying cry became "Reform or Ruin." The fear was not simply of lost souls but

---

condemnation, and contrition" (101; the orthographic marks are in the original). Similarly, he gives advice about the Exhortation: "we usually find, that the clergyman's eye is fixed on the book, and that he utters the words as mere matter of form; but, surely, the truly Christian and affectionate address, with which it commences, from a pastor to his flock, ought to be made with earnestness, and his eyes looking round the whole congregation. 'Dèarly beloved brethren!'= And then should a pause of some length ensue, to give them time to collect themselves, and awaken their attention to the solemn duty they are about to perform. Whereas, in the other way, when the eye is on the book, the congregation cannot feel it as an immediate address to them" (95–6). My thanks to Susan Ford for her personal notes on this volume.

[26]   See Neil on the threat posed to Anglicanism by traveling lay preachers and their propensity to take over "dark" (i.e., unused) churches (190–91).

of losing the country itself to forces of religious and social upheaval. While the Evangelicals such as Hannah More and John Bowles thundered against the luxury and idleness of the Church and its aristocratic and gentry supporters, they were also decrying the possible effect such ills might have on the working classes, now particularly alive to the liberating possibilities of revolution. Most of the social and religious reforms Anglican Evangelicals promoted can be found as issues in Austen's 1816 *Mansfield Park*: non-residency, the abolition of the slave trade, the irreligiosity of urban elites, the importance of family prayers, the distrust of amateur acting, and the call to intense private self-examination.[27] Her favorite brother Henry, ordained in the same year *Mansfield Park* was published, himself became an enthusiastic Anglican Evangelical. Austen did not define herself as an Evangelical, but as her 1814 letter to her niece Fanny Knight makes plain, late in life she had considerable sympathy with their aims and views: "I am by no means convinced that we ought not all to be Evangelicals; & am at least persuaded that they who are so from Reason and Feeling, must be happiest & safest" (*L* 103). One might note, however, that the complex double negatives of the first part of this 15-word declaration indicate something of inevitable gentry suspicion of Evangelical fervor that Austen retained (see Chapter 2 for a further discussion of Austen's attitudes towards Evangelicals).

Evangelicals re-emphasized the ideas of conversion, the supremacy of Scripture, and the centrality of preaching the Gospel (P. Butler 33). Wilberforce, Anglican Evangelicanism's most famous adherent and the guiding light of the Clapham sect (a group of wealthy Evangelical laymen), put great stress on bringing nominal faith into action, through visible and conspicuous reform (Virgin 21). For Wilberforce, the key problem facing the Anglican Church was the "decay of the sense of sin" (Neil 193); from exposing this decay he hoped to abolish the slave trade and enact countless reforms for the underprivileged. One might wonder that a faith with such an emphasis on personal examination, inward holiness, and individual salvation would have been capable of outward action; however, the history of the nineteenth century gives ample testimony to the power of Evangelical-led reform, against slavery, child labor, and prostitution, and for prison and factory reform (Elmen 330). As the historians G. M. Young and W. D. Handcock argue, influenced by Evangelical fervor, "England became, perhaps, more nearly a Christian country than she had ever been before, perhaps more nearly than any comparable community before or since" (335; qtd. in Neil 243).

---

[27] As Macdonagh argues, "Clerical discipline; improvement, moral and behavioral; the priest as gospel-preacher; the duties of the parish and their failure in the city; the challenge of the Wesleyans—these were the burning issues for the serious in 1812–1813; and to each, the response in *Mansfield Park* is, almost classically, moderate. Root-and-branch reform of structures is never canvassed; but individual rectitude and earnestness in one's station are most strongly urged. The clergyman remains central to the order and government of the countryside; but both in and beyond this he is to be a true dispenser of the Word of God. Full-blown Evangelicalism and emotional indulgence in religion are implicitly rejected but . . . the great doctrines which infuse them [are not]—sin, hell, atonement and redemption" (14).

**Higher Criticism and the Reasonableness of Christianity**

England was largely Christian in the early nineteenth century partly because
Evangelical spirit had roused the Church out of lethargy and in part because it had
managed to avoid the earlier threats of Deism and German higher criticism. The
Deist challenge was put most forcefully by Matthew Tindal's *Christianity as Old as
Creation* (1730), but the Established Church responded to the challenge with William
Law's *The Case of Reason* (1731) and Butler's *Analogy of Religion* (1736) (P. Butler
32).[28] Both Law and Butler made rationalist arguments against the acceptance of
a religion stripped of most supernaturalism. Deism, after all, accepted belief in
some sort of God but rejected miracles, the Trinity, and the Incarnation. Both Law
and Butler argued, as had Locke earlier in his *The Reasonableness of Christianity*
(1695), that attention to probabilities, both cosmological and psychological, led
one to affirm Scriptural accounts of both the Old and New Testaments.[29] For
Butler, probability was to serve as "the great guide in life" (McGrade 110). The
analogical thinking Butler proposed set nature as a system imperfectly understood
next to religion as a system imperfectly understood. He argued that many features
of the former provide evidence for the latter: "the marked differences in the life-
stages of many creatures in nature, for example, lend plausibility to the idea that
our earthly life is a stage on the way to an immortal afterlife" (McGrade 110).
Anglican apologetics, based on the values of empiricism, reason, and natural law,
were continued in William Paley's 1794 *View of the Evidences of Christianity*
1794 and his 1802 *Natural Theology*, both widely read works. Austen may not
have read them but she inevitably would have known their arguments, because
they were rehearsed in many an Anglican sermon of her day. While mainstream
Anglican figures were not without their doubts (even that stalwart of orthodoxy,

---

[28]   Henry Sheldon in his 1895 *The History of the Christian Church* notes many of the
main responders to the Deist challenge most forcefully articulated by Tindal:

Lardner's *Credibility of the Gospel History*; Bentley's *Phileleutherus Lipsiensis* . . .
; Edward Chandler's *Defence of Christianity from the Prophecies of the Old Testament*;
Samuel Chandler's *Vindication of the Christian Religion* . . . ; Thomas Sherlock's *Use and
Intent of Prophecy*, also his noted treatise, *The Tryal of the Witnesses of the Resurrection of
Jesus*; Zachary Pearce's *Miracles of Jesus Vindicated*; Richard Smalbrooke's *Vindication
of Our Savior's Miracles*; William Law's *Case of Reason* . . . ; James Foster's *Usefulness,
Truth, and Excellency of the Christian Revelation*; John Conybeare's *Defence of Revealed
Religion*; Bishop Butler's *Analogy* . . . ; John Chapman's *Eusebius* . . . ; William Warburton's
*Divine Legation of Moses Demonstrated*, also his *View of Lord Bolingbroke's Philosophy*;
John Leland's general work entitled *A View of the Principal Deistical Writers*, besides
several specific treatises from his pen. (17)

[29]   As John Tolad, one of Locke's contemporaries, argued, "there is nothing in the
Gospel contrary to reason nor above it; . . . no Christian doctrine can be properly called a
mystery" (Roston 94). Locke himself held that a strict exercise of reason could demonstrate
the existence of God, and that "there were objective, rational grounds for accepting Jesus as
the Messiah" (McGrade 110).

Dr. Johnson, admitted his faith was not easy, and that he himself had worked out the objections held by Hume to religion long before he had read Hume himself [Bogel 51]), apologetics such as Law's, Butler's, and Paley's ensured that the tenor and focus of Anglican debate in the late decades of the eighteenth century and the first decades of the next were not directed particularly at the question of belief or disbelief but rather at the need to reform Church attitudes, practice, and structure. Most Anglicans, including Austen, were sure they had fully reasonable grounds for believing in Christian doctrine and Scripture.[30]

In fact, the British intelligentsia was remarkably incurious about the skeptical Biblical scholarship consuming German theologians of the day.[31] Throughout the eighteenth century, orthodox writers such as Pope and his followers had satirized

---

[30]  An important partial dissent from this proposition can be found in Knox-Shaw's important *Jane Austen and the Enlightenment*. He argues that Austen would have been exposed to and influenced by the skeptical wing of Enlightenment thought. Knox-Shaw's focus, however, is on the emergence of scientific thinking, liberal and/or radical challenges to social orthodoxy and ideas about culture, and evangelical ardor and humorlessness rather than on religious belief as such (for a discussion of the evangelicals and Austen, see Knox-Shaw's chapters five and six in particular). For instance, he and I agree that "though Jane Austen seems to have been influenced by the radical argument that the structure of society had a determining effect on the formation of character, she was not sufficiently impressed by the idea to abandon belief in social hierarchy" (105). Of course, most English Enlightenment figures were orthodox Christians—Newton and Locke being powerful examples. Jocelyn Harris has shown persuasively the traces of Locke's thought in Austen, discernible even if one does not believe Austen read Locke for herself, given his influence over eighteenth-century English philosophy and theology.

[31]  Hans Frei's highly influential reading of the national differences between Germany and Britain in the late eighteenth and early nineteenth century holds that German scholars applied their Enlightenment-powered critical interests to Biblical texts because they had no tradition of realist fiction in which to work out similar issues of probability, cause, and effect. Frei states, "[England and Germany were] two countries in which discussion of the biblical narratives was the most intense in the eighteenth century. In England, where a serious body of realistic narrative literature and a certain amount of criticism of that literature was building up, there arose no corresponding cumulative tradition of criticism of the biblical writings, and that included no narrative interpretation of them. In Germany on the other hand, where a body of critical analysis as well as general hermeneutics of the biblical writings built up rapidly in the latter half of the eighteenth century, there was no simultaneous development of realistic prose narrative and its critical appraisal" (142). Frei adds, "In England the interest in the historical factuality and/or the general themes of the biblical narratives subverted more than the technical appreciation of these writings as realistic narratives. Also pushed out of the way was all concern with what kinds of writings these narratives might be. Their narrative structure and their literary-historical origin and development were largely ignored. Whatever else the fruits of the deist debates [might have been], interest was concentrated from that day forward largely on criticism of the facts and not of the writing of the bible" (151). Austen is thus part of this cultural pattern, with her novels making claims not of representing actuality but human probability, while the same reliance on probability provided the main bulwark of her belief, to the degree she required its rational or evidentiary examination.

those like Tindal, Whitefield, or Wesley, who challenged the existing order in religion (Sutherland 39–40). Elinor Shaffer argues that the only sect interested in higher criticism by the 1790s was the Unitarians. She notes that Thomas Belsham, the founder of the Unitarian Book Society in 1791, was one of the first in England to accept the results of the new scholarship: "composite authorship of the Pentateuch, the unhistorical nature of stories of miraculous birth, the unscientific, that is the mythological nature of the creation story" (26). Radical publications such as *The Monthly Review* and *The Critical Review* greeted his writings, as they did those of the Catholic Alexander Geddes, whose 1792 translation of the Bible severely curtailed its mythological aspects (Shaffer 27), but the Anglican center of opinion was mostly untouched. Later radicals such as Shelley who proclaimed their atheism were often so pilloried that they left England (Shelley first left in 1814 after publishing *The Necessity of Atheism* in 1811). Shaffer argues that "not until the 1830s in England [was] knowledge of the most advanced Continental scholarship [anything other than] a stick [with which] to beat the Anglican academic Establishment, pictured by Unitarian journals as sunk in parochial ignorance, sloth, and obscurantism" (25).

Thus, Austen was little disturbed by arguments attacking the truth claims of Christianity. We know that she endorsed the probabilistic arguments of figures such as Locke, Law, and Butler, because she is on record saying she preferred the sermons of Thomas Sherlock to perhaps any other (*L* 278). His most well-known work in Austen's day was his *Tryal of the Witnesses of the Resurrection of Jesus* (1743). In it Sherlock imagines a group of gentlemen creating a mock trial on the question of the historicity of the Gospel accounts, including the miraculous elements. Repeatedly, the appeal is made to human nature as an argument for scriptural plausibility. For instance, what other than the Resurrection could account for the transformation of the apostles from cowards lurking in an upper room into the world-traveling bearers of the Gospel who, all but one of whom (John) ultimately died for their faith? As Sherlock writes, "The Council for the Apostles insisted . . . that they gave the great Assurance to the World that possibly could be given of their sincere Dealing, by suffering all kind of Hardship, and at last Death itself, in Confirmation of the Truth of their Evidence. . . . [If you] consider that they dy'd for the Truth of a Matter of Fact which they had seen themselves, you will perceive how strong the Evidence is in this Case" (103–4).[32] Austen must have

---

[32]    The summary of Sherlock's argument in this section of the *Tryal* is notable for its reliance on Lockean empiricism:

When a Man reports to me an uncommon Fact, yet such a one as in its own nature is a plain Object of Sense, if I believe him not, it is not because I suspect his Eyes, or his Sense of Feeling, but merely because I suspect his Sincerity; for if I was to see the same thing myself, I should believe myself; and therefore my Suspicion does not arise from the Inability of human Senses to judge in the Case, but from a Doubt of the Sincerity of the Reporter; in such Cases therefore there wants nothing to be prov'd, but only the Sincerity of the Reporter; and since voluntary suffering for the Truth is at least a Proof of Sincerity, the Sufferings of the Apostles for the Truth of the Resurrection is a full and unexceptionable Proof. (104–5)

found such an argument compelling, relying as it does on human probabilities, one of Austen's own strongest commitments in her fiction.[33]

Austen's own brother Henry later made similar probabilistic arguments based on common human motivation to explain why one should take the *Genesis* account of creation as historically accurate. In an 1818 book of apologetics, he argued that Moses, then the assumed author of the Pentateuch (the first five books of the Bible), would have known that saying Eve came from Adam's rib would upset his Jewish readers, and thus included the detail only because it was true and he could not escape it:

> . . . it must occur [to the sober-minded reader] that Moses, whose interest it was to persuade those for whose instruction he wrote, would never, from his own invention, or any other authority short of divine, have made a statement so likely to inspire doubt and disbelief in the minds of the Jews, whom he knew to be a perverse and stiff-necked people. As neither the glory, not profit nor influence of Moses could have induced him to assert such a gratuitous and dangerous falsehood, I must ever consider that his veracity on the above point is sufficiently established by the very singularity of the fact. (24)

In other words, the sheer improbability of the event argues for its probability, given the hostile and skeptical nature of Moses's original audience. Something similar is revealed in the apologetics of Soame Jenyns, noted MP, poet, and popular essayist. Writing in 1776 to prove the truth claims of Christianity, Jenyns argues that Christianity is so implausible that reason requires one to accept it: "For if we have once reason to be convinced, that this religion is derived from a supernatural origin; prophecies and miracles will become so far from being incredible, that it will be highly probable, that a supernatural revelation should be foretold, and inforced by supernatural means" (*View* 5).

---

[33]   Allied to this presumption of reason in the face of seeming unreason is the prodigious work of Isaac Barrow, the seventeen-century divine whose sermons were widely published and republished in the eighteenth century (Jane Austen would have known him and Coleridge often cites his work). As Clayton Koelb explains, Barrow "assumes that the language of Scripture signifies intelligibly on every level and in every conceivable mode of reading. The infinite readability of the biblical text is never an embarrassment for Barrow but is always the occasion for greater feats of scholarly and rhetorical dexterity. The divine authorship of Scripture seems to mean for Barrow that all possible readings of a biblical passage always already exist as part of its intentional structure" (3–4). In other words, because the Bible is presumed to be rational, nothing in it or to be derived from it, no matter how ingenious or even implausible, can be irrational.

## The Book of Common Prayer

The practicing Anglican would have had his or her faith reinforced by the 1662 version of the *Book of Common Prayer*.[34] Cranmer's masterpiece, this work is much more than a volume of church services; Louis Weil makes a common claim when he argues that "in no other Christian tradition does the authorized liturgy take on so great a significance" (55).[35] The *Book of Common Prayer* combines all the texts necessary for the Sunday service, whether Eucharist or Morning or Evening Prayer, the litanies (long prayers of supplication in which the congregation gives set responses such as "Lord have mercy"), daily offices (i.e., daily church services), and services for baptism, confirmations, weddings, ordinations, final unction, and funerals. All the Psalms are there as well, because one or more psalms are part of every service. The collects (short prayers on specific subjects or for each particular day) are also included, partly because they are used in sequence throughout the church year but also because they are to be used in private prayer. Austen's own prayers parallel closely the language and ideas of the collects, focusing on God's mercy and grace as the only forces capable of forgiving the errors and sins of her and her family. Another important part of the *Book of Common Prayer* and central to church dogma and its teaching mission was the catechism, a series of questions and answers that were to guide the young or beginning communicant as he or she learned about the faith prior to confirmation (in Austen's day, the afternoon service on Sundays commonly substituted teaching about the catechism for a sermon).

The *Book of Common Prayer* also contains the lectionary: charts that detail which passages from Scripture (readings from the Old Testament, Psalms, New Testament, and, as its own category, the Gospels) are to be read on which day, given a three-year cycle. Cranmer devised the lectionary so that all of the New Testament would be read every four months and the Old Testament every year, except for certain repetitions (much of the Gospels of Matthew, Mark, and Luke include the same material with only slight variations).[36] Through this system, all of the Psalms would be read each month. The lectionary assumed that the believer would make use of daily offices; otherwise the schedule inevitably loses its force.

---

[34]    There were hardly any changes to the *Book of Common Prayer* between 1662 and Austen's day. Outside the Anglican Church, John Wesley adapted the Anglican liturgy for the Methodists, omitting, for instance, the giving of a ring in the wedding service and the husband's vow, "with my body I thee worship." There were also variants introduced by the Anglicans in the United States, the Episcopalians, in 1790, for their own prayer book (Cuming 179–80).

[35]    Arguably the liturgy of the Eastern Orthodox Church is at least as significant for its practitioners.

[36]    Cranmer also left out, in his own words, "certain bokes and Chapiters, which bee least edifying" (Hatchett 123). Cranmer's omissions are arguably more significant than his own claim might imply. The Jewish tradition poses an interesting contrast, for in a year's worship services, orthodox Jews read the entire Torah, including the horrific, confounding, and/or sexual material regardless of those passages' potential to offend or confuse.

Certainly, as Austen grew up, her own family participated in morning and evening family prayers on a daily basis. George Austen's letter to his son Frank as Frank prepared to go off to sea confirms that this practice was the case in the Austen family. He urged that in lieu of the family gatherings, Frank should continue morning and evening prayers in private as much as he possibly could. "The first & most important of all considerations to a human being is Religion," Frank's father wrote (George Austen, "Memorandum"). Frank evidently remained a highly observant Christian; he won promotion in the Navy in part because Admiral Gambier, an evangelical, was attracted by Frank's piety, as he became known as the "officer who knelt in church" (Hubback and Hubback 144). In the next chapter, we will explore the particulars of Austen's participation in worship and prayer, but it is important to note that the *Book of Common Prayer* was designed as both a private and public resource, and that it knit the private and public religious experiences together: "Thus there was, in the hands of any churchman who could read, a book which linked private with public prayer, which showed the Bible as a text to be used in worship and which embraced the whole range of human life, personal as well as social" (Allchin 315).[37] As Weil notes, "the Prayer Book is first of all the basis for corporate prayer. . . . In addition to this essential role, and as a kind of natural overflow from it, the Prayer Book is also a formative element in the private prayer of Anglicans. Even in solitude, the use of the collects or psalms or the texts of the various rites, links the individual Anglican at prayer with the common prayer of the larger fellowship" (55).

Readers of Austen who not familiar with Anglican worship may not know how much the liturgy shapes religious practice by simple repetition, particularly in an age when daily prayers in the morning and evening were common. As the lectionary schedule makes evident, Austen would have heard and herself recited Morning and Evening Prayer countless times in her life; she would have heard most of Old and New Testaments dozens of times, outside of her own private reading, which would have added to the total. By my conservative calculation, she would herself have said the Lord's Prayer about 30,000 times in her life. It is hard to make exact claims about the effect of all this repetition, especially daily

---

[37] We will return in Chapter 3 to Olivia Smith's important work on the class ramifications of eighteenth-century elite efforts to regulate grammar, pronunciation, speech, spelling, and rhetoric. In reference to the *Book of Common Prayer*, however, it should be noted that its use by Anglicans of all classes provides the one important contrary example to her general point about how vulgar language implied "one was morally and intellectually unfit to participate in the culture. . . . Only the refined language was capable of expressing intellectual ideas and worthy sentiments, while the vulgar language was limited to the expression of the sensations and the passions. Such a concept required making the refined as different from the vulgar language as possible while also requiring that certain types of thought and emotions be advocated to the detriment of others" (2). In other words, even Anglicans who could not read would learn much of the liturgy by the force of repetition, and would in this way participate in elite language (in fact, in the language held up in the eighteenth century as the highest model of propriety and grace—Cranmer's).

repetition, on one's mental landscape and sense of language; I think it is fair to claim that the effect for Austen must have been considerable.

Further, the repetitions of the liturgy presume that collective faith reinforces individual faith and vice versa. Weil argues that for Anglicans, "[f]aith is not seen as a private matter between God and the believer. Faith is corporate: it is the common faith of the Church into which new members are baptized and come to participate in the power of the paschal mystery . . . The Church itself is seen as an article of faith, the fellowship of all those who share a common identity in Christ" (54). The role of the Prayer Book in shaping private prayer and linking it to corporate prayer is vital. The tradition of Anglicanism gives its endorsement to the specific wording of its prayers. Long, heated, and ancient arguments inform many of the choices in these prayers, arguments that are in many cases ongoing—for instance, should the Nicene Creed begin with "I believe" or "We believe"? The exact words matter; one might argue that the dictionary, more than the Bible, is the Anglican book of choice. In fact, Anglicanism has an adage that speaks to this connection between doctrine and wording, *lex orandi legem statuat credendi*—"the law of prayer establishes the law of faith" (Weil 55). So strong is this sense that one says these exact words and not others that the contemporary Anglican writer Annie Dillard explains that "I often think of the set pieces of liturgy as certain words which people have successfully addressed to God without their getting killed" (59).

## Natural Theology and Natural Law

The *Book of Common Prayer* shows the main tenets of Anglican faith as it is expressed in the liturgy and catechism. What it does not completely express is the particular cast of faith, the emphases and stresses, made by Anglican orthodoxy in Austen's lifetime. Orthodoxy did not shift particularly from the Reformation until the Regency, but Church leaders increasingly focused on "natural religion," drawn from natural law and from the presumed lessons of nature. For the eighteenth-century believer, the varieties of landscape gave unambiguous evidence of God's creative power and his merciful hand (we will see this idea clearly in Fanny's rapturous apostrophes to the evergreen and the stars in *Mansfield Park*). The application of reason in the face of nature made God's role plain, and divines spoke often of God's beauty as it was revealed in the created universe everyone could perceive. William Derham, a priest writing in 1714, held that one should "treat all of nature's wonders as signs of the greatness of God, as marks and badges which acknowledge the existence of God to the believer" (Korshin 372). All things were ordered by a divinely rational code. The Church itself presumably was a sign of God's power and mercy; that is, it was assumed to have evidentiary powers about God's nature. Another divine, Edward Reynolds, makes an argument that shows how these two arguments from design were commonly linked: "The sum and total of all God's works are the world and the church; the world is called *kosmos* for the beauty and comeliness of it; in which everything was very good when the Lord took a view of it. But the Lord has chosen his church upon which to bestow more abundant glory. . . . In the world we have the foot-prints of his greatness; but in the church we have the image of his holiness" (Allchin 323).

Theology was thus "natural" and "rational." In 1860, the eminent church historian Mark Pattison held that Locke's title—*The Reasonableness of Christianity* (1695)—would do as a title for much of the sermons and apologetics of the Georgian Church (II. 46; qtd. in Walsh and Taylor 42). This emphasis on reason should *not* be read as a stage in the onward march of secularization; rather, those urging reason "saw themselves not as undermining the foundations of revealed religion, but as strengthening them against the onslaught of skeptics and infidels" (Walsh and Taylor 43). The governing idea of rational theology was that virtue is good for us, and that God has planned for human virtue. As Anthony Hastwell proclaimed in a sermon in the 1790s, "It was plain that every means had been adopted to temper the demands of Christianity to the infirmities of unregenerate human nature, and to promise the consolations of religion to the weakest of its professors" (N. Sykes 260–61).

Those "weakest of its professors" were sure of charitable tolerance, the key feature of eighteenth-century Anglican Latitudinarianism, a frame of mind that valued ecumenism over schism and the wider interpretations of theology over more exacting fundamentalisms. In keeping with the basic tolerance of eighteenth-century Anglicanism, Butler's *The Analogy of Nature* had argued that moral obligation is an essential feature of the rational universe; he concludes that that the rules of nature and heaven, body and spirit, self-love and charity, are not opposed polarities but are supplementary to each other. God's creation makes self-evident within human nature, through the auspices of conscience, the grounds on which morality is to be judged (Elmen 329). As Butler concluded, "Man hath the rule of right within; what is wanting is only that he honestly attend to it" (48; qtd. in Elmen 329). This notion is remarkably congruent with what Fanny urges upon Henry Crawford, when he asks her to act as his own "'rule of right'": "'We have all a better guide in ourselves, if we would attend to it, than any other person can be'" (*MP* 478).

Nature was assumed to follow the Great Chain of Being, a concept derived from a mix of Platonic and Aristotelian thought, admixed with a Christian conception of Godhead, which still held considerable sway. In fact, Arthur Lovejoy's magisterial work on the Great Chain of Being argues that the eighteenth century marked the high point of this idea's acceptance (183). As I will explore further in Chapter 3, the notion of the Great Chain of Being places all of creation in a hierarchy, from God and his angels through human beings in their multitudinous stations through animals, plants, and down to the minerals of the earth. Creation is assumed to be filled with every creature it should have (the doctrine of "plenitude"), to have no gaps (the doctrine of "continuity"), and to be organized in steps in terms of a creature's relative distance from God (the doctrine of "graduation"). Read analogously, the Great Chain of Being argues implicitly that God has designed social hierarchies, and has placed kings and charcoal-burners in their respective places. Virgin argues that "[i]n Georgian England, conventional wisdom held that inequality, far from being a sign of sin, was a proof of virtue. The principle of hierarchy was detected in nature, and it was thought right and fitting that this principle should also be operative in all the affairs of men" (33).

The idea of the Chain also underscored the sense of human limitations and of religious decorum. Dr. Johnson, perhaps the quintessential English Christian of the eighteenth century, nonetheless wrote no religious poetry as such because he felt doing so was hubristic. As Murray Roston argues

> The authors of the Bible were regarded as haloed figures inspired directly from heaven and therefore not to be imitated by mere humans. An age of rules and of Reason is concerned primarily with definitions and hence with limits. In the great Chain of Being, man existed on the narrow isthmus between the beasts and the angels and to attempt to write psalms was rather like trying to fly. One could paraphrase, translate, or even imitate, but to write a new set of psalms based on one's own religious experiences was beyond the limits of man. (103)

Austen too had a clear sense of religious decorum. Unlike almost all of her novel-writing contemporaries, she refrained from citing Scripture, inserting theological passages, creating Biblical parallels with her plots, or even naming her characters after major Biblical figures. As Doody notes, the multitude of Marys in her fiction are there because there were many Marys in her world, not to call forth resonances with the Virgin Mary or Mary Magdalene ("Jane Austen's Reading" 348).

Last of all, understanding Austen's Anglicanism requires understanding its view of history, of its presumptions about the narrative of the cosmos from beginning to end, and the relation of the individual to that cosmic history. In the Christian view of time, history began at the Creation and Fall, was redeemed by Christ's passion and Resurrection, and will end at his Second Coming. This view of the world, *sub specie aeternitatis* (seen under the view of eternity)—inevitably shapes one's view of individual circumstance. If reality is to be found only after death, then the "events of this world become telescoped as one gaze[s] steadfastly towards the world to come" (Roston 43). This steadfast gaze was one of the most common themes of eighteenth-century sermons, and we find Austen's adherence to it in her prayers and in her letters, especially when she writes of the death of friends and family members.

The overall narrative of history's redemption is also signaled in her plots. Gary Kelly has argued that Austen repeatedly writes a kind of "Anglican romance" (169) in which the operations of free will (the characters' choices) conjoin with the intervention of grace (narrative control of the plot) to create an Anglican narrative of redemption that is specifically not deterministic (163).[38] Christian typology

---

[38]   Kelly adds that "her narrative method has historical religious implications, too. The Roman Catholic Church insisted on the authority of priest and church, but many Protestant Dissenting sects based religious authority on individual religious experience and based ecclesiastical authority on the will of the community of believers. The Church of England took a middle way, making salvation the responsibility of the individual, though guided by priest and church doctrine and authorized by an apostolic succession of bishops claiming direct succession from Christ's disciples" (161).

is important here. Though Austen resists typological writing as such, the basic typological parallel between Christ's passion and the individual's struggle for redemption and happiness marks each of her novels, as Michael Giffin has shown in detail. As Frei notes, this idea holds that "though real in his own right, the atoning Redeemer is at the same time a figure or type of the Christian's journey; for this is the narrative framework, the meaningful pattern within which alone the occurrence of the cross finds its applicative sense. What is real, and what therefore the Christian really lives, is his own pilgrimage; and to its pattern he looks for the assurance that he is really living it" (153–4). This way of understanding experience was basic to Anglican discourse, especially Evangelical discourse. By an act of faith, this reading of individual history "raises from . . . the individual happening an affirmation of some kind of [Christian] normativeness" (Caruth 4).[39]

Austen's religious inheritance conjoins orthodox Christian belief with attitudes forged in the crucible of seventeenth- and eighteenth-century religious controversies and cultural changes. Her religious views inevitably are admixed with the complexities of what it meant to have Tory and gentry allegiances. Austen's own particular religious experiences follow from her Anglican upbringing and her Anglican presuppositions, and they in turn provide important guidance in our understanding of how she thought and the words she used.

---

[39]    Joseph Wiesenfarth extends the reading by Christian allegory even further, following the plot elements of romance in Austen's novels back into *mythos*: "A serious interest in structure . . . ought naturally to lead us from *Pride and Prejudice* to a study of the comic form it exemplifies, the conventions which have presented much the same features from Plautus to our own day. The conventions in turn take us back into myth. When we compare the conventional plot of a play of Plautus with the Christian myth of a son appeasing the wrath of a father and redeeming his bride, we can see that the latter is quite accurately described, from a literary point of view, as a divine comedy" (61).

# Chapter 2
# Jane Austen as an Anglican and Anglicanism in the Novels

The benevolence of her heart, the sweetness of her temper and the extraordinary endowments of her mind obtained the regard of all who knew her and the warmest love of her intimate connections. Their grief is in proportion to their affection, they know their loss to be irreparable, but in their deepest affliction they are consoled by a firm though humble hope that her charity, devotion, faith and purity have rendered her soul acceptable in the sight of her REDEEMER.

—from the ledger-stone marking Austen's grave in Winchester Cathedral

Even when contemporary interpreters of Jane Austen attend to the religious contexts of her real and fictional worlds, they are apt to make mistakes. For example, the 1996 film of *Emma* directed by Douglas McGrath includes a scene in which Emma prays before the altar of her parish church, asking God to keep Mr. Knightley from marrying Harriet Smith. First, understanding Austen's premise that none of her heroines could be irreligious as such (as opposed to faulty or selfish) makes plain how unlikely it is that Austen would depict Emma as so spiritually lost as to petition God for thoroughly selfish aims. Second, if the filmmakers had known that "serious reflection" in the novels means praying, they would have known that Austen's characters do indeed pray at key moments of grief, trauma, or thankfulness. They do so, however, in private, at home. Using the parish church as a kind of private chapel would simply not be done by a young woman in Emma's position. The passage from the novel that the filmmakers use as the basis of Emma's prayer does reveal Emma's *desires*. In free indirect discourse, Austen shows that Emma is indulging an "ardent wish"—that Mr. Knightley "remain single all his life"—and is still self-deluded: "Could she be secure of that, indeed, of his never marrying at all, she believed she should be perfectly satisfied" (453). Though Emma is being selfish, she is not so reprehensible as to believe that her wishes constitute an appropriate petition to God. At the novel's end, Emma does pray, "serious in her thankfulness," when Harriet is happily bestowed upon Robert Martin (519).

This miscue in the film is just one of innumerable small errors made by contemporary readers of Austen's works. Readers may sense, indeed, that hers was a world in which Christian belief and values were important, and yet one cannot expect a reader to bring more to their readings than limited or imprecise information about how Jane Austen herself practiced her faith and how her faith governed to some vital degree all her other concerns, including her fiction. In particular, modern readers are likely to mistake the few direct mentions of religious practice in the novels for a sign of religion's relative unimportance. Austen's religious environment and her individual religious presumptions were drawn from the orthodox Anglicanism practiced by the Tory gentry to whom she belonged. Understanding this relationship helps us discern the religious ground of all her fiction. Such detailing even helps explain the religious decorum that itself *prevented* her from making religious material more conspicuous. In a sense, looking for the religious ground in Austen's novels is somewhat like looking through the novels for mentions of the physical ground, the actual dirt of her Georgian landscapes. She refers to the ground on which her heroines walk when it is important to what happens (as when Elizabeth Bennet's walk to Netherfield makes her petticoats muddy, or when a similar muddiness of ground leads Lord Osborne to recommend half-boots to Emma Watson in *The Watsons*); otherwise, the ground is unremarked. Something very similar happens with her treatment of religious belief, but religious belief and its presumptions about human identity, morality, purpose, and history remain underfoot at every moment.

## The Family's Defense

Not surprisingly, after her death, her family members spoke with one voice about Austen's commitment to Christianity in general and Anglicanism in particular, and about her goodness, sweetness, and love for others. Her brother Henry, newly ordained as a clergyman, focused on the depth of her religiosity in his "Biographical Notice of the Author," first published in 1818 as a preface to *Northanger Abbey* and *Persuasion*, but written in December, 1817, about six months after her death in July of that year. His sister, he wrote, was notable for her piety. There was no "sincerer Christian" entombed in Winchester Cathedral, and in her last days, "her love of God . . . [never] flagged for a moment" (6–7). The "Notice" canvasses her life history, her last days, her physical appearance, her accomplishments, her temperament, and her deprecation of herself as an "authoress," but at its end, Henry Austen comes to a paragraph in which he explains what he considers his sister's most important trait:

> One trait only remains to be touched on. It makes others unimportant. She was thoroughly religious and devout; fearful of giving offence to God, and incapable of feeling it towards any fellow creature. On serious subjects she was well-instructed, both by reading and meditation, and her opinions accorded strictly with those of our Established Church. (8)[1]

---

[1]   This ending paragraph also helps remedy the prickly beginning of the "Notice," in which Henry fails to disguise his distaste for Austen's readers: "When the public, which has not been insensible to the merits of "Sense and Sensibility," "Pride and Prejudice," "Mansfield Park," and "Emma," shall be informed that the hand which guided that pen is now mouldering in the grave, perhaps a brief account of Jane Austen will be read with a kindlier sentiment than simple curiosity" (4). The double negative of "has not been insensible" and the conventional but grotesque phrase of "mouldering in the grave" introduces an unexpected harshness to what purports to be a short biography, upbraids readers for their faults in not having been previously *more* sensible to the merits of Austen's works, and makes an appeal to readers that they think about Austen in a graver mode—as a Christian addressing other Christians.

The use of "our" here shows plainly that Henry Austen assumed Austen's readers were also Anglicans, for while his declaration of Austen's *bona fides* as a Christian is meant primarily as a testimony, it also promises religious solidarity between author and audience.

Similar testimony came from her sister Cassandra. Writing to her niece, Fanny, soon after Austen's death, Cassandra described her as a "dear angel":

> If I think of her less as on earth, God grant that I may never cease to reflect on her as inhabiting Heaven & never cease my humble endeavours (when it shall please God) to join her there. . . . May the sorrow with which she is parted from on earth be a prognostic of the joy with which she is hailed in Heaven! (*L* 345–8).

Her oldest brother, James, another priest, wrote verses on the subject of her death that end with lines parallel to Cassandra's perspective, and which speak of Austen's ascension into heaven as a kind of apotheosis of her "Sense, Intelligence, and mind":

> For oh! If so much genuine worth
> In its imperfect state on Earth
> So fair and so attractive proved
> By all around admired and loved:
> Who then the Change dare calculate
> Attendant on that happy state,
> When by the body unconfined
> All Sense, Intelligence and mind
> By Seraphs born through realms of light
> (While Angels gladden at the sight)
> The Atherial Spirit wings its way
> To regions of attendant day. (Selwyn 50)

These early reminiscences are augmented by her nephew Edward Austen-Leigh's view that she was "a humble, believing Christian" (at 18, he was with his father Edward and his uncle Henry as they escorted Austen's bier to her funeral), and by all the later family's evidence, such as Mary Augusta Austen-Leigh who claimed that her piety "ruled her in life and supported her in death" (94).[2] A neighbor of

---

2    Perhaps one of the most compelling testimonies about Austen's character comes from this nephew, James Edward Austen-Leigh, writing over 50 years after her death:

Many may care to know whether the moral rectitude, the correct taste, and the warm affections with which she invested her ideal characters, were really existing in the native source whence those ideas flowed, and were actually exhibited by her in the various relations of life. I can indeed bear witness that there was scarcely a charm in her most delightful characters that was not a true reflection of her own sweet temper and loving heart. I was young when we lost her; but the impressions made on the young are deep, and though in the course of fifty years I have forgotten much, I have not forgotten that 'Aunt Jane' was the delight of all her nephews and nieces. We did not think of her as being clever, still less as being famous; but we valued her as one always kind, sympathizing, and amusing. To all this I am a living witness. (*Memoir* 2–3)

Austen's in Chawton, Mrs. Barrett, also recalled her commitment to her faith: "Miss Austen . . . had on all the subjects of enduring religious feeling the deepest and strongest convictions, but a contact with loud and noisy exponents of the then popular religious phase made her reticent almost to a fault" (Le Faye 233).

As I discuss in the Introduction, many modern critics and biographers find these assertions about Austen's deep religiosity implausible. Piety—even belief—such as Austen's is rare in contemporary life, of course, a factor that no doubt enhances contemporary skepticism. Critics tend to presume that the family's descriptions of Austen's religiosity are actuated by a desire to whitewash unpleasant facts about Austen's character—they imply, in fact, that the family colluded to misrepresent Austen to the world. Voicing distaste for the family's testimony by dismissing it as conventional piety, many critics focus on how the family's presentation of Austen as a firm believer is interlaced with its presentation of her as kindly, incapable of saying a cruel or insensitive word. The argument that usually follows—or at least that is strongly implied—is that since Austen demonstrably wrote cruel words, in her letters to Cassandra and in her fiction, she cannot have been the deeply religious—or kind—figure her family presented.

Basic problems with this argument are clear. As Chapter 4 will demonstrate in detail, Austen's propensity for thinking and writing amusing malice she herself recognized as her chief besetting sin. Her letters to Cassandra were the chief vehicle of her sometimes savage candor—almost all the most uncharitable statements and flashes of caustic wit of her adult life are contained within her correspondence with her older sister. Further, though we do not have Cassandra's letters, Austen gives multiple hints that Cassandra's letters to her were equally full of witty malice.[3] That Austen's malice rarely obtrudes into letters to other people shows she knew how to control her tongue and her pen outside of her relationship with her sister. Austen knew she fell again and again into the enjoyable sin of thinking uncharitably of others; her own prayers make plain how seriously she took this fault.[4] There is no particular reason, however, to disbelieve the family's

---

[3]    For instance, in a letter from 1799, Austen writes to her sister: "You must read your letters over five times in future before you send them, & then perhaps you may find them as entertaining as I do" (*L* 33). Just after Austen's death, Cassandra admitted to having not always been herself perfectly good to other people—an intriguing admission made in her letter to Fanny Knight of July 27, 1817: "I loved her only too well, not better than she deserved, but I am conscious that my affection for her made me sometimes unjust to & negligent of others, & I can acknowledge, more than as a general principle, the justice of the hand which has struck this blow" (*L* 344). That is, Cassandra in part views her sister's death as an appropriate divine punishment for Cassandra's unfair treatment of other people. Most probably, the bond between the sisters sometimes locked others out. What exactly Cassandra meant, however, is unclear, though she writes as if she knows that Fanny will understand.

[4]    Only one sermon written by her father George Austen has survived; his own marginal notations show that he delivered it eight times at Steventon and seven times at Deane, and family members presumably kept it because they thought it was one of his best (Jarvis 19). It is tempting to read something into Austen family attitudes towards wit,

insistence that Austen was kind and loving in her *behavior* to others. In fact, the letters show that Austen commonly allowed herself to proffer a malicious insight to Cassandra about people she knew after she had repressed herself in their presence, and her loving attentions to her family, especially her nieces and nephews, are evident throughout the letters. Those who find it hard to take Austen's Christianity seriously seem to insist on moral perfection from believers, a position far from that taken traditionally by the Church, which presumes that all believers will commit sin after sin throughout their lives, requiring them repeatedly to confess these sins to God and request forgiveness and mercy from Him. The assumption that Austen could not possibly have been a true Christian because her novels and letters demonstrate she was capable of thinking very unkind things—that because she was mean she could not have been pious—lies at the heart of the confusion. Austen was prone to malice, certainly. She was also clearly committed to a faith that taught her to control and repress that malice.

## Austen's Christian View of Death

If we had no record in the novels or in the family documents of Austen's serious commitment to her faith (though we do), there would still be ample evidence within her own letters and other writings to confirm it. In particular, the letters demonstrate that Austen's attitude towards death conformed entirely to Christian orthodoxy—the faithful dead are to be grieved, but since they go to eternal reward, grief should be tempered by Christian consolation. When people important to Austen died—such as her father, George Austen, her sister-in-law Elizabeth Knight, and her mentor and friend Mrs. Lefroy—Austen invariably reflected on their good and godly lives, their certain place in Heaven, the shortness of their suffering, and the needfulness for composure in the face of loss. One record of this attitude is in the letter she wrote to report her father's death to her brother Frank, then departing England as part of his commitment to the navy. Austen follows entirely conventional religious reasoning: one must be consoled by the fact that her father's death was quick and relatively painless, that his life was virtuous and exemplary and that he was such a good father to them, and that he is certain to go to Heaven:

> Our dear Father has closed his virtuous & happy life, in a death almost as free from suffering as his Children could have wished. . . . Heavy as is the blow, we

---

gossip, and malice from the scripture it takes as its text, the ninth verse of Psalm 5: "For there is no faithfulness in their mouth; their inward part is very wickedness; their throat is an open sepulcher; they flatter with their tongue." Collins points out that this sermon "was probably preached . . . on occasions (of which there were two or three every year) where the psalm in question was appointed for recitation by the congregation at Morning Prayer." She adds, "like much of his teaching, it may have ended, as did the psalm itself, on a note of promise to the faithful: 'For thou, Lord, wilt bless the righteous; with favour wilt thou compass him as with a shield'" (*Parson's Daughter* 53).

can already feel that a thousand comforts remain to us to soften it. Next to that of
the consciousness of his worth & constant preparation for another World, is the
remembrance of his having suffered, comparatively speaking, nothing. (*L* 96)

These vital ameliorations themselves require exertion and composure from
the Christian mourner. Regarding Elizabeth, who had died unexpectedly in 1808
just two weeks after the seemingly unproblematic birth of her eleventh child,
Austen wrote to Cassandra, then herself at Godmersham, the Knights' home:
"May the Almighty sustain you all. . . . We need not enter into a Panegyric on the
Departed—but it is sweet to think of her great worth—of her solid principles, her
true devotion, her excellence in every relation of Life. It is also consolatory to
reflect on the shortness of the sufferings which led her from this World to a better"
(*L* 147). Austen was entirely aware of the difficult balance between the need to
feel proper grief and the need for self-composure. After Elizabeth's death, her two
oldest sons came to Southhampton to visit with Austen, their aunt. She reports to
Cassandra that they were much moved by a sermon in church on suffering, but
also that after church they returned to play at "conundrums"—with Austen's clear
approval. Austen writes Cassandra about the boys: "They behave extremely well
in every respect, showing quite as much feeling as one wishes to see, and on every
occasion speaking of their father with the liveliest affection. His letter was read over
by each of them yesterday, and with many tears; George sobbed aloud, Edward's
tears do not flow so easily; but as far as I can judge they are both very properly
impressed by what has happened." Two sentences later, Austen is speaking of their
play: "We do not want amusement; bilbocatch, at which George is indefatigable,
spillikins, paper ships, riddles, conundrums, and cars, with watching the flow and
ebb of the river, and now and then a stroll out, keep us well employed" (*L* 150).
To feel real grief is important, but it seems equally important not to dwell in it.
Likewise, Austen felt for their eight-year-old sister, but was concerned still with
balance: "One must hope the impression will be strong, & yet one's heart aches for
a dejected Mind of eight years old," while for Fanny, Elizabeth's oldest daughter,
Austen urged exertion and resignation:

> Edward's loss is terrible, & must be felt as such, & these are too early days indeed
> to think of Moderation in greif [*sic*], either in him or his afflicted daughter—but
> soon we may hope that our dear Fanny's sense of Duty to that beloved Father will
> rouse her to exertion. For his sake, & as the most acceptable proof of Love to the
> spirit of her departed Mother, she will try to be tranquil and resigned. (*L* 147)

Aware of her own imminent death, Austen asked for and received final unction
and had her last communion.[5] Her last letters are full of gratitude for her loving
family, sorrow at their exertions and troubles, and faith in Heaven to come: "As to
what I owe to [Cassandra] and to the anxious affection of all my beloved family on

---

5    William Jarvis explains that "It is clear that [Austen] expected the approach of
death to summon up thoughts of God's purposes, an attitude of penitence for sin, a desire
to make amends to anyone who may have been offended and a determination to set one's
affairs in order" (121).

this occasion, I can only cry over it, and pray to God to bless them more and more" (*L* 343).[6] Her last words, as reported by Cassandra, were "'God grant me patience, pray for me Oh! Pray for me'" (*L* 344).[7]

---

[6] This same late letter was edited by her brother Henry (we know of it only through the *Biographical Notice*, as there is no remaining manuscript copy), and Henry's edits are in keeping with his sense of Austen's ability to turn from malice to kindness. First, he cuts a section but retains its final statement to demonstrate Austen's virtues: "[*She next touches with just and gentle animadversion on a subject of domestic disappointment. Of this the particulars do not concern the public. Yet in justice to her characteristic sweetness and resignation, the concluding observation of our authoress thereon must not be suppressed.*] . . . But I am getting too near complaint. It has been the appointment of God, however secondary causes may have operated." Henry Austen then adds one final "extract" to "*prove the facility with which she could correct every impatient thought, and turn from complaint to cheerfulness*": "You will find Captain --- a very respectable, well-meaning man, without much manner, his wife and sister all good humour and obligingness, and I hope (since the fashion allows it) with rather longer petticoats than last year" (*L* 343). Henry does not note how Austen's last characterization of a minor figure in her life manages subtly to dismiss him and his female relatives (Austen's turn to petticoats almost always rhetorically stood for dismissal, as in her famous statement on Byron: "I have read the Corsair, mended my petticoat, & have nothing else to do" [*L* 257]).

[7] Even the one example of art criticism we have from Austen supports her view of Christian death. Visiting her ill brother Henry in London in 1814, Austen saw Benjamin West's *Christ Rejected* at its first exhibit [Fig. 1]. She wrote Martha Lloyd that this work had the "first representation of our Saviour which ever at all contented me" (*L* 273). The comment is revealing. Austen implies that she has seen many figures of Christ before but found something lacking in all of them. In this large-scale painting, West depicts the moment when the High Priest rends his garment and calls for Christ's execution. What is notable about West's depiction is that Christ's face is so composed and tender. The exhibit's catalogue, which Austen would certainly have read, focuses on Christ's composure, resignation, and tranquility in the face of his coming death:

The Saviour whom the Pencil has wished to represent as standing with a divine composure, while with a dignified and mute pensiveness and resignation, he is absorbed in the grandeur of the end for which he 'came into the world' –evincing this tranquility amidst the thoughtless and savage tumult of men who were condemning him to the most cruel and lingering death. (Jarvis 90)

This composure and tenderness is entirely in keeping with Austen's own view of how death should be faced. These qualities are moreover the only qualities Austen ascribes directly to Christ in her third prayer, the one I believe is partly in her handwriting, in which she speaks of Christ's "Forbearance and Patience" (see Chapter 2, note 87).

Not everyone admired West's depiction of Christ. The very qualities of tenderness and resignation Austen seems to have preferred annoyed the critic William Hazlitt into sniping at West in indecorous terms. Hazlitt wrote in the June 26, 1814 issue of *The Campion*: "Mr. West has presented us with a naked, shivering dough-baked figure, that looks 'like a sick girl.' In aiming to give the extremes of sublimity and pathos, the artist has missed both; and for the awful tranquility of the Saviour of the World, has given the mawkish insensibility of the hero of a whining love-tale!" (Jarvis 90).

## Austen's Religious Practice and Reading

Austen's everyday experience of religion made the foundation of this life-long piety. First, it is important to note how thickly clerical was the atmosphere in which she lived. Austen lived in and among the church all her life. She was intimately connected with scores of clergymen, including her father, her grandfather, her great-grandfather, two of her brothers, two nephews, her sister's fiancé, and several of her cousins. She agreed to marry another clergyman, the Rev. Harris Bigg-Wither, before changing her mind, and, according to the family, was seriously attached to another clergyman before he died (M. Butler, "History" 202–3). She practiced her faith carefully. We know that she, like her creation Emma, was charitable to the poor, distributing foodstuffs and handiworks from her needle such as mittens or socks; she attended church regularly; she read religious texts commonly; she prayed more than daily.[8]

It is hard for modern readers to grasp how thoroughly religious practice permeated Austen's life. Anne Richards notes that "by the standards of this century, Austen's every day was overfull of duties and rituals" (142). The ordinary course of a weekday would have included morning and evening prayers, usually conducted with the family together, as well as briefer prayers Austen would have said privately both upon arising and going to bed. Grace was said before each meal and thanksgiving was said afterwards (Giffin 28). By my reckoning, she would have said the Lord's Prayer at least 30,000 times in her lifetime. On Sundays, she would have usually attended church twice, in the morning and in the late afternoon, each time for two to three hours (if she could not attend the afternoon service because of weather or illness, she would have taken part in evening prayers with her family, with a sermon read out loud in addition).

Her church attendance would have been in keeping with that of her gentry and clergy neighbors, and unexceptional. Austen's home county of Hampshire was by all measures one of the most observant and faithful shires in Britain. The Religious Census of 1851 showed that Hampshire was still the strongest in England in terms of measures such as sittings, attendances, and numbers of places of worship. In "worship density," defined as the density of places of worship per 10 square kilometers, Hampshire ranked among the top two counties, and its levels of occupancy (that is, the total attendances divided by its total sittings) were also very high. Austen lived in the Anglican heartland, one of its core areas of strength, where attendance at service, especially for clergy families, was taken for granted (Snell and Ell 59–71).[9] Church attendance was central to Austen's society.

---

[8]    In a letter to Cassandra in 1798, Austen details her Boxing Day charities (the letter was finished on December 26th): "I have given a pair of Worsted Stockings to Mary Hutchins, Dame Kew, Mary Seevens & Dame Stapes; a shift to Hannah Staples, & a shawl to Betty Dawkins; amounting in all to about a half a guinea" (*L* 31).

[9]    See also Jarvis, pp. 14–8, for a compendium of the places in her letters in which Austen mentions attending church.

It bound the rural world of the parish together, and presented its members with a chance to come together, dressed in their best. As Addison decades before noted in the *Spectator*:

> It is certain the country people would soon degenerate into a kind of savages and barbarians, were there not such frequent returns of a stated time in which the whole village meet together with their best faces and in their cleanliest habits, to converse with one another upon different subjects, hear their duties explained to them, and join together in adoration of the Supreme Being. Sunday clears away the rust of the week. (I.460)

Austen supplemented her church-going and religious observations at home with religious reading. We think of Austen as a reader chiefly of novels, but while she indeed read many, she also read many sermons. Irene Collins points out that Austen was "an assiduous reader of sermons and a sharp critic of those she heard from the pulpit" (*Parson's Daughter* 52), and she was as likely to be reading "serious" (i.e., religious) literature as she was to be reading the latest novel. We know she read the sermons of Thomas Sherlock, Thomas Gisbourne, Hugh Blair, James Fordyce, Robert Lowth, Robert South, Thomas Secker, Edmund Gibson, and Edward Cooper, among others, and it is highly probable she read such widely available and influential works such as Bishop Law's *A Serious Call to a Devout and Holy Life* (1728), Bishop Butler's *Sermons* (1726), and Vicesimus Knox's *Family Sermons* (1799).[10] She evidently had clear likes and dislikes. Margaret Doody argues that Austen did not much care for the highly fashionable Blair, a point of view intimated by the scene in *Mansfield Park* in which it becomes plain that the unregenerate Mary Crawford knows Blair's work but has not profited by it (Mary asserts that sermons can have little effect): "'How can two sermons a week, even supposing them worth hearing, supposing the preacher to have the sense to prefer Blair's to his own, . . . govern the conduct and fashion the manners of a large congregation for the rest of the week?'" (*MP* 108; cited by Doody 349). There is even clearer evidence Austen did not like the sermons of her cousin, the Rev. Edward Cooper—they were both too fervent and too intolerant for Austen's tastes, in violation of Anglican steadiness and latitudinarianism. In her letter of September 8, 1816, she writes to Cassandra that "We do not much like Mr. Cooper's new Sermons; --they are fuller of Regeneration & Conversion than ever—with the addition of his zeal in the cause of the Bible Society"; of his earlier collection of sermons in 1809, Austen could only praise the third volume

---

[10]     Austen brings Fordyce into that comic scene in *Pride and Prejudice* when Mr. Collins selects his *Sermons to Young Women* as family reading for the assembled Bennets. Though Kitty and Lydia yawn, they might well have attended to the start of Sermon XIV, "On Female Meekness," which asserts that "Dress and show will never captivate any but superficial minds. The reign of youth and beauty are necessarily short. Mere vivacity may amuse in a girl, but in a woman [it] cannot give lasting delight; and trifling accomplishments are all too feeble to fix the heart" (269).

in that these were "professedly practical" (*L* 167), and she had complained in a letter of 1808, after Elizabeth Knight's death, that one could only expect "cold comfort" from one of his letters of condolence (*L* 148). Thomas Gisbourne's work Austen also found useful. In a letter of 1805, she thanks Cassandra for sending her a book of Gisbourne's sermons, saying she was "pleased with it, and I had quite determined not to read it" (*L* 114). Gene Koppel suggests that she found material in Gisbourne to praise because Gisbourne focused on "habitual principles," the need for daily exertion as a guidance and preparation for life's vicissitudes (9). Certainly, the lack of "habitual principles" is what causes the moral downfall of figures like Willoughby, Maria Bertram, Henry Crawford, Lydia Bennet, and Mr. Elliot. Austen's religious vision focuses on daily exertion, goodness by habit, a point of view confirmed toward the end of her life when she wrote to her beloved niece Fanny praising her many virtues, sustained despite "so much Imagination, so much flight of Mind, such unbounded Fancies," and concludes, "Religious Principle I fancy must explain it" (*L* 334).

Austen's favorite writer of sermons seems to have been Thomas Sherlock. Of Sherlock, she said in a letter to her niece Anna that "I am very fond of Sherlock's Sermons, prefer them to almost any" (*L* 278). She would certainly have approved of Sherlock's insistence on the same habitual principles Gisbourne endorsed; Sherlock writes, "The love of God, and the love of our neighbour, if carefully attended to, will easily grow into a complete system of religion" (*Discourses* 232). Sherlock was tolerant and undogmatic; when advising his readers about confessing their sins, he endorses a generalized confession and argues that trying meticulously to account for each misdeed, known and unknown, could lead to morbid introspection and a lack of faith in God's mercy (Collins, "The Rev. Henry Tilney" 157). In surveying Sherlock's sermon on Luke 13:23–4 (in which Jesus tells his followers that many will try but few will enter the Kingdom of Heaven), the Anglican priest and Austen scholar William Jarvis characterizes Sherlock's argument as one proceeding with "leisurely dignity and solemnity, a refusal to rush to superlatives, . . . [with] a respect for natural religion, for reason, and for Scripture, and a [preference for] sense rather than sensibility" (20). Sherlock was not overly rationalistic in his sermons; in fact, one key passage in his *Discourses* holds that "faith has ever been the principle of religion, and must ever continue to be so; for, when all other gifts shall cease, faith, hope, and charity will be the only gospel graces which time will not destroy" (232). His sermons stressed self-examination (Richards 12); in one, he focuses on "sins committed in ignorance, sins we have fallen into through habit, and sins we have simply forgotten" and reminds the Christian reader that "for every idle word, how soon soever it slips from our memory, for every vain imagination of the heart, how soon soever it vanishes away, we shall give an account on the day of judgement" (Knox 176–80; qtd. in Collins, "The Rev. Henry Tilney" 155). This warning about the idle sins of speech probably spoke to the core of Austen's moral sensibility and to her sense of her own greatest failing, and, as Collins notes, the sin of speaking ill of others is one of the few sins Austen singles out for particular mention in her prayers ("The Rev. Henry Tilney" 155).

Even when she read novels instead of sermons, she read them seriously, that is, with regard to their religious content. For instance, while working on *Emma* in 1815 we have this reflection to Anna Lefroy on the novel *Rosanne, or a Father's Labour Lost* by Laetitia Matilda Hawkins: it is "very good and clever, but tedious. Mrs. Hawkins' great excellence is on serious subjects. There are some very delightful conversations and reflections on religion" (*L* 289). The novel deals with a young woman who converts her atheist father, a French freethinker; they both ultimately become Anglicans. Another "serious" text she read was the one novel attempted by Hannah More, the Evangelical writer and reformist, *Coelebs in Search of a Wife* (1809). She had misgivings about the work, mocking the "pedantry & affectation" of the hero's name (why should it not be the more honest "Caleb"?) (*L* 172). Maggie Lane has argued that in this case Austen's suspicion of Evangelicals was probably yoked to professional pique, since compared to Austen, More was an inferior novelist, but here More was successfully publishing a work in a genre she herself had earlier castigated as immoral, while Austen had yet to be published at all (162–3).[11] A few months later, Austen was happy enough to report that More's *Practical Piety*, a non-fictional treatise on religious behavior, was a success.

Austen's religious reading would have been supplemented by the *Book of Common Prayer*, which served as a resource for both communal and private worship and prayer. Austen must often have read through the "Forms of Prayer to be Used at Sea" as she directed her thoughts towards her two sailor brothers on missions in the Atlantic and the Mediterranean. The "Forms of Prayer to be Used at Sea" are powerfully poetic, with their invocation of the "terrible things, and wonders in the deep" and their assurance of God's mercy: "Great is the Lord, and greatly to be praised; let the redeemed of the Lord say so: whom he hath delivered from the merciless rage of the sea" (363). She would also have known the Commination, the service that denounces "God's anger and judgments against sinners" with its refrain from the congregation of "Amen" to such proclamations from the minister as "Cursed is he that removeth his neighbour's landmark," "Cursed is he that lieth with his neighbour's wife," and "Cursed is he that putteth his trust in man, and taketh man for his defence, and in his heart goeth from the Lord" (346–7).[12] She must have been amused by the extraordinary foresight of the "Table of Kindred and Affinity," which bars relations of certain degrees from marrying, wherein she would have read that a man may not marry his "wife's father's mother," nor his "son's son's wife," nor many other kin of improbable relation. (The Table did, however, allow one to marry one's first cousin, a common practice in Austen's day, which she depicts as occurring between Fanny and Edmund in *Mansfield Park*.)

---

[11] Lane also argues that Austen may have written *Mansfield Park* in response to *Coelebs in Search of a Wife*, taking up its plot of a young man searching for the ideal mate and finding her, at last, in his own home (164–5).

[12] A recent biographer of Austen's, David Nokes, takes as a key text for understanding Austen the comic curse on the Winchester races she wrote a few days before her death. I will examine this curse in Chapter 4, but it bears pointing out here that the poem makes more sense in context of the Anglican commination, understanding it as a parody of that rite.

## Austen's Experiences in Church

Religious services, religious reading, religious self-examination: these practices were core to Austen's daily life. This immersion in religious practice had profound effects, as we will see. *How* Austen worshipped is also important. Most importantly, Anglican worship, then and now, is liturgical. Liturgical worship means that the exact words for each service are used every time the service is said; there is very little that is improvisational in liturgical Anglican services, and there were far fewer improvisational elements in Austen's day than in contemporary Anglican practice.[13] The variants in a given service come in very specific ways: first, through the lectionary, which provides readings from the Old and New Testament in a predetermined cycle; second, through options about which collects and "sentences" (short selections from scripture) will be employed; and third, through the sermon (though even here there was a good deal of repetition, as we will see).[14] Austen heard the service of Evening Prayer, for instance, most Sunday afternoons and most weekday and Saturday evenings of her life. Again and again, she not only heard but herself said thousands of times the same words, such as this beginning of the General Confession:

> Almighty and most merciful Father; We have erred, and strayed from thy ways like lost sheep. We have followed too much the devices and desires of our own hearts. We have offended against thy holy laws. We have left undone those things which we ought to have done; And we have done those things which we ought not to have done; And there is no health in us. (*Book of Common Prayer* 33)

It is hard to demonstrate exactly the effect on Austen's consciousness of all this repetition, all this immersion in Scripture and the words of invocation, confession, petition, and creedal confirmation that comprise the liturgy. But while the effects cannot be quantified, it is hard to imagine that they were not powerful. If nothing else, as Doody notes, Cranmer's balanced and coordinated clauses, at least as much as Dr. Johnson's, served as models for the architecture of her own sentences (347). But the effect must have been more than stylistic. Admittedly, while we have no evidence on this count, Austen was probably not always attentive in the pews and at home in family service; she would have been superhuman not to have

---

[13] When Henry Crawford gives his considered opinion that the liturgy has too many "'redundancies and repetitions'" (*MP* 393), Austen is providing yet another clue about his moral vacuity, not proffering a serious critique. Henry goes on to admit that his attention often strays during prayers: "'nineteen times out of twenty I am thinking how such a prayer should be read, and longing to have it to read myself'" (393–4).

[14] As Hatchett notes, the whole of the Scriptures are covered by the Lectionary. Given daily offices (i.e., Morning Prayer and Evening Prayer each day, with the exception of those Sundays reserved for Holy Communion), the New Testament would be read in its entirety every four months (leaving aside repetitions such as found in the synoptic material of Matthew, Mark, and Luke) and the Old Testament every 12, while all of the Psalms would be read in a given month (123).

sometimes thought of other things while the service was going on. But that she was conscientious about her religious duties is clear. Her well-thumbed copy of William Vickers's *Companion to the Altar*, given to her at the age of 18 prior to her confirmation, testifies to her interest in soul-searching and private confession, since this volume promoted intense self-examination prior to attending church and, especially, prior to receiving communion. Collins notes: "to carry out all William Vickers's advice would have required several hours of meditation" ("The Rev. Henry Tilney" 156).[15]

There was not much in the church experience of Austen's day to draw the attention away from the liturgy, no aesthetic lures for the imagination beyond the words spoken and heard. Rural churches, like the one in Steventon Austen attended as a child and adolescent, were plain.[16] Inside, the twelfth-century building was whitewashed—partly to signify purity and partly because whitewash was cheap (Sykes 232). There were no stained glass windows nor any of the Gothic ornamentations that became so popular after the Oxford Movement and Pugin's calls for aesthetic and spiritual reform. It was common practice to post the Ten Commandments on the east end, with other key texts such as the Nicene Creed or the Lord's Prayer. The altar would have been plain, with white linen and two candles—crosses were rare, as were flowers (Sykes 233). The one opulence of the church at Steventon was the high pew reserved for the squire's family, in Austen's day filled with the members of the Digweed family, long-standing tenants of Thomas Knight, the absentee squire (Jarvis 11). For those without pews, there were mats or hassocks (Sykes 235). There was also a three-decker pulpit, rising high above the altar; its prominence was in keeping with the importance of the Sunday sermon, the most popular and entertaining feature of Anglican worship. It is difficult to know how much singing took place in Austen's church experience. Metrical psalms were certainly sung, led by the parish clerk (and sometimes accompanied by a village band or choir) (P. Butler 34). While hymns had received official sanction in 1792, they were slow to replace the psalms (the first Anglican hymnal was not issued until 1827, though Evangelical parishes incorporated hymns much earlier) (Cuming 194).[17] Instead, the heart of worship was composed

---

[15]    Austen's lifetime comprised a period, of course, in which devotional material was enormously popular, especially as an aid to family and private prayer. Bishop Gibson's *Family Devotion* (1705), for example, had gone through 22 editions by 1800 (Walsh and Taylor 25). Further, the *Book of Common Prayer* was itself used for private prayer and family services (as discussed in Chapter 1).

[16]    The Anglican homilies adapted by the Church in 1662 (the second Book of Homilies) as part of the Articles of Religion include strong language against church decoration, condemning the "gay gazing sights, as [Catholics'] grosse phantasie was greatly delighted with" (*Book of Common Prayer* Eskimo.com).

[17]    This singing of the psalms was more often than not a rather unmusical performance. In arguing for what would become the Methodist practice of ample hymn-singing, John Wesley noted the droning and off-tune performance of most parish clerks in their leading of the psalms. The choir of "unawakened striplings" who supported the clerk also came in for attack (Sykes 240).

of repeating and hearing very well-rehearsed prayers and scriptural passages; the liturgy was drummed into one's consciousness.

The services themselves took approximately two to three hours, including about an hour for the sermon; in the afternoon, commentary on the catechism often replaced the service, and in consequence attendance was lighter, since the sermon was considered to exercise the greatest draw upon congregational attention (Boswell marveled, for instance, at Dr. Johnson's willingness to attend church when there were only prayers and no sermon; he did so, Johnson said, to set an example to others "as the people required more an example for the one than the other, it being much easier for them to hear a sermon than to fix their minds on prayer" [340]). No Anglican of Austen's day expected the minister himself to compose more than an occasional sermon, since there were so many fine sermons written by eminent divines that had been published widely. Nor did parishioners mind hearing the same sermons repeated (that sermon of George Austen's that he preached 13 times at two churches was not over-used by contemporary standards; see 44n). Popular favorites were repeated and heard with pleasure; after all, the sermon was still at this time one of the "most popular and important of literary forms" (Walsh and Taylor 14). In this as in so many other respects, repetition was a key element of Austen's church-going experience.

Holy Communion was usually celebrated only four times a year, at Christmas, Easter, Pentecost (50 days after Easter), and after the ingathering of the harvest in the fall (Sykes 250). Monthly communion became more the usual practice later in the nineteenth century, and by the middle of the century, Evangelicals and other church reformers commonly denounced the rarity of communion-delivery in Austen's day as one of many signs of earlier laxity (Walsh and Taylor 10).[18] But though a serious Anglican would not have taken communion often in the first decades of the nineteenth century, when he or she in fact did so, it was done with a high sense of purpose and obligation. The *Book of Common Prayer* sets out the dire consequences of taking communion without proper spiritual preparation, as the priest instructs his congregation:

> Therefore if any of you be a blasphemer of God, an hinderer or slanderer of his Word, an adulterer or be in malice, or envy, or in any other grievous crime, repent you of your sins, or else come not to that holy Table; lest, after the taking of that holy Sacrament, the devil enter into you, as he entered into Judas, and fill you full of all iniquities, and bring you to destruction both of body and soul. (250)

Thus, the threat of damnation "through unworthy reception" prompted many to exit the church after the Antecommunion (the prayers leading up to communion)

---

[18]    An early promoter of communion was the Rev. William Grimshaw, who in 1742 became the rector of Haworth, later to be the home of the Brontës (Neil 191). He built his congregation from a dozen or so parishioners to more than a thousand, and was reported to have used more than 35 bottles of wine for each communion service ("England's Christian Heritage").

when communion was offered.[19] While in Southampton, Austen herself notes how shocked she was to see a noted adulteress staying behind to receive Communion (*L* 131). Austen took communion seriously, and asked for and received communion on her deathbed (as her brothers James and Henry, both priests, were in attendance, this last communion would have been a family affair).

Communion was not the only important sacrament Austen experienced regularly; she attended weddings, baptisms, and ordinations. She did not go to funerals, however; it was customary for only men to attend, presumably to protect women from the emotional hardship of the occasion (for this reason, Cassandra did not attend Jane's funeral in 1817). Austen would have, however, witnessed the sacrament of final unction, a ceremony intended for the sick in preparation for death. As a teenager, Jane Austen acted as witness for several of the Steventon weddings officiated by her father. Her role as matrimonial witness must have provoked her, sometime when she was about 16, into a piece of juvenile high jinks: the fictional entries into the marriage register at Steventon, announcing the banns of marriage between herself and Frederick Howard Fitzwilliam of London, then between herself and Edmund Arthur William Mortimer of Liverpool, and then between herself and Jack Smith, place unmentioned (Jarvis 12).[20] She attended weddings often herself, though never, of course, as a bride. Her knowledge of the service is evidenced by the joke at the end of *Pride and Prejudice*, when the reader is informed that Mr. and Mrs. Collins are expecting a "young olive branch," "olive branch" being a term Mr. Collins had used earlier in his rhetorically inept letter of introduction to the Bennet family (*PP* 403). Austen certainly knew that one of the two Psalms ordained for the marriage service suggests that the bearing of children is the first goal of matrimony: "Thy wife shall be as the fruitful vine: upon the walls of thine house; / Thy children like the olive-branches: round about thy table" (*Psalms* 128:3–4).

---

[19]   In fact, as Walsh and Taylor argue, "among the lower orders, these fears were accentuated by a belief that only the more educated or respectable members of society could be worthy" (23).

[20]   Here in evidence is Austen's common comic technique of bargaining down from the high to the low, as seen perhaps most famously in the dialogue between Mr. and Mrs. John Dashwood in the second chapter of *Sense and Sensibility*. Austen would ultimately give the names of her imaginary London betrothed to three of her heroes (in *Persuasion, The Watsons,* and *Pride and Prejudice*, respectively), while the names of her Liverpudlian beau become attached to the hero of *Mansfield Park* (Edmund), the selfish brother of *Sanditon* (Arthur), and the good brother in *Mansfield Park* as well as the cad in *Persuasion* (William); "Mortimer," the last appellation, she never used in the major works. Jack Smith is the lowest and last—his common name is attached to the socially marginal Harriet Smith and Mrs. Smith of *Emma* and *Persuasion*, respectively, but also to Willoughby's wealthy relative Mrs. Smith in *Sense and Sensibility*.

## Clergymen in the Novels

Austen's rich experience with church rites, doctrine, and liturgy, however, tends not to be represented fully in the fiction—the above example is one of the few liturgically based moments of humor in the novels. For the most part, Austen seems to have been operating within a code of religious decorum, which held that serious subjects were exactly *too* serious to be treated within novels. But clergymen are thick on the ground, as they were in Austen's own life. In *Northanger Abbey*, Catherine's father is a priest (and a mild pluralist, with two livings), while James, her older brother, is about to be ordained. Henry Tilney, the hero, is a clergyman whose living was bequeathed him by his father; when we meet him he is something of an absentee priest, riding over to Woodston, his rectory, on the weekends to conduct parish business and to lead the services. In *Sense and Sensibility*, Edward Ferrars is a clergyman without a living; the happy ending comes about in part because of Colonel Brandon's uncommon generosity in giving Edward, a man he barely knows, the living at Delaford. Mr. Collins is Austen's first fully unflattering depiction of a clergyman, whose "'kind intention of christening, marrying, and burying his parishioners whenever it were required'" strikes Elizabeth from the first as the mark of an unserious man (*PP* 71). The insult to the cloth he represents is only partly mollified by the treatment of Mr. Wickham, who, as we learn, was to have had the living attached to Pemberley. In the letter to Elizabeth in which Darcy explains his conduct, he tells her he acceded to Wickham's request to trade the church for the law, noting, with commendable understatement, "I knew that Mr. Wickham ought not to be a clergyman" (*PP* 223). Later, after Wickham has been forced to marry Lydia, Elizabeth mocks him—"'How should you have liked making sermons?'"—but Wickham cannot be shamed, for he replies, "'Exceedingly well. I should have considered it as part of my duty, and the exertion would soon have been nothing'" (363).[21] In *Mansfield Park*, the late Mr. Norris was a clergyman; so too are Dr. Grant, whose gluttony casts the priesthood in a poor light, and Edmund Bertram himself, whose ordination provides one of the novel's preoccupations.[22] *Emma* showcases another reprehensible clergyman, Mr.

---

[21]    In this view of a clergyman's duties as nominal, Wickham is thus aligned with Mr. Collins. In after-years, Austen made a redress to the cloth; she told her family that Kitty ultimately marries a clergyman near Pemberley (James Austen-Leigh 148)—presumably the holder of the very living Wickham would have sullied had he been allowed to take it.

[22]    Critical consensus is divided about whether or not Austen actually stated that the subject of *Mansfield Park* was ordination. In January of 1813, she writes, after speaking of cropping *Pride and Prejudice*, "Now I will try to write of something else; --it shall be a complete change of subject—Ordination" (*L* 202). Deidre Le Faye warns that readers should not assume Austen was just beginning her composition of the novel, since a prior letter of the same January refers to Austen's queries about the Commissioner's House in Gibraltar, a minor detail that emerges in chapter six of volume two (*L* 411). At any rate, in the first three chapters of volume two Austen has at her narrative fore the subject of Edmund's ordination, as he journeys to Peterborough before Christmas to take his vows.

Elton, while in *Persuasion*, Wentworth's brother is a curate, as is Charles Hayter, Henrietta's beau; Charles Hayter, like many curates, longs for his superior, Dr. Shirley, the rector of Uppercross, to retire so that he may be given the living by his soon-to-be father-in-law.[23] While there are no clergymen in *Lady Susan* or *Sanditon*, in *The Watsons,* Emma's father is a sickly rector, while the putative hero is the Rev. Mr. Howard. In one of the few explicit references Austen makes to church practice, we learn in this novel fragment that Emma's father attends a Visitation, an occasion in which the bishop or archdeacon calls the local clergy together for a conference. Mr. Howard himself preaches the sermon at the service honoring this ecclesiastical gathering and wins the Rev. Mr. Watson's approval. This moment, incidentally, allows Austen to dilate briefly on the best ways to give a sermon, a subject she returns to in *Mansfield Park*, when Henry Crawford holds forth at length about the best styles in sermon-giving.[24] Morally, Austen's clergymen are a very mixed bag, but she knew that the Articles of Religion, included in the *Book of Common Prayer*, held that faulty clergymen did not ultimately damage the Church: "Neither is the effect of Christ's ordinance taken away by their wickedness, nor the grace of God's gifts diminished from such as by faith and rightly do receive the sacraments ministered unto them, which be effectual because of Christ's institution and promise, although they be ministered by evil men" (*Book of Common Prayer*, Eskimo.com). Her clergymen were like the men she knew, mostly devoted servants of the Church: some were model Christians, some were not.

---

Jarvis points out that the traditional time for ordination was right before Christmas, as evidenced by the timing of Ember Days, "when prayer was to be offered for those about to be ordained, [which] were the Wednesday, Friday, and Saturday following 13 December, according to the *Book of Common Prayer*" (78).

[23]   *Persuasion* also includes the fatuous musings of Mrs. Clay on the burdens of being a clergyman—at least in terms of what might injure his personal beauty, a presiding concern for Sir Walter: "'and even the clergyman—' she stopt a moment to consider what might do for the clergyman; --'and even the clergyman, you know, is obliged to go into infected rooms, and expose his health and looks to all the injury of a poisonous atmosphere'" (23).

[24]   The two passages offer notable contrasts. Mr. Watson values "'great propriety'" "'without any Theatrical grimace of violence'": "'I own I do not like much action in the pulpit—I do not like the studied air and artificial inflexions of voice, which your very popular and most admired Preachers generally have. –A simple delivery is much better calculated to inspire Devotion, and shews a much better taste.'" Mr. Watson sums up his verdict, praise probably in keeping with Austen's own views: "'Mr H. read like a scholar and a gentleman'" (*LM* 113). Henry Crawford, by contrast, focuses on the "'capital gratification'" of a "'thoroughly good sermon,'" praising the "'eloquence of the pulpit'": "'The preacher who can touch and affect such a heterogeneous mass of hearers, on subjects limited, and long worn thread-bare in all common hands; who can say any thing new or striking, any thing that rouses the attention, without offending the taste, or wearing out the feelings of his hearers, is a man whom one could not (in his public capacity) honour enough. I should like to be such a man'" (*MP* 394). Austen surely wants the reader to note the moral fault of Crawford's focus on the "new or striking" and his judgment that Gospel passages, the subject of all sermons, are by inference "limited" and "long worn thread-bare."

## Church-going and Sacraments in the Novels

Nor do the novels lack references to church-going, though such moments are usually spare. Austen assumes her characters all go to church, and do so regularly. Michael Giffin argues that

> . . . [a]lthough religious observance is muted in all of Austen's novels, we can assume it is pervasive. According to custom and obligation, Austen's characters would regularly perform liturgical duties and attend liturgical services, even if this occurs with varying degrees of commitment or enthusiasm, and even if the reader does not actually 'see' them doing so (27–8).[25]

Even Henry and Mary Crawford go to church, for Henry is right on the spot in Portsmouth to escort the Price family to Sunday services, and when Mary complains about family prayers, she does so in a way that makes plain she has experienced tedium in the pews herself: "'Every body likes to go their own way— to choose their own time and manner of devotion. The obligation of attendance, the formality, the restraint, the length of time—altogether it is a formidable thing, and what nobody likes'" (*MP* 101–2). (Edmund's rebuke must speak for Austen herself: "'Do you think the minds which are . . . indulged in wanderings in a chapel, would be more collected in a closet?'" [102]). In *Northanger Abbey*, Isabella and Catherine rejoice to learn they are to attend the same theatre at night and the same chapel in the morning, and Catherine attends church when she visits the Abbey (though without Henry, who is conducting his own services at Woodston several miles away). In *Persuasion*, once Anne goes to visit Lady Russell, she expects to see Wentworth every Sunday, as they are now residing in the same parish, and her expectation is unfulfilled only because Wentworth has gone off to visit his curate brother, avoiding as best he can the imputation that he is to marry Louisa Musgrove. The one explicit exception to regular church-going occurs in *Pride and Prejudice*, when we learn that Mr. Collins has preached only twice before Lady Catherine de Bourgh in a period of time that stretches from Easter to mid-October—a detail that suggests that for all her oversight of her parish, Lady Catherine neglects to go to church herself. A related transgression is referenced in *Persuasion*, when we learn that Mr. Elliot has been given to Sunday-traveling, a practice condemned by the church (and implicitly by the Fourth Commandment). Similarly, when in

---

[25]   Jarvis provides a useful summary of all the moments in the novels and in the letters in which Christmas and Easter are referenced, for instance in *Emma*, when church-going on Christmas Day is made impossible by a snowstorm, and in her two Easter Day letters, especially that of her last Easter to her younger brother Charles, which ends "God bless you all!" (51–2). Most of the Christmas references, both in the novels and in the letters, speak of festivities, eating "turkies," and giving to the poor.

*Northanger Abbey* General Tilney sends Catherine home by herself on a Sunday, the timing of her dismissal worsens the already black nature of that act.[26]

Other church events in the novels, beyond ordinary Sunday worship, are weddings and ordination. Emma escorts Harriet to church to marry Robert Martin the month before she herself will marry Mr. Knightley. Austen tells us, "Perhaps, indeed, at that time she scarcely saw Mr. Elton, but as the clergyman whose blessing at the altar might next fall on herself" (*E* 527)—a signal improvement over Emma's perspective at the novel's first wedding, that of Miss Taylor and Mr. Weston, when she had improperly fantasized about finding a match for Mr. Elton herself: "'I thought when he was joining their hands to-day, he looked so very much as if he would like to have the same kind office done for him!'" (12). Emma later will quote the marriage ceremony from the *Book of Common Prayer* as she looks forward to her own joining with Mr. Knightley. She tells him she will call him by his Christian name only once, "in the building in which N. takes M. for better, for worse'" (505). The novel ends with this wedding, "very much like other weddings, where the parties have no taste for finery or parade"; one great good is that though Mr. Elton must be present to officiate, Mrs. Elton seems not to have been invited, for she renders her jealous verdict on the inadequate show with its "very little white satin" after gaining "the particulars detailed by her husband" (528).

An even more consequential invocation of the wedding service occurs in *Mansfield Park*, at Sotherton chapel, when Julia mischievously notes that Maria and Mr. Rushworth are in tableau before the altar, "'standing side by side, exactly as if the ceremony were going to be performed. . . . Upon my word, it is really a pity that it should not take place directly, if we had but a proper license, for here we are altogether, and nothing in the world could be more snug and pleasant'" (103). Julia knows how provoking this speech must be to her sister, who hopes to trade Mr. Rushworth for Henry Crawford, but she plows on to cause further consternation—this time, in Mary Crawford, who has up to this point not known that Edmund is slated for the cloth. Julia's sisterly malice strikes an unintended target: "'If Edmund were but in orders! . . . How unlucky that you are not ordained, Mr. Rushworth and Maria are quite ready'" (103). Pamela Regis argues that "[i]n the abandoned chapel Austen invokes for the first time the sacred vows of marriage and ordination that will trump all other vows in this novel" (169). When Maria does marry Mr. Rushworth, months later, the ceremony's description is meant to contrast with what readers knew of the serious and religious vows required by this rite, found in the *Book of Common Prayer*. The bride must affirm her duties to her husband, for she is asked, "Wilt thou obey him, and serve him, love, honour, and keep him in sickness and in health; and, forsaking all other, keep thee only unto him, so long as ye both shall live?" (309). Maria cannot affirm any of these

---

[26] Anne sees Mr. Elliot's Sunday-traveling as just one of the proofs that "there had been a period of his life (and probably not a short one) when he had been, at least, careless on all serious matters" (*P* 174); as I discuss below, "serious matters" explicitly means religious matters.

statements in conscience, for we learn in Austen's mordant summary why Maria intends to marry: "In all the important preparations of the mind she was complete; being prepared for matrimony by an hatred of home, restraint, and tranquility; by the misery of disappointed affection, and contempt of the man she was to marry. The rest might wait" (236). The wedding ceremony thus is "very proper" and "[its] etiquette . . . might stand the strictest investigation"; we also learn that the "service was impressively read by Dr. Grant"—but readers are to register that the ceremony makes a travesty of the marriage vows (237).[27]

Edmund's ordination, by contrast, confirms his heartfelt commitment to God, even though someone like Mary Crawford cannot understand his act. We learn much about Mary Crawford when she describes his ordination as a heathen sacrifice (126), and goes on to accuse him of taking orders because he has a comfortable living waiting for him, and because he is indolent (she is judging from the behavior of her brother-in-law, Dr. Grant). Mary in fact voices many of the criticisms made by church reformers in the late eighteenth and early nineteenth century of the clergy (as discussed in Chapter 1): "'A clergyman has nothing to do but to be slovenly and selfish—read the newspaper, watch the weather, and quarrel with his wife. His curate does all the work, and the business of his own life is to dine'" (128). Later in the novel, Sir Thomas, speaking for Edmund (and for Austen as well, I am certain), rejects the earlier models of pluralism and non-residence that Henry and Mary Crawford assume set the pattern for clergy behavior:

'A parish has wants and claims which can be known only by a clergyman constantly resident, and which no proxy can be capable of satisfying to the same extent. Edmund might, in the common phrase, do the duty of Thornton, that is, he might read prayers and preach, without giving up Mansfield Park; he might ride over, every Sunday, to a house nominally inhabited, and go through a divine service; he might be the clergyman of Thornton Lacey every seventh day, for three or four hours, if that would content him. But it will not. He knows that human nature needs more lessons than a weekly sermon can convey, and that if he does not live among his parishioners and prove himself by constant attention their well-wisher and friend, he does very little either for their good or his own.' (288)

Henry's response to the speech is to bow "his acquiescence"; he is certainly silenced. Mary in her turn sees Sir Thomas as a "destroyer" of her hopes to "shut out the church, sink the clergyman, and see [in Thornton Lacey] only the respectable,

---

[27] Regis points out that "Austen's audience would have been familiar with this service" and that "Austen herself would have had the volume containing this service in her hand, at least weekly, from the moment she could read" (172). Thus the irony of the wedding's depiction "relies on the reader's knowledge of the religious foundation of the event" (172). As Regis notes, all then-contemporary readers would also have known that the service includes the priest's injunction: "Those whom God hath joined together, let no man put asunder" (311). Henry Crawford will "put asunder" Maria and her husband in fairly short order.

elegant, modernized, and occasional residence of a man of independent fortune" (289). Only the respect Sir Thomas commands keeps her from "throwing ridicule on his cause" (289).

Edmund's vows when he becomes ordained set his religious seriousness against Mary and Henry's worldliness and callow religiosity. Regis notes the far greater length of the ordination service in comparison to the marriage service, found, like the marriage service, in every Anglican's copy of the *Book of Common Prayer*; in particular she notes the gravity and momentousness of the vows (172). Again and again, the bishop queries the ordinand as to his "faithful diligence," diligence to his faith, to the Church and its authority, to the Scriptures, to his parishioners, and to his family. In particular, the priest-to-be is asked to "[lay] aside the study of the world and the flesh," a vow that itself makes it very difficult to accede to Mary Crawford's view of how to be a clergyman. True to the dictates of religious decorum, Edmund's vows take place off-scene, but Austen's readers would have known what Edmund was pledging himself to do, and would have judged him, Mary, and Henry accordingly.[28]

## Prayer in the Novels

Austen's assumption that her characters (and readers) go to church regularly and are accustomed to its key rites and sacraments, including marriage and ordination, is paralleled by her assumption that her characters (and readers) pray in private. She rarely uses the word "prayer" as such, however, and only twice to refer to the actions of her characters are doing. Wentworth engages in "prayer and reflection" with his "folded arms and face concealed" in the aftermath of Louisa's accident (*P* 121), while Fanny, distraught at Edmund's love for Mary Crawford, tries to subdue her own feelings with "fervent prayers for his happiness" (*MP* 307). By far the most frequent use of the word "pray" occurs as an informal interjection or as a synonym for "please," as in Mr. Woodhouse's request to Emma: "pray do not make any more matches" (*E* 10). But her characters do pray, particularly at moments of high gratitude. As Stuart Tave has noted, the word that denotes religious content in Austen's vocabulary is "serious," and its presence should alert us to specifically religious events (12).[29] For instance, when Mrs. Smith confesses

---

[28]   Regis notes that the true vows, Edmund's ordination vows in Peterborough, and Fanny's and Edmund's betrothal in the gardens of Mansfield Park, both take place unseen. On the other hand, we do see false or morally askew vows enacted, including in the aborted rendition of *Lovers' Vows* and Mary's vow never to dance with a clergyman. See also Macdonagh on the centrality of ordination to the plot and themes of *Mansfield Park*, including his extended discussion of what he identifies as four "master-scenes" in the novel and their "calibration on the measures of seriousness and ordination" (15).

[29]   K. C. Phillipps argues that this use of "serious" to mean "religious" was a relatively recent development in the English language, occurring first in the *Oxford English Dictionary* in 1796 (58). However, William Law's *A Serious Call to the Devout Life*, a strongly influential and much re-published Anglican text, had yoked "serious" with "religious" since its introduction in 1729 (Macdonagh 12). Law's book, incidentally, focuses on those

with great emotion to Anne that "'there are so many who forget to think seriously till it is almost too late,'" she is thinking of her husband, irreligious until the moment of his deathbed (*P* 169). "Serious" reflection or meditation in Austen thus means prayer. We see it in the scene in which Anne returns home overwhelmed by happiness after she and Wentworth have confessed their love to each other: "an interval of meditation, *serious* and grateful, was the best corrective of every thing dangerous in such high-wrought felicity; and she went to her room, and grew steadfast and fearless in the thankfulness of her enjoyment" (*P* 266; my italics). Her steadfastness and fearlessness arise from her having acknowledged and properly thanked God as the author of her happiness. After Harriet has become engaged to Robert Martin, Emma too engages in thankful prayer: "Serious she was, very serious in her thankfulness, and in her resolutions" (*E* 519), and again, Austen is telling the reader that Emma has been praying. Other words that almost always have a religious connotation for Austen include "principle," as in religious principle, and "exertion," which means struggling to do the right thing out of a sense of religious duty; "duty," of course, at heart usually means religious duty (Tave 112–3).[30] Of course, for Austen, there is no greater indictment than to say someone is "irreligious," and thus it is important when Elizabeth Bennet, reforming her ideas about Darcy, notes that she had never known him to be "irreligious," a verdict confirmed by the close of his letter to her: "God bless you" (*PP* 230, 225). At the close of the novel, we see that Elizabeth has not forgotten Darcy's finishing invocation of God's blessing: "'The letter, perhaps, began in bitterness, but it did not end so. The adieu is charity itself'" (409). "Adieu," she remembers, is a farewell that commends the other to God.[31]

---

"habitual principles" discussed above relative to Gisbourne and Sherlock, for his book is a guide to the daily practice of Christian principles. Dr. Johnson reported that reading Law was instrumental in turning him into a serious Christian: "I began to read it expecting to find it a dull book (as such books generally are), and perhaps to laugh at it. But I found Law quite an overmatch for me; and this was the first occasion of my thinking in earnest of religion, after I became capable of rational inquiry" (Boswell 29).

[30]   Tave argues that "[o]f the three duties, to God, to one's neighbors, to oneself, specified in the Book of Common Prayer [in the catechism] and innumerable sermons and moral essays, duty to God would not be for Jane Austen the proper subject of the novelist; but the other duties are, and they become gravely important, not as they might be in a later nineteenth-century novelist, because they are substitutes for religion, but because they are daily expressions of it in common life" (113).

[31]   Joseph Wiesenfarth cites the close of Darcy's letter in support of his contention that the novels are "seldom explicitly religious, though some Christian instances do peep through" (61). See also Willis, who argues that "the fact that [Elizabeth] has registered [the end of Darcy's letter] so deeply tells us much about Elizabeth—and about Jane Austen" (67).

**Religious Decorum in the Novels**

The periphrastic or subdued markers of religious practice that Austen prefers make it far more likely that contemporary readers will miss her original meaning, though the audience of her day could see the Christian markers despite their indirection or subtlety. Writing an unsigned review of Austen in an 1821 issue of the *Quarterly Review*, Archbishop Whately noted that she was "evidently a Christian writer" but that "her religion [was] not at all obtrusive. She might defy the most fastidious critic to call any of her novels, (as *Coelebs* was designated, we will not say altogether without reason,) a 'dramatic sermon.' The subject is rather alluded to, and that incidentally, than studiously brought forward and dwelt upon" (325).[32] Allusions and incidental reference are indeed Austen's preferred mode of introducing specifically religious material. For example, when Colonel Brandon speaks of how he found the first Eliza on the point of death, he tells Elinor, "'Life could do nothing for her, beyond giving time for a better preparation for death; and that was given'" (*SS* 235). "Better preparation for death" means the rite of "The Communion of the Sick," otherwise known as final unction, contained within the *Book of Common Prayer*, knowledge familiar to Austen's original readers (Jarvis 57), but contemporary readers may assume that this "better preparation for death" refers vaguely only to personal introspection or a settling of accounts. It is worth noting that Austen's periphrases extend to other important matters not specifically religious. She does not call a pregnancy a pregnancy, nor does she call a duel a duel. Colonel Brandon explains that he and Willoughby have fought a duel, but many contemporary readers miss his meaning: "'we met by appointment, he to defend, I to punish his conduct'" (*SS* 239). Similarly, most twenty-first century readers miss that Fanny is pregnant at the end of *Mansfield Park*, because Austen is so understated in her signaling of the event: "the acquisition of Mansfield living . . . occurred just after they had been married long enough to begin to want an increase of income, and feel their distance from the paternal abode an inconvenience" (*MP* 547).

Austen's most explicit treatment of religious commitment and personal conversion in the novels comes not in *Mansfield Park*, despite its concern with ordination, religious vows, and the proper role of the clergy. Rather, we find the most sustained language about religious feeling in *Sense and Sensibility*, after

---

[32] Whately proffers a plausible explanation for Austen's reserve, one focusing on the uselessness of obvious didacticism: "In fact she is more sparing of [religious subjects] than would be thought desirable by some persons; perhaps even by herself, had she consulted merely her own sentiments; but she probably introduced it as far as she thought would be generally acceptable and profitable: for when the purpose of inculcating a religious principle is made too palpably prominent, many readers, if they do not throw aside the book with disgust, are apt to fortify themselves with that respectful kind of apathy with which they undergo a regular sermon, and prepare themselves as they do to swallow a dose of medicine, endeavouring to *get it down* in large gulps, without tasting it more than is necessary" (325; italics in original).

Marianne has recovered from her near-fatal illness. Marianne admits that she had almost committed "'self-destruction,'" i.e., suicide, an act clearly forbidden by the Church as a sin (391).[33] In her desire to make amends for her past behavior, Marianne speaks specifically of "'atonement to my God'" and the narrator tells us she has a "self-reproving spirit" marked by "frankness and contrition" (391–3). She informs Elinor that she intends to overcome the memory of Willoughby by "'religion, by reason, by constant employment'" (393). Her plan of reformation is to "'divide every moment between music and reading,'" and to "'enter on a course of serious study'" (388); Austen's audience would, of course, have known that "serious study" means religious study, not secular education. Marianne intends to read sermons, not works of history or philosophy.

Marianne's language of religious reform is to be contrasted with that of Willoughby, whose "confession" to Elinor in chapter eight of volume III is marked by more explicit and sustained religious diction than occurs anywhere else in Austen's fiction. As Richards points out, Willoughby "utters the word God four times; the devil, twice; soul, three times; heart, six times; guilty, twice; blessed, twice; and also diabolical, saint, heaven, faith, temptation, and atonement" (147). This extravagantly religious vocabulary underlines the fact that Willoughby knows the depths of his sins, but his deep-laid egotism has kept him from ever choosing the right action over the self-serving one. As Elinor later notes to Marianne: "'The whole of his behavior . . . has been grounded in selfishness'" (397–8). However, the terms Austen uses at the close of the novel to describe Willoughby's status imply that Willoughby is still a Christian. She notes that he "lived to exert" himself (again, for Austen, "exertion" implies spiritual and moral effort); further, she claims one "need not [doubt]" that "his repentance of misconduct, which thus brought about its own punishment, was sincere" (430).

The larger question of Austen's use of religious language involves interesting complications. Many characters, both good and bad invoke God, sometimes thoughtlessly (Jarvis 56), as with Mrs. Jennings' violation of the Third Commandment ("Thou shall not take the name of the Lord your God in vain"): "Oh! Lord, I am sure your mother can spare you very well" (*SS* 176). Like Ms. Jennings and other vulgar characters, Lydia Bennet uses "La" (a shortened form of "Lord"), "God," "Lord," and "Heaven" commonly as interjections. In *Northanger Abbey*, John Thorpe actually swears, and frequently, though his "damns" are rendered in the text as "d---." Jarvis notes, however, that Austen diminishes her use of these casual callings upon the divine and of swearing considerably in the last

---

[33]  St. Augustine's directives in *The City of God*—"that Christians have no authority for committing suicide in any circumstances whatever"—still governed the Anglican Church (and the Christian Church more generally) in the nineteenth century (26). Consequently, those who had killed themselves were not eligible for burial in consecrated ground. Like later Church divines, Augustine cites passages of Scripture in support of his position, such as this one: "Do you not know that your body is a temple of the Holy Spirit, who is you, whom you have received from God? You are not your own; you were bought at a price. Therefore honor God with your body" (*1 Corinthians* 6:19–20).

three novels. These three, one might note, were written entirely in the 1810s, while the first three novels were drafted in the 1790s—the novelist's standards about such language evidently tightened. These later novels do include more appropriate invocations, when characters are under great stress. "'Oh God! that I had never seen her!'" cries Emma after learning that Harriet believes Mr. Knightley returns her affections (*E* 448); likewise, when Wentworth learns from Anne that she would have married him eight years before when he returned to England, he cries, "'Good God! . . . you would!'" (*P* 268).

Words like "sin" and "evil" are also employed, both in religious and secular ways. Frank Churchill describes some of his exploits in Highbury, for instance, as "having sinned against Emma Woodhouse," forgetting or ignoring that one cannot sin against another person but only against God (*E* 478). In the same novel, we are told that Emma, in thinking of leaving her father, "even wept over the idea of it, as a sin of thought" (474). "Evil" is a word Mary Crawford uses in *Mansfield Park* to describe the "foolish precipitation last Christmas"—that is, Edmund's ordination (*MP* 502), an inversion of meaning that indicts Mary instead. But Austen herself often uses the word "evil" to describe purely secular concerns. For instance, when Fanny learns that Henry Crawford cannot come to dinner with the Prices in Portsmouth, she is "in a state of actual felicity from escaping so horrible an evil!" (472).[34] "Evil," in fact, rarely carries the full moral weight we might expect it to. Mrs. Norris, for example, feels "some evil from the passing of the servants behind her chair" when dining in a cramped room (*MP* 278), while Elizabeth Elliot in *Persuasion* finds the Baronetage an "evil" because her own name has yet to be supplemented by the name of a husband (7). If "evil" often means simply a social mistake or an ill, real evils are sometimes called by far less, especially by the morally obtuse. When Mary Crawford describes Henry's running away with Maria as a "moment's *etourderie*" (in other words, a blunder or careless mistake), she is not only using what was for Austen the suspect language of French but she is also showing that she has no conception of the irremediable step her brother has taken (506). Fanny herself terms it a "horrible evil" (510), a moment in which the word has its full religious force.

Austen very rarely quotes Scripture. Margaret Doody claims that, other than one quotation of the Psalms by Miss Bates in *Emma*, "the great serious texts do not enter at all into her novels" (348). Miss Bates quotes the sixteenth Psalm: "'We may well say that 'our lot is cast in a goodly heritage''" (174). As Doody notes, Miss Bates has no real heritage at all except the kindness and charity extended her by her Highbury neighbors, and the quotation should be read as revealing the gap between the drawbacks of Miss Bates's situation and her panglossianism. There is one other direct citation of Scripture in Austen's novels, however. In *Mansfield Park*, Henry Crawford claims that "'I do not like to eat the bread of idleness'," a phrase from *Proverbs* 31:27, originally about a careful housewife: "She looketh

---

[34] See Phillipps, 22ff, for further examples of Austen's use of the word "evil," often with less serious meanings than we might expect.

well to the ways of her household, and eateth not the bread of idleness." The novel includes two idle housewives, Lady Bertram and her sister, Mrs. Price, and one housewife who annoys precisely because of interference, Mrs. Norris; this context helps undermine Henry's hint that he has domestic, godly, and matronly virtues. These two citations of Scripture in the novels are in keeping with Austen's sense of religious decorum, in that both share a prudential rather than spiritual focus.[35]

Austen did not use religious language lightly in her private writings, either. As William Jarvis notes, she used the phrase "God bless you" in less than a dozen of her more than 150 letters. He also documents her even rarer use of "Thank God": once on the occasion of her father's death (the thankfulness was for the brevity of his suffering), once after a fire in Southampton in 1808 that could have spread to the rooms the Austens were renting but did not, once after the death of Elizabeth Knight (again about the brevity of suffering), and once in a late letter regarding Cassandra's response to Jane's own suffering: "Thank God! She does not seem the worse for it yet. . . . I have so many alleviations & comforts to bless the Almighty for" (*L* 340).

Two reasons loom for Austen's insistence on keeping explicit religiosity at bay in her novels. First, she knew she would bore, and possibly lose, her readers if she was too religiously didactic. Her playful jest in 1816 to her nephew Edward, himself a beginning novelist, shows her sense of the ridiculousness of inserting religious material into fiction: "Uncle Henry [her brother] writes very superior Sermons. –You & I must try to get hold of one or two & put them into our Novels; --it would be a fine help to a volume" (*L* 323). Her correspondence that same year with the Prince Regent's secretary, James Stanier Clarke, and his absurd suggestions for her next novel led her to compose a parodic "Plan of a Novel," in which the insertion of clerical material is openly mocked. The hero, a clergyman, "perfect in Character, Temper & Manners," is obsessed with the need to replace tithes with income (*LM* 226). On his deathbed in Kamschatka (*sic*; a region at the eastern end of Siberia), he "expires in a fine burst of Literary Enthusiasm, intermingled with Invectives against Holder's of Tythes" (*LM* 228–9). Most critics of her day were certainly tired of explicitly enthusiastic and Evangelical novels. The anonymous reviewer of *Emma* in the *British Critic*, for instance, was relieved to find the novel did not "dabble in religion," adding that "of fanatical novels and fanatical authoresses we are already sick" (Southam 71), and Mary Russell Mitford, writing in 1814 about *Pride and Prejudice*, argued that Austen

---

[35]    John Wiltshire notes in his introduction to the Cambridge edition of *Mansfield Park* that Austen does invoke phrases from the King James Bible without quoting it as such: "Austen's prose frequently carries a biblical allusion, though without deliberate or ostentatious reiteration of phrasing" (liii). He gives several examples of such echoes, including Edmund's appraisal of Fanny as having a "heart which knew no guile," a revision of *Psalms* 32.2, which blesses those "in whose spirit there is no guile" (liv).

was superior to Maria Edgeworth because "she preaches no sermons" (I. 300).[36] And, as we have seen, Archbishop Whately also praised Austen's discretion, sure that she might have put in more religious material had she thought it would be efficacious to do so.

Austen probably also kept religious material to a minimum because she felt serious subjects belonged in wholly serious venues, not in the popular arena of fiction.[37] Her friend Mrs. Barrett, who knew her at Chawton, spoke of her reticence: "I think I see her now defending what she thought was the real province of a delineator of life and manners and declaring her belief that example and not 'direct preaching' was all that a novelist could afford properly to exhibit" (Chapman 173). Mrs. Barrett also noted that Austen was shocked at the suggestion that a certain real clergyman was the model for Mr. Collins, on the grounds that using a real person, especially a man of the cloth, as a figure in fiction violates both decorum and privacy (Chapman 172). The most serious moments, such as deathbed scenes, she excludes. Mrs. Churchill's death in *Emma*, for instance, occurs off-stage, allowing Austen to treat it comically: "The event acquitted her of all the fancifulness, and all the selfishness of imaginary complaints" (387). The closest we come to a deathbed scene occurs in the first chapter of *Sense and Sensibility*, when Mr. Dashwood

---

[36]   A similar verdict was recorded in an 1815 letter from the Scottish poet Anne Grant to a friend: "I am glad you approve so much of Mansfield Park, it being a great favourite with me, on account of its just delineation of manners and excellent moral, which is rather insinuated than obtruded throughout—the safest and best way, I think" (II. 84).

[37]   Austen's sense of decorum also operated at another level, enforcing different standards for what can be spoken about in novels as opposed to in family correspondence. For instance, her letters, especially to Cassandra, are filled with details about dress—the lengths of hems, the trims of bonnets, the material for gowns or tippets. But the novels only discuss clothing when it is useful for characterization, as when we learn about Mrs. Thorpe's elaborate gowns or Fanny Price's plain white dress at the ball given in her honor. See Norman Page on the issue of novelistic decorum: "In her private writings, as the Letters repeatedly demonstrate, Jane Austen was quite capable of finding a source of lively interest in the pattern of a new gown. In the novels, on the other hand, there is a carefully-guarded frontier between the serious use of abstract language by the narrator and those characters who command respect, and the foolish or absurd or suspiciously frivolous use of the concrete" (59). Page notes that the letters include many colloquialisms (170), but that Austen shows by her tone exactly how such playful diction is to be understood: "she habitually endows social and domestic trivialities with a sense of style. They are retailed in a spirit of fun which both conveys a sense of values—the awareness that this is trivial enough in all conscience, as if the writer were laughing at herself for bothering to mention it—and, at the same time, by its wit and originality, gives gossip an unusual distinction" (171). One other marker of Austen's sense of textual decorum stands as noteworthy: while in the letters she shows great flexibility in what she calls friends and relatives, making up nicknames and having fun with titles, in the novels she is scrupulously accurate about the then-conventional modes of address (Phillipps 288ff).

exacts a promise from his son. It is given only in summary, as Austen refuses any scenic rendering.[38]

Austen also clearly believed that her novels could indeed show the most important choices about serious values, through an attention to common life, attention to the way ordinary people choose to behave on a daily basis. As Stuart Tave notes, Austen agreed with the dictates of Thomas Secker, whose 1769 *Lectures on the Catechism of the Church of England* she owned, that the "common Duties of common Life . . . make far the greatest Part of what our Maker expects of us" (113). Sherlock, her favorite sermon writer, concurred: "In all cases, . . . where your duty to your neighbour is plain and clear, depend upon it your duty to God concurs with it" (qtd. Koppel 8). Tave's summary of Austen's view has stood the test of time:

> Of the three duties, to God, to one's neighbors, to oneself, specified in the Book of Common Prayer and innumerable sermons and moral essays, duty to God would not be for Jane Austen the proper subject of the novelist; but the other duties are, and they become gravely important, not as they might be in a later nineteenth-century novelist, because they are substitutes for religion, but because they are daily expressions of it in common life. (112)

Austen's religious values are imprinted everywhere in the novels. The ordinary behavior of her characters shows their moral and spiritual status, and their ability as free creatures to change and grow into greater Christian maturity, an ability especially vouchsafed her heroines and heroes. The world of her novels is a Christian one in which worldliness competes against traditional orthodoxy and moral precepts. Living in the real world, Austen shows, is the best test of one's Christian values, and the novels rest on this foundation of Christian purpose.

### Austen's Own Prayers

One can find Austen using explicit religious language without reserve in one place only: her prayers.[39] These prayers, three in number, were copied out by the family and kept for posterity, with a notation from one of her brothers or sisters (possibly

---

[38] Nonetheless, Austen's then-contemporary readers would have felt the force of a death-bed promise more fully than readers today. When John Dashwood and his wife selfishly bargain down the commitment he made to his father to support his stepmother and stepsisters, readers then would have known that he was not merely violating a promise to his father but a promise to God, as death-bed vows were understood to be sanctified and authorized by God's presence.

[39] The scholarship on these prayers is limited. Stovel (196–201) and Dabundo have the most detailed discussions of their importance and literary features. Lambdin and Lambdin also discuss the prayers at some length (286–9), but absurdly find Deist undertones in their theology. Doody's treatment of the prayers is brief but highly recommended ("Jane Austen's Reading" 346–7), as is the much fuller explication in the Introduction to the *Later Manuscripts* volume of the *Cambridge Edition of the Works of Jane Austen* by Janet Todd and Linda Bree, cxviii–cxxvi.

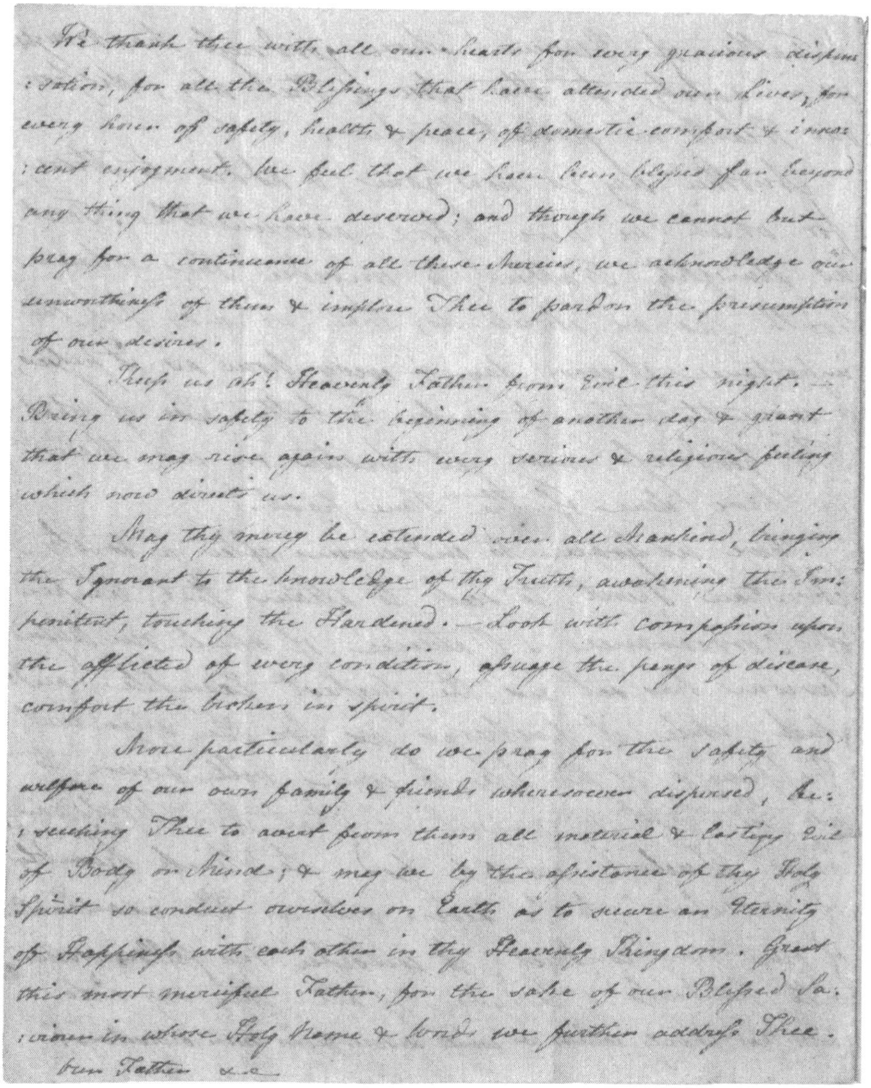

We thank thee with all our hearts for every gracious dispensation, for all the Blessings that have attended our Lives, for every hour of safety, health & peace, of domestic comfort & innocent enjoyment. We feel that we have been blessed far beyond any thing that we have deserved; and though we cannot but pray for a continuance of all these Mercies, we acknowledge our unworthiness of them & implore Thee to pardon the presumption of our desires.

Keep us oh! Heavenly Father from Evil this night. — Bring us in safety to the beginning of another day & grant that we may rise again with every serious & religious feeling which now directs us.

May thy mercy be extended over all Mankind, bringing the Ignorant to the knowledge of thy Truth, awakening the Impenitent, touching the Hardened. — Look with compassion upon the afflicted of every condition, assuage the pangs of disease, comfort the broken in spirit.

More particularly do we pray for the safety and welfare of our own family & friends wheresoever dispersed, beseeching Thee to avert from them all material & lasting Evil of Body or Mind; & may we by the assistance of thy Holy Spirit so conduct ourselves on Earth as to secure an Eternity of Happiness with each other in thy Heavenly Kingdom. Grant this most merciful Father, for the sake of our Blessed Saviour in whose Holy Name & words we further address Thee.

Our Father &c

Fig. 2.1 Facsimile image of prayer attributed to Jane Austen. Special Collections, F. W. Olin Library, Mills College.

Charles or James or Cassandra Austen): "Prayers Composed by my ever dear Sister Jane." The first two are in Charles's or James's hand, while the third continues with that hand, shifting with the last line on the first page to Jane Austen's own.[40]

---

[40]  I have studied facsimile copies of the original manuscripts (now at Mills College in the Elinor Raas Heller Rare Book Room) and agree in general with the conclusion come to by Todd and Bree that, contrary to Chapman and others following his lead—such as Austen's bibliographer, David Gilson—the first two prayers are in either Charles's or James's hand (without seeing the manuscripts, Chapman asserted that the first is in Cassandra's, the second in Henry's, and the third in both Henry's and Jane's [Chapman 453, Gilson 384]), though I believe it is entirely possible that the third prayer, written half in one hand and half by another, may be written by Charles or James first and then Jane herself, not Charles/James and Cassandra as Todd and Bree argue. The question of handwriting is complicated, but I do not believe the question of authorship is as problematic as Todd and Bree submit (as they note, "[i]n terms of attribution, these are the works that most trouble us" [cxxv]. It is true that the attribution of "Prayers Composed by my ever dear Sister Jane" is on only the first of the two large sheets that have come down to us through the family of Charles Austen (for the details of provenance, see Todd and Bree, "Introduction," cxviii–cxxvi). But not only had the papers been kept together by the heirs of Charles Austen, but also the particular flavor and the concerns of these prayers are very similar, as I discuss in detail in the larger text; in particular I argue that while it is true that the prayers represent traditional Anglican orthodoxy and that "they echo in simplified extemporized form aspects of the intercessional collects of the Book of Common Prayer" (Bree and Todd cxxiii), the specific attention the prayers give to the fault of pride and uncharity and to the idea of "fellow-creatures" as well as many other points of similarity mark them as written by the same person, and thus by Jane Austen, as Charles (or perhaps James or perhaps even Cassandra) noted on the first sheet. There are two sheets. The first, beginning "Give us grace, Almighty Father," is folded so as to make four pages, and begins on the recto side, continues onto the verso side of the back, and concludes on the back's recto side. The inscription, "Prayers Composed by my ever dear Sister Jane," is on the front side, verso. Underneath this inscription, in a different hand, is written "Charles Austen" (this notation was most likely made by one of Charles Austen's family members). This sheet is watermarked 1818. The second sheet is also large (though not the same size as the first) and is also folded. It contains two prayers, in two distinctly different hands. The second prayer (by Chapman's reckoning), beginning "Almighty God!," is on the front recto side, continuing onto the back verso side. The third prayer (again, by Chapman's reckoning), beginning "Father of Heaven!," begins on the recto side of the back; all but the very last line on this part of the sheet is in Charles Austen's hand (or, again, perhaps James's). The last line, beginning "with that charity which we would desire from them ourselves," is in a more precise and smaller handwriting, as is the rest of that third prayer, which continues on the verso side of the front side. I find that this handwriting is more like Jane's than Cassandra's, and readers may make the comparison for themselves by viewing an example of Austen's mature hand (as evidenced, for example, in the cancelled manuscript chapters of *Persuasion*—see *P*, 281–313) and Figure 1, a facsimile copy of the last page of the second sheet of the prayers. Chapman evidently did not consult the manuscripts, as he himself admits, as his edition of the prayers in *Minor Works* omits most of the capitalizations and some of the exclamation marks and alters some of the spellings (*MW* 453–7). Accurate transcriptions of the prayers are now available in *LM* 573–676. Chapman is also wrong about the division of the prayers

These are not private prayers; rather, they were evidently composed as evening prayers to provide as shorter occasional replacement for the rite of Evening Prayer as found in the *Book of Common Prayer*.[41] Bruce Stovel argues that they were probably composed after 1805, the year Austen's father died, as the Rev. George Austen would have been in charge of leading prayers while he lived. These are prayers for her family, to be read aloud in the circle of nightly piety, a practice very likely followed by Austen all her life (her father expected it, and Gisbourne and Vickers's *Companion to the Altar* urged it; most clerical families, like Austen's own, would have had morning and evening prayer regularly except on Sunday [Stovel 200]). As Janet Todd and Linda Bree also suggest, shorter prayers would have been helpful at Chawton, when the illness of one or another family member made church attendance impracticable (cxxiii–cxxiv).

Each prayer follows the ordained sequence of a collect (that is, a prayer designed to express the "collected" petitions of the group in a general way). Collects begin with an address to God, followed by a characterization of God's attributes; then follows a petition and a statement of the expected result (for example, "give us peace that we may live in harmony with each other"). Last, the collect states that the prayer is made in Christ's name (for example, "through Christ our Lord") and then concludes with an "Amen." Anglican collects were translated from the Latin Catholic Mass by Cranmer, and he set one at the beginning of each Sunday's service in the year. In the service for Evening Prayer, there are three collects. The petition in each varies: the first asks for pardon for sins, the second for God's peace, and the third for defense "against all perils and dangers of this night" (*BCP* 41).

---

on the manuscripts, believing incorrectly that the first two prayers were on the 1818 quarto sheet and the last on the undated sheet. I will follow Chapman's ordering of the prayers because, with the exception of Todd and Bree, the (limited) scholarship on the prayers does so; however, I should note that if I am right about the handwriting being Austen's, the second and third prayers may have been copied in Austen's lifetime, before the "first" prayer, copied, we know, sometime during or after 1818. More importantly, the prayers are so similar in tone and content that their chronological order is probably not particularly consequential. Chapman's errors may have proceeded from his sense that the prayers were relatively unimportant; as Laura Dabundo notes with asperity, he put them at the very end of *Minor Works*, preceding only the solutions to Austen's charades (243). Bree and Todd also examine in detail the question of when these prayers might have been composed and used. Following Deidre Le Faye, they consider that the prayers may have been written (though not yet copied) anytime after 1809 (cxxiii–cxxiv), and I can see no reason to find problematic the idea that the Austen family women would have used these prayers in lieu of prayers, psalms, and a sermon (the more usual practice of Evening Prayer), since they are shorter but perform most of the functions of evening prayer, including a collect, confession, intercessions, and the Lord's Prayer. What they omit is scriptural reading and the hortatory and expository function of the sermon. Many thanks to Janice Braun, Special Collections Librarian, Mills College, Oakland, California, for her help with these manuscripts.

[41]   In composing these prayers, Austen was not following, as she so commonly did, Dr. Johnson's strictures, for Johnson is on record as saying, "I know of no good prayers but those in the Book of Common Prayer" (Boswell 1292; qtd. Stovel 194).

Austen's prayers follow the form of the collect, though they are longer than the ones in the rite for Evening Prayer, one presumes because they were meant to replace the whole service. It is for this reason that each of these prayers also includes a sustained confession of sin and a request for forgiveness, a central part of Evening Prayer. That the prayers are to be a briefer replacement for Evening Prayer is evidenced as well by the fact that all three of the prayers ends with the Lord's Prayer, with an appropriate introduction at each prayer's close, such as this language from the first prayer: "Hear us Almighty God, for His sake who has redeemed us, & taught us thus to pray" ("Prayers Composed").[42]

The language of the prayers is closely modeled on the language of the *Book of Common Prayer*. Its Latinate vocabulary, sonorous cadences, and parallelisms heavily influenced Austen's diction and style. Specific phrases, directly quoted or only slightly altered, also reappear.[43] A few examples from the dozens of clear echoes include "thy faith and fear" (from the prayer for "the whole state of Christ's Church militant" in the Communion service [248]), "thy fatherly goodness" (from the "Thanksgiving for deliverance from the Plague or other common sickness" [63]), "thought, words and actions," a slight change from the "thought, word, and deed" of the General Confession in the Communion service (253), and "from thee no secret can be hid," a revision of the Collect in the Communion service, "Almighty God . . . from whom no secrets are hid" (242). The echoes are not merely verbal. The theology of the prayers is entirely orthodox relative to Anglican Christianity (though if we remember Henry Austen's "Biographical Notice" in which he claimed Austen's "opinions accorded strictly with those of our Established Church," we will not be particularly surprised [8]). As Wiesenfarth notes, in these prayers Austen attends closely to the doctrines of "the Trinity, the Incarnation, redemption, providence, and the fallen state of man" (60).

Yet these prayers are also clearly Austen's, marked by her own concerns and personality.[44] First, unlike the *Book of Common Prayer*, her prayers are rigorously

---

[42]  I follow here and elsewhere the manuscripts' capitalizations and spellings, rather than Chapman's.

[43]  Stovel (197–201), Dabundo, and Lambdin and Lambdin list further echoes or repetitions (the parallels cited by Lambdin and Lambdin are in some cases far-fetched [286–9]).

[44]  There is only one moment in which a notable phrase occurs in both the prayers and in the novels. In the third prayer, Austen thanks God for every hour of "innocent enjoyment." "Innocent enjoyment" also describes Fanny's pleasure in the Mansfield theatricals, contrasted with the morally compromised ambitions of all the other characters: "Fanny believed herself to derive as much innocent enjoyment from the play as any of them" (*MP* 193). Note that even here Austen does not affirm Fanny's judgment about her own "innocent enjoyment," and given the highly complex moral calculations concerning the theatricals, this refusal on the author's behalf to endorse the idea of "innocent enjoyment" directly only adds to the interpretive quandaries of this section of the novel.

devoid of figurative language.[45] There are no colorful phrases such as that found in the Prayer of Humble Access: "We are not worthy so much as to gather up the crumbs under thy Table" (257). There is also more direct emotion in Austen's invocations of God than in the prayerbook, for repeatedly the prayers are punctuated with an "Oh God!"—exclamation point included—a form of address not to be found in Cranmer's text. She also in five instances and in all three prayers uses the term "fellow-creatures" to refer to other people, a usage not found in the *Book of Common Prayer*, but one that reinforces the sense that Austen understood herself and other human beings chiefly as God's creation, an awareness that we explore in detail in Chapter 3 (as Austen prays, "Be Thou merciful, Oh heavenly Father! to creatures so formed and situated").[46] The prayers also emphasize the value Austen placed on the Anglican Church as such, asking God "to quicken our sense . . . of the value of that Holy Religion in which we have been brought up, that we may not, by our own neglect, throw away the Salvation Thou has given us, nor be Christians only in name." All three prayers remind their listeners that their family and friends are dispersed and in potential danger, as they ask God's protection from the evils of night and all the other ills that befall ordinary people, as in the second prayer: "For all whom we love & value, for every Friend and Connection, we equally pray; However divided & far asunder, we know that we are alike before Thee, and under thine Eye." Austen prays for self-knowledge, forgiveness, protection from evil, gratitude for God's grace, and ultimate redemption in heaven; she never prays for goods or services or any particular mark of fortune, instead marveling at the fortune she has already received ("We feel that we have been blessed far beyond any thing that we have deserved; and though we cannot but pray for a continuance of all these mercies, we acknowledge our unworthiness of them & implore Thee to pardon the presumption of our desires").

The third prayer was probably written last, as it demonstrates the clearest sense of the weight of time passing and the weight of divine judgment for wrongs committed; as Austen notes, "Another day is now gone, & added to those, for which we were before accountable." Her ultimate desire, the pinnacle of her hopes, becomes clear in the third prayer: to be reunited with her family in heaven after death. Noting the dispersal of "our own family and friends," Austen moves to her last petition: "may we by the assistance of thy Holy Spirit so conduct ourselves on Earth as to secure an Eternity of Happiness with each other in thy

---

[45]  Stovel notes that in this respect, Austen is following the dictates of Dr. Johnson: "I do not approve of figurative expressions in addressing the Supreme Being; and I never use them" (Boswell 1293; qtd. Stovel 198).

[46]  Dabundo discusses D. A. Miller's sense of Austen's "creatures" as sexless entities (Miller 101 [20n]), noting that it is more in keeping with Austen's worldview to see the term as rendering everyone "equivalent on a common plane" (250). She goes on to say that the "fellow" of "fellow-creatures" "adds to this usage a sense of joint plight or circumstance," reminding Austen's listeners of their two kinds of shared identity: standing before God, and standing together in the tradition of the Anglican Communion (251).

Heavenly Kingdom."[47] With this continual goal in hand, Austen was shielded from being devastated by the worldly disappointments she endured—lack of money, relative lack of recognition for her artistic achievements, spinsterhood, and illness. Instead, she asks in the third prayer for "that temper of Forbearance and Patience of which our Blessed Saviour has set us the highest Example, and which, while it prepares us for the spiritual Happiness of the life to come, will secure to us the best enjoyment of what this World can give."[48] We recognize here the hard moral evidenced most clearly in the portrayal of Mrs. Smith in *Persuasion*: forbearance, patience, lead to happiness—eternal and immediate (Mrs. Smith's "disposition to be comforted" and her "power of turning readily from evil to good" Anne views as "the choicest gift of Heaven" [*P* 167]).

The most important defining mark of Austen's prayers, however, comes in her awareness of human fault, particularly her own, and the commensurate greatness of God's mercy.[49] The most idiosyncratic feature of her prayers is their appeal for greater self-knowledge and greater charity.[50] It is hard to read the prayers without thinking of Austen's own propensity for malice, for the prayers seem to address her own consciousness of the wrongs she may have committed on a regular basis, a subject we will return to in Chapter 4. In the first prayer, she asks, "Teach us to understand the sinfulness of our own Hearts, and bring to our knowledge every

---

[47]    Even by 1817, the immediate Austen family, despite its size and the actuarial probabilities of death in this period, had suffered few losses, with the exception of Austen's father. Read in context, this prayer seems less a petition to join those who have already died than one to be joined ultimately by all the family members, now living and dead, in Heaven—in other words, to reform the happy Steventon domestic circle in God's kingdom.

[48]    This moment is the only one in the prayers in which Austen characterizes Christ, noting his "temper of Forbearance and Patience," the very qualities she found so appealing in West's "Christ Rejected" (see note 46).

[49]    Laura Dabundo usefully catalogues the characteristics Austen ascribes to human beings, her "fellow-creatures," in the prayers—they are "fallen, distracted, irresolute, irreverent, disobedient, slothful, weak, and evil souls, in a world where many are distressed, ill, afflicted, orphaned, widowed, captive, and imprisoned, as the night's shadows fall and loss and separation loom" (249). God, on the other hand, is characterized as "merciful, charitable, gracious, omniscient, omnipresent, [a] generous and good Father, afflicted with vexing children, deserving chiding and destruction, but Himself disposed, to instruct them how to be redeemed" (251).

[50]    Bruce Stovel argues that in her petitions for self-knowledge Austen is not relying on any model in the *Book of Common Prayer* (204), but I would point to the Collect in the Communion service, which makes this request: "Almighty God, unto whom all hearts be open, all desires known, and from whom no secrets are hid; Cleanse the thoughts of our hearts by the inspiration of thy Holy Spirit, that we may perfectly love thee, and worthily magnify thy holy Name" (242). One might also point to the long strictures read before the reception of Communion, which asks communicants "diligently to try and examine themselves" (252) and to "examine your lives and conversations by the rule of God's commandments" (250).

fault of Temper and every evil Habit in which we have indulged to the discomfort of our fellow-creatures, and the danger of our own Souls" ("Prayers Composed"). She continues, "have we . . . willingly given pain to any human Being?" and concludes, "Incline us to ask our Hearts these questions Oh! God, and save us from deceiving ourselves by Pride or Vanity." In the second prayer, Austen writes, "We remember with shame and contrition, many evil Thoughts & neglected duties; & we have perhaps sinned against Thee & against our fellow-creatures in many instances of which we have no remembrance." In the third prayer, she voices a similar sentiment: "Incline us Oh God! to think humbly of ourselves, to be severe only in the examination of our own conduct, to consider our fellow-creatures with kindness, & to judge of all they say and do with that Charity which we would desire from them ourselves." Stovel is correct to argue that these prayers feature "the sins to which Jane Austen felt she was most inclined" (204). Thus Austen's prayers provide powerful testimony about her orthodoxy as well as her own sense of her particular propensities regarding sin. Her readership, then and now, cannot really be surprised to learn that Austen thought her own worst sins were pride and an uncharitable disposition to judge her faulty "fellow-creatures," for her extraordinary intelligence and talents were sure to awaken a sense of personal pride, and her disposition to judge with wit rather than charity is one of the main reasons she has been read with such pleasure for almost two centuries.

# Chapter 3
# Austen and the Anglican Worldview

Above all other blessings Oh! God, for ourselves, & our fellow-creatures, we implore Thee to quicken our sense of thy Mercy in the redemption of the world, of the value of that Holy Religion in which we have been brought up, that we may not, by our own neglect, throw away the Salvation Thou has given us, nor be Christians only in name.

—Austen, "Evening Prayer"

## The Great Chain of Being

Austen's experience of Anglican Christianity during the late Georgian period underlies her presumptions about society's moral order; the "value of that Holy Religion" manifests itself in all Austen's presumptions about how the world is put together. However, even deeper in its effects than her contemporary religious experience runs the influence of Christian cosmology, a worldview dominated by the Great Chain of Being and natural law, those twin syntheses of Christianity and classicism. These interrelated explanations for nature, morality, social organization, and history—indeed, for all of space and time—dominated Western Christian thought from its beginnings until at least Austen's day, even though Enlightenment ideas had begun to challenge their rationale as early as the sixteenth century. While by the eighteenth century, French and German philosophers and scientists such as Diderot, Voltaire, and Schelling had joined British freethinkers, pantheists and deists, Unitarians, "levelers," and other heterodox religious figures to question the orthodoxy of natural law and the Great Chain, people in Austen's world—home county Anglican gentry and clergy—and Austen herself felt very little of these disruptions. One key reason for the relatively placid acceptance of these ancient ideas by Austen's milieu is that the British poets and thinkers of the eighteenth century who constituted much of the intellectual heritage of the English gentry largely accepted the ideas themselves. As Donald Greene argues about eighteenth-century authors, "[i]t is evident, as one makes one's way through the writings of the standard authors of Enlightened England, that their view of man and his place in the universe and his destiny is essentially that of such earlier Christian writers as Spenser and Milton, Donne and Herbert, rather than that of Voltaire and Diderot" (*The Age of Exuberance* 93). Arthur Lovejoy, whose 1936 study of the Great Chain is one of the most important works of intellectual history of the twentieth century, goes further: "There has been no period in which writers of all sorts—men of science and philosophers, poets and popular essayists, deists and orthodox divines—talked so much about the Chain of Being, or accepted more implicitly the general scheme of ideas connected with it" (183).[1] Thus the Great Chain was a key component of Austen's Christian and neo-classical inheritance.[2] The deep embeddedness of the Great Chain of Being and natural law in Austen's views of language, social hierarchy, nature, and history underpins the worldview of all her fiction. The evidence and consequences of her reliance on these governing cosmological ideas and the evidence and consequences of her modest challenges to their hegemony, particularly as they apply to the "natural" hierarchies of social rank, rewards investigation.[3]

At the heart of the Great Chain of Being are the presumptions that God created the universe and everything in it, that everything that has been created has a reason for existence, and that the created world is complete, orderly, and hierarchical. The three governing principles of the Great Chain are *plenitude, continuity*, and *gradation. Plenitude* originates with Plato; the doctrine holds that the created world contains every form of being that could be possible (the obverse, that some form of existence might exist but does not, would undermine the premise that the universe is perfect and that God failed to express His creativity completely). The idea held sway in the Christian tradition largely because its predicate, the infinite goodness, creativity, and reasonableness of God, made its logic seemingly unanswerable. Augustine, Abelard, and Aquinas in turn agreed that if God's perfection is manifested in part by His creativity, then every possible form, every

---

[1]    Lovejoy continues: "Addison, King, Bolingbroke, Pope, Haller, Thomson, Akenside, Buffon, Bonnet, Goldsmith, Diderot, Kant, Lambert, Herder, Schiller—all these and a host of lesser writers not only expatiated upon the theme but drew from it new, or previously evaded consequences. . . . Next to the word 'Nature,' 'the Great Chain of Being' was the sacred phrase of the eighteenth century, playing a part somewhat analogous to that of the blessed word 'evolution' in the late nineteenth" (183–4). Lovejoy's seminal text sets out the intellectual heritage of the Great Chain from Plato and Aristotle through Augustine, Aquinas, and others up to the eighteenth and early nineteenth century. Importantly, Lovejoy tracks the challenges to and modifications of the idea, particularly in the late Enlightenment, primarily by continental thinkers but also by British figures such as Hume and Smellie. An important re-assessment of Lovejoy's work can be found in Bynum.

[2]    Winthrop Jordan notes that "[i]t is instructive to remember that the concept could never have gained such widespread popularity during the eighteenth century without having roots thrust deep in men's conception of the world. . . . To put the matter boldly and hence to overstate it, the Chain of Being was only one (unusually specific) projection of a profound sense of and yearning for hierarchical arrangement" (510).

[3]    Michael Giffin puts the case for her immersion in the ideologies of natural law most plainly: "Austen conducts her critique as a devout Christian believer within the Anglican church; and as a Georgian believer in classical metaphysics—that is, in the metaphysics synthesized from the classical Greek, ancient Hebrew, and Christian world-views. Her metaphysical attitude, which is both implicit and explicit in her novels, sets her apart from the postmetaphysical attitude of many of her literary descendants. Austen accepts the deposit of mainstream Anglican 'truth' as she sees it reflected in the web of human relationships that make up her family, her society, and her church; and as she sees it reflected in the natural world" (2).

idea God could have imagined, in fact exists (Formigari 326).[4] *Continuity* and *gradation* emerge as concepts in Aristotle. *Continuity* holds that among all the creation there are no gaps.[5]

The doctrine of continuity thus holds that all nature forms a chain in which each entity is connected and linked to those above and below.[6] Importantly, the chain presumes overlaps; no creature or created thing exists in discontinuity with others. The third principle, *gradation*, is closely allied to continuity. It premises a hierarchy of value in the chain of nature, running from the angels down to humans down to animals, plants, and inanimate nature, such as that lowest of minerals, lead. The idea of gradation is primarily expressed through the metaphor of up and down, often as a ladder that runs from the height (angelic beings) to the depth (amoebas, lice, minerals). In the middle ages, this view of nature as a hierarchy received intense and detailed calibration. Indeed, our popular culture still has lingering memories of these medieval hierarchies, for everyone "knows" that the

---

[4]   As Leibniz argued in *De rerum originatione radicali* (1697), "In possible things, or in their very possibility or essence, there is an exigency to exist, or (so to speak) claim to exist" (qtd. in Formigari 328). It is not until the eighteenth and nineteenth centuries that the idea of plenitude happening *over time* arises with any strength; at this historical juncture, scientists and philosophers begin to argue that, yes, all creatures that could exist do, but do so across the fullness of time, from the primeval past through an unknown future. This shift to seeing plenitude through the panoply of time allows room for understanding the skeletons of dinosaurs, for example. See Lovejoy, chapter 9. In general, early paleontology posed a devastating threat to all tenets of the Great Chain, but the crisis regarding plenitude was created chiefly through the increasingly popular idea of species (the idea of species also raised difficulties for the premise of continuity; see 6n below).

[5]   Aristotle argued that nature passes so gradually from the inanimate to the animate that their continuity renders the boundary between them indistinguishable; and there is a middle kind which belongs to both orders: "For plants come immediately after inanimate things; and plants differ from each other in the degree in which they seem to participate in life. For the class, taken as a whole, seems clearly animate; but compared with animals to be inanimate. And the transition between plants and animals is continuous; for one might question whether some marine animals are animals or plants, since many of them are attached to the rock and perish if they are separated from it" (486a).

[6]   The idea of continuity underwrote many eighteenth-century rejections of the idea of species, such as that made by the French naturalist Buffon: "There will be found a great number of intermediate species, and of objects belonging half in one class and half in another. Objects of this sort, to which it is impossible to assign a place, necessarily render vain the attempt at a universal system" (qtd. in Lovejoy 230). Oliver Goldsmith, whose popular compendium of natural history Austen very likely knew (at 16, she parodied his *History of England* with her own, and later referred to other well-known works of his, including "The Deserted Village" and *The Vicar of Wakefield*), also argued that all divisions among nature's creatures "are perfectly arbitrary. The gradation of one order of beings to another, is so imperceptible, that it is impossible to lay the line that shall distinctly mark the boundaries of each" (283–4). For more on Goldsmith's views of nature's laws, see Lynskey and Pitman.

lion is king of beasts, the eagle king of birds, the oak the king of trees, and gold the king of the elements. Humankind's position was particularly interesting, caught midway between angels and beasts, a theme Shakespeare returns to incessantly, as in Hamlet's speech:

> What a piece of work is a man! how noble in reason!
> how infinite in faculty! in form and moving how
> express and admirable! in action how like an angel!
> in apprehension how like a god! the beauty of the
> world! the paragon of animals! (II, ii, 304–8)

English thought of the eighteenth century largely still accepted gradation, despite the socio-political challenges posed to its dominance by revolution, democracy, and capitalism. Humankind is peculiarly posed as the nexus of creation, as Addison argued: "[h]e who, in one respect, is associated with angels and archangels, and may look upon a being of Infinite Perfection as his Father, and to the highest order of Spirits as his brethren, may, in another respect, say to Corruption, Thou art my Father, and to the Worm, Thou art my Sister" (Lovejoy 195).

Gradation in particular gave divine authority to hierarchical social structures, most importantly, feudalism and the assumption of "the divine right of kings." But though feudalism had in large part disintegrated by the eighteenth century, the orthodox presumption that society's order has a divine sanction persisted. Pope's *Essay on Man* (1734), for instance, assumes the justice and self-evident rightness of hierarchic gradation:

> Order is Heav'n's first law; and this confest,
> Some are, and must be, greater than the rest,
> More rich, more wise: but who infers from hence
> That such are happier shocks all common sense.
> Heaven to mankind impartial we confess,
> If all are equal in their happiness:
> But mutual wants this happiness increase;
> All Nature's diff'rence keeps all Nature's peace.
> Condition, circumstance, is not the thing;
> Bliss is the same in subject or in king. (IV, ll. 49–58)

Soame Jenyns, member of Parliament and writer, also set out (in 1757) the self-affirming virtues of social rank, approving the entire system with the relish common to those near the top of this structure:

> Thus the Universe resembles a large and well-regulated Family, in which all
> the officers and servants, and even the domestic animals, are subservient to
> each other in a proper subordination; each enjoys the privileges and perquisites
> peculiar to his place, and at the same time contributes, by that just subordination,
> to the magnificence and happiness of the whole. It is evident therefore that the
> Evils of Imperfection, proceeding from the necessary inferiority of some Beings
> in comparison to others, can in no sense be called any Evils at all. (40)

The Anglican catechism contained in the 1662 *Book of Common Prayer* enshrines this principle of subordination as a moral duty; four of the 14 tenets of "thy duty to thy Neighbour" recited by the devout initiate concern accepting one's place in the social order ("to submit myself to all my governors, teachers, spiritual pastors and masters," "to order myself lowly and reverently to all my betters," "not to covet nor desire other men's goods," and "to do my duty in that state of life, unto which it shall please God to call me" [298–9]).

## Natural Law

Closely allied to the Great Chain of Being is natural law, first set out by Aristotle and then "Christianized" by Aquinas.[7] Natural law holds that everything in creation has a reason and purpose, and that reason itself, made by God, is the central mode by which we can understand the purpose of the universe. Locke's 1695 *The Reasonableness of Christianity* thus prefigures the approach of almost all British theology of the eighteenth century, because reasonableness is presumed to follow from God's design and in turn to allow us to discern it. Natural law holds that the reason and purpose of humankind is to do good, avoid evil, and to work to know and love God. Since, as Aquinas held, the one rational goal of humankind was to join God in the next life after death, one's behavior rationally should accord with that goal. God is the logical ground of all moral sanctions, as St. Augustine argued (Burke 4), and the best exercise of our reason is to praise the God who gave it, in Locke's view (Harris 1). As Locke explained in Book IV of his *Essay on Human Understanding*, "Reason is natural revelation, whereby the eternal Father of light, the Foundation of all knowledge, communicates to mankind that portion of truth which he has laid within the reach of their natural faculties; Revelation is natural reason enlarged by a new set of discoveries communicated by God immediately, which reason vouches the truth of, by the testimony and proofs it gives that they come from God" (289).[8] These central principles of natural law endure and even

---

[7]    Daston and Stolleis give the antecedents in detail:

In both law and science, historians have drawn attention to ancient roots and medieval precedents. Historians of law cite Aristotle in the *Nicomachean Ethics*, Cicero in *De legibus*, Romans 2:13–15 in the New Testament, Gratian in the *Decretum*, Aquinas in the *Summa theologiae*–all speak of a natural law that has normative force and is variously derived from universal human nature . . . the dictates imprinted by God in the human heart, or the participation of rational creatures in the divine *lex aeterna*. For their part, historians of science point to Seneca's reference to a possible 'law' of comets in the *Questiones naturales*, Pliny's call for a 'law' of the maximum elongation of Venus and Mercury from the sun in the *Historia naturalis*, Roger Bacon's 'law' of refraction, and the *lex contradictionis* of thirteenth-century logic as evidence of a long lineage for the natural law concept in the sciences. (2–3)

[8]    Colin Brown explains: "What Locke was doing here was to combine the traditional apologetic approach, which stressed fulfilled prophecy and miracles as divine attestation of Christian truth claims, with his empirical approach to knowledge. . . . In taking up this

thrive throughout the eighteenth century. As late as 1830, the (by this point) entirely orthodox Coleridge would declare: "to divinity belong those fundamental truths, which are the common ground-work of our civil and our religious duties, not less indispensable to a right view of our temporal concerns, than to a rational faith respecting our immortal well-being" (51).

Natural law holds that Scripture, nature, and even human activity give forth evidence of God's reason. Most eighteenth-century divines agreed with Locke that Scripture both reveals divine revelation and records the human reasoning that approaches the divine (Giffin 14). Eighteenth-century belief rested on an understanding that Scripture's authority derived less from its canonicity—the authority given it by church dictate—than from the way "its revelation is reflected in society as well as in nature; and its truth is empirically verifiable to the believer who has been made in the image of God, who has been given the faculty of reason, and who has the ability to reflect on experience" (Giffin 15).[9] Eighteenth-century theologians such as Butler, Law, and Gisbourne followed the traditions of natural law by commonly treating nature's wonders as signs of God's majesty and as proofs of God's existence (the latter is known to us as the argument from design—that is, nature shows the marks of design, and these marks thus prove the existence of a Designer). One did not need raptures or visions to see God's plan—it was evident in all nature, including its most ordinary and lowliest aspects. David Hartley, a Christian philosopher, argued in 1749 that nature was analogous to Scripture, proffering self-evident confirmation of God's design: "[a]ll the works of God, the parts of a human body, systems of minerals, plants, and animals, elementary bodies, planets, fixed stars, etc. have various uses and subserviences, in respect to each other; and, if the scriptures be the word of God, analogy would lead one to expect something corresponding hereto in them" (160). All things in nature were understood to be ordered by a divine rational code. William Derham, Canon of Windsor and natural philosopher (he was, incidentally, the first person to

---

position Locke was adopting a form of foundationalism which argues that there had to be a rational foundation for belief. Acceptance of divine revelation was rational because there were rational grounds for believing that the revelation (understood in terms of unverifiable proposition) had come from God" (224–5).

[9]    Giffin further notes that "natural law dominated mainstream Anglican morality in the Georgian period because it complemented the scientific and empirical spirit of the age" (25). As Hans Frei argues, in the British eighteenth century, Biblical narratives were presumed to embody divine truths, while the realist outlook "never shaped in the study of the Bible the same kind of imaginative and analytical grasp applied to the writing and reading of the novel. Realism in regard to the Bible meant . . . its treatment in the spirit of Bolingbroke's dictum about history, 'philosophy teaching by example.' . . . The Bible's perennial themes were taken to be descriptive of the solid, real, and mundane world and its God taught by eighteenth-century science, and of the solid, real, and mundane virtues inculcated by history and philosophy" (151–2). See also Chapter 1, n. 31, for Frei's contrast between the demands of realist inquiry in Germany and Great Britain relative to Scripture and the novel.

measure the speed of sound) held in 1714 that it was rational and natural to treat all of nature's wonders as signs of the greatness of God, as marks and badges that acknowledge the existence of God to the believer, flatly proclaiming that "the Universality and Uniformity of the Figure of the several Globes of the Universe is a sign of their being the Work of GOD, not of Chance or Necessity" (124). [10] Even the affairs of men can manifest God's plan, design, and reason.[11] Moralists made much of the individual histories of great men when the lesson could be drawn that those who lived in accord with natural law thrived and those who defied it by living outside of God's law were doomed (Plutarch's *Lives* provided useful examples).

Further, the doings of men and women living in the here and now were also understood to be governed by natural law. Each of Austen's novels illustrates this idea; repeatedly, selfish and irreligious people create their own unhappy destinies by their behavior, while the moral education of faulty protagonists works to align their behavior with natural law. After all, natural law cannot be evaded, as figures such as Mary Crawford and Willoughby learn to their sorrow; even the bad characters that seem to prosper, such as Lucy Steele, live in hells of their own

---

[10]  See also Wasserman, "Nature Moralized," on the widespread assumptions of the "divine analogy," that correspondence between spiritual reality and nature: "In one fashion or another, most eighteenth-century philosophic roads led to the divine analogy" (67). Wasserman concludes by noting the breakdown of the analogy by the mid-nineteenth century, when "the union . . . between the intellectual and material world . . . is to be created by the mind instead of found" (76).

[11]  Natural law holds that human intercourse, properly conducted, shows God's reason, while the far more numerous examples of improperly conducted human affairs also bear evidence in that wrong behavior brings punishment. Even conversation can lead and should lead to God, even though it so often does not. In a long poem on "Conversation" (1782), Cowper, Austen's favorite poet, first records and dissects the many faults of conversation as practiced in his contemporary society (the discussion of common faults comprises almost all of the poem) and then moves to a much briefer section on what God-given conversation should be: "Conversation, choose what theme we may, / And chiefly when religion lead the way, / Should flow, like waters after summer show'rs, / Not as if raised by mere mechanic pow'rs" (254). Here, Cowper holds that conversation comes from heaven and is designed to follow the course that "truth and nature teach" (Korshin 382). The poem closes by comparing conversation to a lyre played by artful hands: "tun'd at length to some immortal song / It sounds Jehovah's name, and pours his praise along" (265). Austen's sense of religious decorum forbids her from attempting to reproduce such heavenly conversation in her novels, though she does intimate that the best and most proper conversations will take place between her lovers once they have come to a romantic understanding of each other. The closest example the novels provide of such high-flown discourse occurs in *Mansfield Park*, when Edmund finds out that Fanny has always loved him: "His happiness in knowing himself to have been so long the beloved of such a heart, must have been great enough to warrant any strength of language in which he could clothe it to her or to himself; it must have been a delightful happiness!" (545). For more on the moral complexities of Austen's conversations, see the careful and discerning analysis in Tandon.

making.[12] Similarly, when essentially good characters like Emma go wrong, they do so because they are acting lawlessly, without attention to the need for humility, charity, truthfulness, or self-examination, and in pursuit of vain triumphs—as Emma's behavior at Box Hill evidences most clearly.[13] Properly pursued, relations between people can reveal God's truth and the moral underpinnings of the universe. Christians were trained to find evidence of God's providential rule in their own lives, and the proper role of meditation and self-examination was to rehearse this process of discerning God's will and to discover and rectify one's variance from it (Williams 54–5). The undeniable and painful evidence of unreason in actual human history could also be explained by natural law, partly by the presumption that heavenly justice ultimately rights all earthly injustices (so the wicked only *seem* to prosper) and partly by the popular trope (continued from the Renaissance) of *concordia discors*—that is, reconciled extremes. We see lingering hints of the idea of *concordia discors* in Elizabeth's regret-filled rationale for why she and Mr. Darcy could have had perfect "connubial felicity":

---

[12]   In the closing pages of *Sense and Sensibility*, Austen tells us of the fate of Mr. and Mrs. Robert Dashwood, a fate that follows from the tenets of natural law: "They settled in town, received very liberal assistance from Mrs. Ferrars, and setting aside the jealousies and ill-will continually subsisting between Fanny and Lucy, in which their husbands of course took a part, as well as the frequent domestic disagreements between Robert and Lucy themselves, nothing could exceed the harmony in which they all lived together" (428). In other words, despite their financial security, they live in complete disharmony, a disharmony they create themselves.

In meting out a similar dispensation for Henry Crawford in *Mansfield Park*, Austen takes care to distinguish between the punishment in the here-and-now and the "juster appointment hereafter": Henry will not suffer as much as Maria in the public view, because women's sexual sins earn a disproportionately harsher rebuke, but he will have "no small portion of vexation and regret—vexation that must rise sometimes to self-reproach, and regret to wretchedness" (542). By contrast, Austen's earlier cad, Willoughby, undergoes a "repentance of misconduct [that is] sincere" and "live[s] to exert himself" (SS 430); that is, Willoughby undergoes Christian redemption. There is no sign that the same happens to Henry Crawford, for he is allotted the "wretchedness" assumed to be allied with that worst of Christian sins, despair.

Austen could be playful about her devotion to the principles of natural law relative to poetic justice. Writing to her young niece Caroline in 1814 about a story Caroline had submitted for her aunt's review, Austen advised that "the good for nothing father, who was the real author of all [the heroine's] Faults & Sufferings, should not escape unpunished. –I hope he hung himself, or took the sur-name of *Bone* or underwent some direful penance or other" (*L* 288). "Bone" would have been a dreadful punishment because it was a variant of "Bonaparte."

[13]   Gene Koppel notes this unswaying role of natural law in *Emma*: "[A]lways, . . . there is Christian natural law, demanding that . . . Emma should stop thinking and acting like a spoiled child and becomes what God wants her to be" (56–7).

On lying as a particular transgression against natural law, Locke writes, "[lying introduces] confusion, disorder and uncertainty into the Affairs of Mankind; and if not destroyed, yet in great measure [renders] useless, those two great Rules, Religion and Justice" (*Essay* III. x. 12; qtd. in Harris 21).

> She began now to comprehend that he was exactly the man, who, in disposition and talents, would most suit her. His understanding and temper, though unlike her own, would have answered all her wishes. It was an union that must have been to the advantage of both; by her ease and liveliness, his mind might have been softened, his manners improved and from his judgment, information, and knowledge of the world, she must have received benefit of greater importance. (344)

*Concordia discors* provides a means of rationalizing the oppositions in nature, human and otherwise; it further implies that the reconciling of opposites is a sign of natural balance, that oppositions all have their order in God's plan and fit a God-given harmony.[14] That by 1813 Austen sees how easily *concordia discors* may be undone is perhaps evident by Elizabeth's reflection that follows the above: "[n]o such happy marriage could now teach the admiring multitude what connubial felicity really was. An union of a different tendency, and precluding the possibility of the other, was soon to be formed in their family" (344). Another opposition comes to mind—Elizabeth and Darcy vs. Lydia and Wickham—and Elizabeth is forced to see how irreconcilable the two extremes are. (We note that Elizabeth is wrong, and that both unions do take place, providing clearly contrasting didactic examples of good and bad marriages, but not of reconciled extremes.)

## Providence

One key concept of natural law provides a reason for everything that happens to human beings, good or bad: Providence. Providence denotes God's creation of the world with its ultimate redemption in view, his sovereignty over history and events, and his continual agency in ordinary people's lives. As the Anglican divine George Horne argued in a 1775 sermon, "a proper survey of the great scheme of Providence . . . must take its rise from that gracious purpose of saving mankind, and bringing them to glory, which appears to have possessed the first place in the designs of heaven" (*Providence of God* 3). Anglican conceptions of Providence, derived both from Augustine and Aquinas on the one hand and from Calvin on the other, focus on God's election of those who choose him freely (this seeming paradox, of course, is at the root of all the difficulties inherent in Calvinist doctrines of predestination). The Catechism Austen memorized prior to her confirmation at age 18 explains the function of God's Trinity in human life in this manner:

---

[14] See Bogel, pp. 35–7, on the eighteenth-century treatments of *concordia discors*, especially in Pope. The concept's power declined, inevitably, as the vision of the universe's order decayed. See also Wasserman for a detailed discussion of the progressive loss of explanatory power *concordia discors* held in the eighteenth century (*Subtler Language*, chapter 5). However, some Romantic (and partly secularized) versions of the idea held, as in Goethe's 1809 *Elective Affinities*, a novel which expresses the idea that "opposite dispositions are the best basis for a very close union" (40).

First, I learn to believe in God the Father, who hath made me, and all the world.
Secondly, in God the Son, who hath redeemed me, and all mankind.
Thirdly, in God the Holy Ghost, who sanctifieth me, and all the elect people
    of God.
(*Book of Common Prayer* 297)

This is what Austen believed: God made, redeemed, and sanctified her and other believers; further, his plan—laid before the universe was created—was that she would be part of this cosmic plan for creation and redemption. As her prayers make plain, she expected God's providential care for her and her family. Sickness and death were understood as part of God's plan. Anglican theology, especially as inflected by Evangelical ideas, assured each Christian that suffering was the believer's walk of the Cross, a parallel experience of Christ's passion that helped prepare one for heaven.

The Christian insistence on Providence is allied with its understanding of human experience as typological. Typology is a term for a kind of reading practice, in which the earlier events of Biblical history (as represented in the Old Testament) are rendered intelligible by the Gospel narrative.[15] In the Gospels, Christ himself often proffers typological readings on the multiple occasions he quotes Hebrew Scripture so as to point to himself as the fulfillment of that Scripture's promises. He does so particularly on the one occasion when he gives a comprehensive exegesis of how he fulfills scripture, as related in the story of the road to Emmaus from the *Gospel of Luke*. The story takes place after the Resurrection. Having appeared to two of his own disciples who are fleeing Jerusalem for the safer haven of Emmaus (they do not recognize him), Christ rebukes them for their lack of understanding about his passion: "'O foolish men, and slow of heart to believe all that the prophets have spoken! Was it not necessary that the Christ should suffer these things and enter into his glory?' And beginning with Moses and all the prophets, he interpreted to them in all the Scriptures the things concerning himself" (*Luke* 24:23–7). Christian writers developed the typological idea with extraordinary detail, no one more so than Augustine, who famously noted that "The New Testament lies hidden in the Old and the Old Testament is revealed in the New" (*City of God* XVI, 26). Thus Adam, Job, and Jonah could be understood as "types" in the Old Testament whose full meaning becomes revealed in their "antitype," Christ, in the New Testament, while Noah's Ark, the "type," becomes understood more completely once one identifies its "antitype," the Church.

---

[15]   Typology is a longstanding branch of Christian theological study, one that can easily consume a lifetime of research. For a good introduction, see Charity, *Events and Their Afterlife*. Charity defines typology "as either the broad study, or any particular presentation, of the quasi-symbolic relations which one event may appear to bear to another—especially, but not exclusively, when these relations are the analogical ones existing between events which are taken to be one another's 'prefiguration' and 'fulfillment.' Christian typology is the science of history's relation to its fulfillment in Christ" (1).

Typological thinking was most widespread in the middle ages, but it persisted through Austen's day (and beyond).[16] For instance, the philosopher David Hartley wrote in 1749 that "there is an Aptness in the Types and Prophecies, to prefigure the events, greater than can be supposed to result from Chance, or human Foresight. When this is evidently made out from the great number of the Types and Prophecies and the Degree of Clearness and Preciseness of . . . will rather prove the Divine Interposition rather than exclude it" (160). Eighteenth-century minds were particularly bent to adopt a certain inflection of typology, in which individual believers themselves are understood to enact the passion narrative by moving through life with its sufferings and moral trials.[17] This species of typological view became especially popular among Evangelicals, Anglican and dissenting alike. Each believer was thought to hold his or her own Cross, so that Christ becomes the type and the individual becomes the antitype: "this narrative framework [provides] the meaningful pattern within which alone the occurrence of the cross finds its applicative sense. . . . What the Christian really lives is his own pilgrimage, and to its pattern he looks for the assurance that he is really living it" (Frei 153–4).

Eighteenth-century British literature is full of typological tropes and plots, particularly in its employment of the idea of the protagonist as a Christian pilgrim, who, as in Bunyan's work, walks along the way Christ had prepared for him. As Paul Korshin notes, British narratives of this period are replete with "scenes that recall the beginning of Christian's pilgrimage [which] occur hundreds if not thousands of times in the structures of narrative beginnings" (370). Defoe, Richardson, Goldsmith, Fielding, Sterne, and even Johnson presented typological plots.[18] For example, Defoe's defense of *Robinson Crusoe* in the novel's seldom-read third volume makes evident the typological meaning of his protagonist's trials. Defoe compares them directly to those of Bunyan's Christian: "The telling or writing a parable, or an allusive allogorick [*sic*] History . . . is design'd and effectually turn'd for instructive and upright Ends, and has its Moral justly apply'd: Such are the historical Parables in the holy Scripture, such the Pilgrims Progress, and such in a Word the Adventures of your fugitive Friend, *Robinson Crusoe*" (115–6).

---

[16]  Korshin, for instance, argues that "[t]he view that God was the author of the types, as he was the author of the book of nature, may be found in eighteenth-century theology as clearly as in that of Augustine" (390).

[17]  Gerhard von Rad, the most eminent Old Testament typologist of the twentieth century, has argued that this analogical kind of reading of human experience, natural to artists, follows from and seems to prove natural law: "in the passing of the years and the days, in the most elementary relationships of man with man, in simple mechanical performances—in everything regularity 'reveals' itself to the poet, and hints at an order that dwells deep within things" (17).

[18]  See Damrosch for a thorough treatment of the development of the eighteenth-century novel as a mode of Puritan religious sensibility, especially Puritan self-searching and providentialism. Damrosch finds an end to providentialism in Fielding's *Tom Jones* (1749).

Austen's use of typology is very subdued, for two reasons: religious decorum and utility. As we have seen in Chapter 2, she consciously excluded explicitly religious material because it was improper, she felt, to include such entirely "serious" material within the world of the popular novel and because she was also aware that subtler messages were more likely to succeed than straightforward didacticism or preaching. She does not write explicit Christian allegory, though some narrative sequences, such as the visit to Sotherton in *Mansfield Park*, which features a garden in which humans choose to wander and sin, invite allegorical explanations.[19] Nonetheless, the plots are in accord with Christian teleology, as Gary Kelly argues: "[the plots] are consistent with an Anglican reading of human history as a form of romance journey in which an omniscient yet benevolent deity presides over a historical plot of human error, fall, and redemption by both free will and grace, and which instructs the reader to hope for and aspire to redemption" (165).[20] The novels display the workings of Providence, as engineered by a sub-creator, whose values are meant to be in complete accord with the Creator himself.[21]

The novels provide invaluable evidence about Austen's views of Providence. For instance, as a Christian, she was bound to disbelieve in chance or fortune as such, and it should not surprise that characters who bind themselves to the operations of chance (by choosing an irreligious principle) thus choose poor outcomes (as natural law dictates). As Stuart Tave shows, characters such as Charlotte Lucas (who avers, "Happiness in marriage is always a matter of chance" [*PP* 25]) or Frank Churchill (who relies on "any thing, every thing—to time, chance, circumstance" [*E* 476–7]), expose themselves to unhappy consequences exactly because they believe in the random effects of chance rather than Providence (15–6).[22] Further,

---

[19]  Michael Giffin's work most thoroughly advances an allegorical reading of the novels, arguing that reading the novels within an "overarching frame of Christian humanism," readers will find an author who "writes Christian stories in which heroines who fall, as do we all, have to imitate Christe [*sic*], loving their enemies, turning the other cheek, denying themselves, taking up their crosses, and . . . making their way to their metaphorical crucifixion" (27). I would hold that Austen's motives of religious decorum (see Chapter 2) militate strongly against her advancing allegory as such, but the typological parallels between her heroines' stories and that of the Christian passion are indeed in evidence.

[20]  Kelly continues: "Austen's narrative structure can be read as a secularized homology for the Anglican position. In this homology the protagonist is responsible for her worldly 'salvation,' or moral condition and social destiny, guided by a sympathetic yet critical narrator, who allows the reader to identify with the protagonists' struggle, and thus to experience that struggle vicariously, again guided by the narrator" (161).

[21]  The formal and moral difficulties that arise as a consequence of this elision between God's values and the implied values of Austen's narrator are discussed in detail in Chapter 5.

[22]  Tave further notes that characters who use the word "odd" often reveal themselves as "simpletons." Harriet and Mr. Martin's birthdays are only 15 days apart "'which is very odd'" (*E* 29); "'How very odd!,'" Miss Bates exclaims when she finds there is but one step into the Crown Inn, though she had thought there were two (*E* 356); and Mrs. Bennet cannot understand the entail: "'Things are settled so oddly. There is no knowing how estates will

the happy endings for Austen's heroines are rarely the result of the heroine's own direct dealings; Providence in the form of the author must intervene. In *Northanger Abbey*, Elinor's marriage to a titled gentleman softens the General's heart so that he allows Catherine and Henry to wed; in *Sense and Sensibility*, Lucy Steele clears herself away as competitor to Elinor for Edward; in *Pride and Prejudice*, Darcy's intervention with Lydia and Wickham and Lady Catherine's intervention with Elizabeth are the primary causes of Elizabeth and Darcy's engagement; in *Mansfield Park*, Henry and Maria's absconding results in Edmund turning his attention to Fanny; and, last, in *Emma*, Frank and Jane's engagement clears up confused motives so that Emma and Mr. Knightley may come to understand each other. Only in *Persuasion* does the heroine propel the happy ending into being, finding an indirect way to let Wentworth know she loves him, and even in this case, a rival must first remove herself from the field, as Louisa does by turning her attentions from Wentworth to Benwick. Tave rightly notes that Austen's moral is clear, that one must be prepared to accept suffering to be ready for joy:[23]

> All the heroines find happy endings and they all deserve them, as each has, in one way or another, worked, suffered, learned. But . . . they seem to arrive at, or be helped to, the happy ending by a stroke of luck. . . . The happy ending is not guaranteed by their actions. What seems to be more important than the sudden and fortunate event, however, because it precedes the ending again and again, . . . is that the heroine is prepared to accept unhappiness. . . . She must really see it as a loss, absorb it as an irreversible fact, and then come to terms with herself and go ahead with what she must do now. . . . What is important is that at the time [the reward] is granted the heroine is worthy of a happiness that has a meaning. (18–9)

---

go when once they come to be entailed'" (*PP* 178). Their worldviews are so limited that anything that disrupts their expectations seems random and entirely accidental, though of course there is nothing accidental, for instance, about how entails operate (Tave 44). Tave argues that the moral life "turns upon probabilities," but that Austen allows us to judge her characters in part by the degree to which they allow self-interest to shade their sense of the probable: "Emma Woodhouse's easy equation of 'desirable, natural, and probable' is always tempting" (*E* 35, 74; Tave 54).

[23] Kelly makes a parallel point: "Austen's plots are resolved by neither the protagonist's rational will nor the force of systemic injustice, by neither a *deus ex machina* nor coincidence, but by a convergence of will and circumstance, or something like grace" (163). Active protagonists like Elizabeth Bennet or Emma Woodhouse err repeatedly, but act correctly and somewhat unexpectedly at the decisive moment. Passive protagonists have correct judgment but seem unable to act, and destined to endure rather than to prevail, until circumstances unexpectedly present the occasion to receive their merited happiness. The turning point for the active protagonists is a moment of profound Christian humility. As Donald Greene has written, "The great climactic scenes . . . are of self-recognition, where a central character reaches the stage of being able to confess as Jane Austen's Book of Common Prayer put it, 'I have left undone those things which I ought to have done, and I have done those things which I ought not to have done, and there is no health in me'" ("Jane Austen's Monsters" 263). The passive heroines are already humble, but the mistaken selfish actions of others bring about their happiness.

Merit does not guarantee happiness; rather grace, that instrument of God's Providence, governs the final allotments of justice and reward (Kelly 164).[24]

The two novels which refer to Providence directly are, unsurprisingly, *Mansfield Park* and *Persuasion.* In *Mansfield Park*, on learning that Fanny is not pained to have lost Henry Crawford, Edmund exclaims, "'Thank God! . . . We were all disposed to wonder—but it seems to have been the merciful appointment of Providence that the heart which knew no guile, should not suffer'" (527). While Fanny does not miss Henry's attentions, Edmund is wrong that she has not suffered, and the reader will be aware of this irony. In fact, Fanny had hoped for a different providential outcome on learning that Henry and Maria have run off together: "it appeared to her, that as far as this world alone was concerned, the greatest blessing to every one of kindred with Mrs. Rushworth would be instant annihilation" (511). Fortunately, Austen's own Providence is less apocalyptic. Hers will bring Edmund and Fanny together, instead, and Austen notes the perfection of its workings: "exactly at the time when it was quite natural that it should be so, and not a week earlier, Edmund did cease to care about Miss Crawford, and became as anxious to marry Fanny, as Fanny herself could desire" (544).[25]

Providence also plays an important role in *Persuasion.* Providence made Sir Walter a baronet, we learn, but his many failings threaten his God-given appointment; he is a "foolish, spendthrift baronet, who had not had principle or sense enough to maintain himself in the situation in which Providence had placed him" (270). That Sir Walter's view of his responsibilities to Providence is corrupt has been established much earlier, for Austen describes his squandering of his estate in language that parodies the language of Providence and God's call: "he had done nothing but what Sir Walter Elliot was imperiously called on to do" (10). Providence's plan can be temporarily waylaid by other human failings as well, as Anne notes about Lady Russell's early caution: "How eloquent could Anne have been . . . against that over-anxious caution which seems to insult exertion and distrust Providence!" (32).

The most important treatment of Providence in *Persuasion*, however, comes in the management of plot. Throughout the novel, Austen explores the gap between faulty human arranging and Providence's better order through the motif of missed opportunities and meetings. The novel is replete with small occasions on which

---

[24]    Kelly notes that Austen's treatment of Providence is both more nuanced and more in tune with Anglican theology than many other religious narratives written in her day: "[her] linking of merit and circumstance seems to lack the sense of inevitability or determinism found in both reformist novels and many didactically religious novels of the period" (165).

[25]    See also the discussion of providential orderings for the reader's own good in Harris, 166ff. Harris argues that the novel abounds with debatable questions for the reader to ponder: "the method . . . is ultimately Socratic. It lures the reader to predetermined ends" (166). When Fanny, "a Christ-like sufferer [is] rewarded by almost-transcendental happiness, religious teaching combines with realism" (167). Harris wryly notes, "We may no longer be able to admire the conjunction" (167).

the reader—and Anne—are led to expect that she or someone else will meet someone or go somewhere or that someone will come to them; again and again, these expectations are unfulfilled. These many missed meetings serve as an object lesson about impermanence, chance, and luck and implicitly give the moral that "There's a divinity that shapes our ends / rough hew them how we will" (*Hamlet* V, ii,10–11). We begin this pattern at the famous end of chapter three, where Austen plays with the reader's romantic expectations by allowing Anne a "gentle sigh" as she walks along a "favourite grove": "'a few months more, and *he*, perhaps, may be walking here'" (27). The reader is invited to conjecture prematurely about whom this romantic "he" might be (the start of the next chapter humorously upbraids us by relating, "*He* was not Mr. Wentworth, the former curate of Monkford, however suspicious appearances may be, but a captain Frederick Wentworth, his brother" [28]). More importantly, however, we are being led to expect that at some happy moment in the plot, Anne will walk through these favorite groves with this beloved, even if he is at the moment unknown. But this walk in the groves of Kellynch never happens, or at least, if Wentworth ever strolls there while he is staying with the Crofts, Austen never tells us about it, and Anne and Wentworth certainly never stroll there together.

The pattern of missed meetings continues apace. Anne stays away when the Crofts first tour Kellynch in the role of prospective tenants ("Anne found it most natural to take her almost daily walk to Lady Russell's, and keep out of the way till all was over" [34]). She almost meets Captain Wentworth on his first visit to Uppercross, but the fall of her nephew prevents her from her usual morning visit to the Great House. That next evening, while Mary and Charles abdicate their parental responsibilities and leave her to tend to their wounded son, Anne is left to ponder, "what was it to her, if Frederick Wentworth were only a half mile distant, making himself agreeable to others!" (62–3). Wentworth himself is the agent of the next missed encounter, as he arranges things so that the breakfast occurs at the Great House rather than at the Cottage. A few days later, by pleading a headache, Anne also misses the dinner at which Henrietta and Louisa vie for Wentworth's attentions. Nor does Anne see Wentworth while she is at Lady Russell's, though she expects to: "[Being there] would place her in the same village with Captain Wentworth, within half a mile of him; they would have to frequent the same church, and there must be intercourse between the two families" (100). The seemingly guaranteed contact, however, comes to nothing, because the intervening visit to Lyme and the accident there disrupt everything: Wentworth goes to visit his brother to create distance, both emotional and physical, between himself and Louisa. Thus Anne's anxiety about their renewed proximity comes to nothing. The narrator notes, "So ended all danger to Anne of meeting Captain Wentworth at Kellynch-hall, or of seeing him in company with her friend. Every thing was safe enough, and she smiled over the many anxious feelings she had wasted on the subject" (139). If Anne is not to expect Captain Wentworth, she is to expect Captain Benwick. Charles Musgrove gives Anne every reason to expect a visit from this newly ardent admirer. However, as Elizabeth Elliot found with Mr.

Elliot many years earlier at Kellynch, the ardor of a suitor becomes suspect when he never shows up. Benwick is expected and expected, but never comes:

> Lady Russell could not hear the door-bell without feeling that it might be his herald; nor could Anne return from any stroll of solitary indulgence in her father's grounds, or any visit of charity in the village, without wondering whether she might see him or hear of him. Captain Benwick came not, however. (145)

Only many chapters later will the reader learn that his non-appearance followed from his fickle new attachment to the convalescent Louisa.

The vagaries of human connections are also reinforced by meetings that are unexpected. Such chance meetings include Mr. Elliot's visit to the very inn at which Anne's party is staying at Lyme, or Wentworth's entrance into the same tea shop that holds Anne, her sister, and Mrs. Clay at Bath. Austen's role as providential author is sufficient to bring both Mr. Elliott and Captain Wentworth within speaking distance of the woman they desire. Authorial providence seems to play a role as well when Wentworth catches Anne alone as she tends her injured nephew, or when the ladies' walk to Winthrop happens to converge with the walk of the returning sportsmen, Wentworth and Charles Musgrove. In her role as one who guarantees providential meetings, Austen has been kind enough to provide a too-young dog, which prematurely spoils the hunters' chances of killing the birds they had in view.

In one telling moment, Austen explicitly invokes Providence as the cause of such near-misses or unexpected meetings. When Mary makes a great fuss about missing an opportunity to be introduced to Mr. Elliot at the inn in Lyme, she laments the mourning requirements that made it impossible for her to discern the Elliot livery as well as the greatcoat that happened to obscure the Elliot arms displayed on the coach's door. Wentworth's commentary is ironic: "'Putting all these extraordinary circumstances together, . . . we must consider it to be the arrangement of Providence, that you should not be introduced to your cousin'" (115). His speech reminds us of Austen's own role as the creator of providential circumstances, arranging the plot as she does to amplify the uncertainties of human contact. Further, Austen *has* played a providential role in this particular instance of plot, for had the introduction Mary sought taken place, the incident that follows Mary's complaint, Louisa's fall, might not have occurred, and Louisa's fall is key to the ultimate reunification of Anne and Wentworth.

## Language

The complementary concepts of the Great Chain of Being, natural law, and Providence had highly consequential effects on Austen's views of the world. Her plots re-enact the workings of Providence, as discussed above. Further, her views of social hierarchies, nature, and history were all inflected by her religious and ontological inheritance. Most dramatically, perhaps, is the effect these Christian and neo-classical ideas had upon her use of language. Austen's preference for moral abstractions and aphorisms, her avoidance of metaphor and periphrasis, and her assumption that "best chosen language" (*NA* 31) can discriminate among otherwise confusing moral and social predicaments all arise from her basic acceptance of natural law, while her habit of describing social relations with metaphors of spatial hierarchies, even when practiced with ironic intent, follows from the residual force of the Great Chain of Being.

Natural law's presumptions governed the linguistic preoccupations and habits of eighteenth-century literature and prose. Abstractions and generalizations dominated, because natural law presumed that the universe was under the sway of regular, uniform commandments. As Dr. Johnson insisted, poetry deals with the recurring thoughts and feelings of the human race: "great thoughts are always general . . . those writers who lay on the watch for novelty could have little hope of greatness; for great things cannot have escaped former observation" (*Lives* I.22). Neo-classical aesthetic theory assumed that the universal and the uniform, rather than the individuated and local, was of greatest value (Lovejoy 291), while originality was suspect. The word "originality" first appears in dictionaries in 1787 (Sutherland 18), not coincidentally about the same time as the words "sincerity" and "authenticity," with all their proto-Romantic presumptions about the self, come into prominence.[26] Neo-classical poets and thinkers looked suspiciously upon new ideas; Addison, writing in the *Spectator* on December 20, 1711, gives a particularly clear précis of this view: "Wit and fine writing doth not consist so much in advancing things that are new, as in giving things that are known an agreeable turn. It is impossible in us, who live in the latter ages of the world, to make observations in criticism, morality, or in any art or science, which have not been touched upon by others" (qtd. in Sutherland 18). "Behind the neo-classicist's search for ultimate criteria of literary excellence," Murray Roston argues, "lay the conviction that all men were fundamentally alike, that Reason was the supreme touchstone, and that therefore the standards of taste established by Reason would be acceptable to the entire civilized world" (78). The fact that not all men (or women) had a chance to achieve the standards "civilization" had agreed upon did not seem to undermine this consensus about reason's pre-eminence.

Natural law also underwrites the age's predilection for personification, classical allusions, and periphrasis. If the universe can be best understood by generalized and supra-historical abstractions, then personification becomes one reasonable and artful strategy by which abstractions can be clothed. Roston concludes, "eighteenth-century faith in the uniformity of mankind demanded such generalization, and both personification and a pretended belief in ancient mythology could be exploited for the same ends. The individual submerged himself in abstractions or donned the

---

[26]   Lionel Trilling's treatment of this subject is worth reading by every new generation of scholars. See *Sincerity and Authenticity*, esp. chapter 1, "Sincerity: Its Origin and Rise" (1–23).

guise of a mythological figure" (33).[27] Thus, Justice, Beauty, Judgment, Fancy, and so on appear as human figures, with countenances, figures, and costumes in accord with their characteristics.[28] Classical allusions also imply the stability of human experience, as it is assumed that Horace's verdicts on human affairs, for example, are as pertinent to the then-contemporary reader as anything written within more recent memory. Periphrasis, that trope of substituting playful elaborations for common nouns, is also to be expected to occur in the writings of those who take natural law (and the general, uniform nature of experience) for granted. Invention, deprived of new ideas as such, must lavish itself on substitution. Thus fish will always be fish, but one can call them a "finny tribe," as does Pope, while rats, for the poet Grainger, become "the whiskered vermin race" (Boswell II. 453). The example of the rats reminds us also of the central role of decorum in these aesthetics, which required that unpleasant or low subjects be softened or cloaked by rhetoric.[29] Schoolboys were taught to look up Latin words and find elegant and ameliorating replacements, so that death became "perpetual night" or "the dark day" (Roston 29–30). Periphrasis was thus valued in part as a distancing and elevating device.

Austen also inherited the assumptions about language held by language reformers of the late eighteenth century, for "by her day, the grammarians had been hard at work prescribing, proscribing, and pontificating about English usage for some fifty years" (Phillipps 13). By the days of Austen's youth, language had become a central socio-political battlefield. Just as the explosion of etiquette books in the post-Civil War United States testifies to increased numbers of middle-class citizens, each hopeful and anxious about his or her prospects for social ascent, the plethora of grammars, dictionaries, stylebooks, and the like in the late eighteenth century tells of the period's politically charged clashes over culture and class. There were over 200 titles on grammar and spelling published between 1750 and

---

[27]    Bronson notes the historical anomaly that other aesthetic fields such as sculpture have identified the taste for the abstract with maturity, but that the post-eighteenth-century movement towards the concrete in literature instead is understood to stand for a greater and more serious grappling with reality—that is, a more mature approach (136ff). See also Wasserman ("Inherent Values"), who argues that personification was viewed in the eighteenth century as a mode of rhetorical and emotional intensification, since "the eighteenth century . . . tended to accept the theory that the creative function of the higher forms of imagination is to idealize matter, not by transcending it, but by seeking out the universal" (443).

[28]    Margaret Doody muses that "Augustan poets frequently employ personifications, and (what now seems to some even more strange) readers of the time evidently enjoyed them" (163). She goes on to defend the neo-classical rage for personifications, arguing that personifications were "embodiments of energies, . . . real and significant presences" (165) and concludes that "the Augustan love of personification was not the effect or a mild liking for a shallow artifice" (166).

[29]    Chesterfield, for instance, cautions his son that elegance is prerequisite in language and behavior: "Whether for better or worse, no matter; but we are refined; and plain manners, plain dress, and plain diction would as little do in life, as acorns, herbage, and the water of the neighboring spring, would do at table" (qtd. in Sutherland 88).

1800, as compared with fewer than 50 from 1700–1750 (Leonard 12). Many were written and published to fulfill a regulatory function, to marshal and codify the use of English. The idea that the English language needed such control arose from the dizzying outbreak of print publications in the eighteenth century, made possible by technological innovations in bookbinding, printing, and the production of paper on the one hand and rising literacy rates on the other.[30]

Three of the most influential of these works to exercise linguistic (and social) management were Bishop Lowth's *Short Introduction to English Grammar* (1762), Johnson's *Dictionary of the English Language* (1755), and James Harris's *Hermes: A Philosophical Inquiry Concerning Universal Grammar* (1751). In Olivia Smith's important work on the relation between politics and language from roughly 1750–1830, she argues that these works, meant for elite audiences, helped impose the hegemony of elite standards, admixing language with moral and cultural value:

> 'The vulgar and the refined,' 'the particular and the general,' 'the corrupt and the pure,' 'the barbaric and the civilized,' 'the primitive and the arbitrary' were socially pervasive terms that divided sensibility and culture according to linguistic categories. The baser forms of language were said to reveal the inability of the speaker to transcend the concerns of the present, an interest in material objects, and the dominance of the passions. Those who spoke the refined language were allegedly rational, moral, civilized, and capable of abstract thinking. . . . Civilization was largely a linguistic concept, establishing a terrain in which vocabulary and syntax distinguished the refined and the civilized from the vulgar and the savage. (3)[31]

Each of these authors wrote in part to help speakers and writers conform to standards they saw as God-given and universal. Lowth, the Bishop of London, a professor of poetry at Oxford, and a scholar of Hebrew, held that language was a gift from God, and that correctness in grammar was a form of practicing

---

[30]   It is telling that, while patronized by the Earl of Chesterfield, Johnson's *Dictionary* was first commissioned by a consortium of wealthy London printers.

[31]   The grammars did not always have the elite audience their authors intended. Lowth, for instance, presumed his readers had an extensive classical education and were denizens of "polite society," but the radical William Cobbett not only read but studied and memorized Lowth's book, all the better to equip him to challenge elite attitudes about class and power (Smith 6–7). Cobbett would write his own grammar in 1817 for an audience of workers and the self-educated. This "act of class warfare," Smith posits, was "intended to forestall intellectual intimidation deriving from the assumption that only those who knew the learned languages could write English accurately" (1). In the 1790s, evangelical reformers such as Hannah More who championed education for the poor had been careful to couch their arguments in terms of the benefits of religious learning; they held that the more the poor could read, the more religious they would become, and the more religious they became, the more likely they were to be socially quiescent (Smith 12). Such logic was not to be borne out in practice, as the various working-class upheavals of the early nineteenth century demonstrate.

God's intentions.[32] Dr. Johnson, who incidentally also wrote a book on the claims of natural law, the preface of which claims that "Religion is the first inherent Principle of Reason's action in Nature, pure, simple, and easy to be comprehended and practiced" (*Philosophick Mirrour* ix), wrote his *Dictionary* to condemn "cant" and the language of the "laborious and mercantile part of the people" as well as to define authoritatively the language of the educated classes.[33] Harris' *Hermes* sought to discover the universal structures of thought at the level of the sentence (long before Noam Chomsky's efforts along the same lines). For Harris, vulgarity "meant a language excluded from God's order" (Smith 29). Later in the century, Hugh Blair, Scottish divine and professor of rhetoric at Cambridge, wrote a popular composition guide (*Lectures on Rhetoric and Belles Lettres* [1783]), which held that the principles of rhetoric evolved from the principles of nature. Like Lowth's, Johnson's, and Harris's work, Blair's *Lectures* helped dismiss writing to or from a vulgar audience: "Anger, vehemence, a non-abstract vocabulary, and an abundance of metaphor could be dismissed according to Blair . . . as primitive both morally and intellectually" (Smith 30).

There were some authors who wrote with more egalitarian missions, such as Thomas Sheridan, who felt that uniform standards for pronunciation "would eventually eliminate the distinction of region and social class [and would] foster

---

[32]    Lowth's *Grammar* was highly influential; 22 editions were published before 1795, the year his work was overtaken by a new grammar written by Lindley Murray. Olivia Smith demonstrates that both Lowth and Murray associate virtue with good grammar inferentially by their examples. For sentences that show good (that is, correct) grammar, the content often concerns people behaving in accord with moral and spiritual laws, while the sentences for bad grammar often concern people behaving badly. For instance, the use of strong, active verbs (which Murray commends) is accompanied by this sentence: "Patriotism, morality, every public and private consideration, demand our submission to lawful government" (Murray 93), but his example of a problem of agreement in number is illustrated thus: "The Normans, under which general term is comprehended the Danes, Norwegians, and Swedes, were a people accustomed to slaughter and rapine" (Murray 88). Smith concludes: "Grammar, virtue, and class were so interconnected that rules were justified or explained not in terms of how languages was used but in terms of reflecting a desired type of behaviour, thought process, or social status" (9).

[33]    Johnson saw no difficulty in applying the Great Chain to human society: "Sir, I am a friend to subordination, as most conducive to the happiness of society. There is a reciprocal pleasure in governing and being governed," he told Boswell in 1763 (208). However, he was aware that custom rather than God's precepts held more sway in the development of language. His plan for the *Dictionary* notes that "I shall therefore, since the rules of stile, like those of law, arise from precedents often repeated, collect the testimonies of both sides, and endeavour to discover and promulgate the decrees of custom, who has so long possessed whether by right or by usurpation, the sovereignty of words" (*Plan* 27). The metaphor of *sovereignty* speaks to a presumption that language has God-given order; the metaphor of *usurpation* speaks to Johnson's acknowledgment that humans change languages themselves.

linguistic upward mobility and egalitarianism" (Bailey 186).[34] James Elphiston's radical proposal for spelling reform (*A Miniature of Inglish Orthoggraphy* [1796]) was also meant to unseat class divisions, but even he in his preface spoke of linguistic purity and polish; adherents to his cause would "secure alike dhe purified language from relapsing into' barbarism, and from degenerating into' corrupcion [and] raiz her to' her just rank among polished languages" (*sic*; qtd. in Bailey 187). Most of these language levelers had little effect on elite opinion. Horace Walpole dismissed, for instance, the efforts of one John Pinkerton, who, like Elphinston, hoped to change society by changing grammar (among other reforms, Elphinston wished to add vowels to the ends of all words and eliminate the use of "s" for plural nouns). Walpole wrote to Pinkerton explaining that "when a country has been polishing itself for two or three centuries, and when consequently authors are innumerable, the most supereminent genius . . . possesses very limited empire, and is far from meeting implicit obedience" (Bailey 189). Walpole was confident no further innovation was necessary or possible in language; his trust on this count was entirely in keeping with the consensus of the age.

Jane Austen's fiction accommodates and appropriates most of these religiously based neo-classical values about language (and culture). She prefers aphorisms and universal truths to the concrete and particular, assigning significantly lesser moral value to the latter. She gives colloquialisms and non-standard grammatical constructions to her most vulgar characters, and implies that their misuse of language is allied to their moral faultiness. However, she does reject those elements of eighteenth-century literary practice most tied to the classical education—an education she of course had no means of obtaining.[35] Her works betray no interest

---

[34]    In Sheridan's *Lectures on the Art of Reading* (a volume owned by Austen, now at the Chawton House Library), Sheridan notes the egalitarian effects of speech training: "All who are desirous of opening the way to honour and preferment to their children, will not fail to have them so instructed, while the ear is uncorrupt, and the organs of speech are flexible. Thus all public speakers, will become uniform in their use of accents; and their auditors, accustomed to this uniformity, will of course catch it: and thus, a musical speech, will, in time, spread through a whole people, and uniformly prevail, among all ranks and classes of men" (71–2). My thanks to Susan Ford for her personal notes on this volume.

[35]    Because Austen never had any classical education, she was not in a position to feel for herself the force of the common claim made in the eighteenth century on behalf of classical languages and especially on behalf of Hebrew—that it was the "first" language, the language of God (this position was taken by Cowper, for example). She knew French well enough to read French texts easily, and had a little Italian, according to her family. In an 1809 letter, she makes fun of the idea that she would be writing Latin; having sent her young nephew Edward Knight some playful verses, she writes to Cassandra, "I am sorry my verses did not bring any return from Edward, I was in hopes they might—but I suppose he does not rate them high enough. –It might be partiality, but they seemed to me purely classical—just like Homer & Virgil, Ovid & Propria que Maribus" (*L* 170). "Propria que Maribus" is the opening phrase of one of the first lessons in the Eton Latin Grammar, a book Austen would have known, though not have studied *per se*, in her youth when her father tutored her brothers and the paying boarding students at Steventon. For a general survey of Austen's education, see McMaster.

in elaborate periphrasis, classical allusions, or mythological reference (the moment when Fanny speaks of Cassiopeia as she and Edmund star-gaze constitutes one interesting exception).[36] To see how prose ought not to be written—in Austen's estimation—one need only refer to the notice in the London paper that tells of Maria Rushworth's running off with Henry Crawford: ". . . it was with infinite concern the newspaper had to announce to the world, a matrimonial *fracas* in the family of Mr. R. of Wimpole Street; the beautiful Mrs. R. whose name had not long been enrolled in the lists of hymen, . . . [has] quitted her husband's roof in company with the well known and captivating Mr. C" *(MP* 509). The hyperbole of "infinite concern," the periphrasis of "had not long been enrolled in the lists of hymen" (made all the more egregious with its clichéd use of the classical trope, "hymen"), and the pretentious (and French) *fracas* mark the passage as a morally slippery production—one Austen could ventriloquize if only to condemn.

Austen's distrust of metaphors and hyperbole also follows from her inheritance of an eighteenth-century worldview and the Anglican commitments towards social quietism. After all, highly figurative language in the eighteenth century still bore the marks of seventeenth-century enthusiasm, and was understood as the "rhetorical counterpart of fanatical religion" (Irlam 23).[37] She does use metaphors, but in general holds to the dullest and most conventional of figures. For example, Emma compares her piano-playing to Jane Fairfax's: "'My playing is no more like hers, than a lamp is like sunshine'" (250). When she realizes she loves Mr. Knightley, the recognition comes "at the speed of an arrow" (444). But the conventionality of these metaphors is not meant to mark a dull moment. After all, at the climax of *Persuasion*, Wentworth writes to Anne: "you pierce my soul" (257). When Austen uses more striking tropes, she tends to blunt their effects. For instance, after the news of Wickham's misdeeds reach Meryton, we learn "[a]ll Meryton seemed striving to blacken the man, who, but three months before, had been almost an angel of light" *(PP* 325). The use of "seemed" and "almost" dampens the rhetorical strength of this talk of blackness and angels (Babb 20). The mildest rhetorical novelty seems suspect, as Mr. Collins's invocation of an "olive branch" in his introductory letter to the Bennets evidently marks him as one whose language is too flowery and pretentious. Howard Babb notes Austen's particular

---

[36]    There is the occasional use of a Latin tag in the juvenilia; for example, Austen placed the inscription *ex dono mei patris* at the top of the Contents page in her *The History of England* (written when she was 16). Margaret Doody rightly points out that Austen is singular in her avoidance of classical allusions, myths, or characters: "there is no other novelist, male or female, of her time, of whom this is true. Other women writers as various as Burney and Edgeworth, West and Wollstonecraft, exhibit a respect for the ancient public tradition of letters—a respect apparently absent in Austen" ("Jane Austen's Reading" 355).

[37]    As Clement Hawes argues, "manic rhetorical style is constituted, above all, by its rebellious stance toward traditional hierarchies of socio-economic privilege and their related hierarchies of discourse"; manic speech, associated with political rebellion of the seventeenth century, was understood in Austen's day as a natural ally of revolution, the natural enemy of "patrician hegemony" (2–3).

antipathy towards extended metaphors; she assigns, for instance, a woefully inapt one to Sir Thomas when he views his plan to send Fanny to Portsmouth as a "medicinal project" (*MP* 425; Babb 21). Vladimir Nabokov argues that the moment in *Mansfield Park* in which Mrs. Norris is "entirely taken up in fresh arranging and injuring the noble fire which the butler had prepared" (*MP* 317) constitutes the "one really original metaphor" in her work (41). All in all, Austen liked her metaphors dead (Phillipps 65).

Austen repeatedly demonstrates her agreement with the eighteenth-century consensus that the best writing incorporates correct grammar and exact and standard diction—and that the "best chosen language" comes from the operations of reason, virtue, religion, and taste. That good taste was seen as the self-evident practice of those operating in accord with natural law only reinforces the more general point that neo-classical reasoning was little disturbed by the argument—the current consensus of modernity—that taste is governed by the accidents and self-serving character of elite choice. Furthermore, Austen seems to accept most of the embedded class assumptions the idea of "the best chosen language" implies. She consistently employs substandard language—bad grammar and slang—to confirm the moral laxity of "vulgar" characters. The slang used by Lydia Bennet, the Steele sisters, Mrs. Norris, John Thorpe, and Mrs. Jennings, for instance, bears out other validating suggestions of their social and moral deficiencies. For example, Austen provides corroborative evidence of Lucy Steele's dearth of virtue and gentility by making plain that Lucy is an ungrammatical and slangy writer (Phillipps 20). As Edmund laments to Elinor after showing her Lucy's letter in which he is released from his engagement: "'In a sister it is bad enough, but in a wife! –how I have blushed over the pages of her writing! . . . –this is the only letter I ever received from her, of which the substance made me any amends for the defect of the style'" (*SS* 414). Conversely, a lower-class character can demonstrate his true worth by writing with taste and correctness, as Robert Martin does in his letter proposing marriage to Harriet. Emma is disconcerted to see that he is worthier than she had thought, but the evidence of the letter's language is powerful: "There were not merely no grammatical errors, but as a composition it would not have disgraced a gentleman; the language, though plain, was strong and unaffected, and the sentiments it conveyed very much to the credit of the writer. It was short, but expressed good sense, warm attachment, liberality, propriety, even delicacy of feeling" (*E* 53). That a member of the yeoman class could have "delicacy of feeling" is particularly noteworthy, as elite opinion was sure that the lower classes had but a rough range of emotions. One might also note that these sentences of judgment (Emma's, through indirect discourse) are themselves crafted in accord with neo-classical ideals; they are comprised by series of balanced clauses that conclude with a list of carefully chosen abstractions that express moral judgment.

Austen's distaste for slang follows eighteenth-century standards as well. Dr. Johnson had condemned slang as a threat to the stability and purity of the English language, and Blair had argued that "purity" lay in avoiding words or phrases that are "new-coined, or used without proper authority" (118). The dividing line seemed self-evident to Blair, as it did to so many of his contemporaries: "Propriety is the selection of such words in the language, as the best and most established usage has appropriated . . . It implies the correct and happy application of them . . . in opposition to vulgarisms, or low expressions" (Blair 118). Austen inherited the common idea that deviating from standard linguistic practice was immoral as well as dangerous to morality and class stability.[38] The "low" register of prose represents all the ills then associated with the unvirtuous poor: indolence, uneducated and sloppy thinking, the propensity to treat all subjects casually, and careless morality. For example, Lydia Bennet's reliance on "fun" (then a slang term) tells the reader a great deal about her laziness, ignorance, unseriousness, and willingness to broach social mores.

The residual strength of natural law theories about language also governs Austen's proclivity to associate the concrete with the trivial (Page 59). When Emma complains, for instance, that Miss Bates is capable of "fly[ing] off, through half a sentence, to her mother's old petticoat" (248), she is complaining not merely about Miss Bates's unsteady command of decorum but also about the spinster's commitment to petty material concerns.[39] Mrs. Elton, Mrs. Norris, Harriet, Lydia, Mrs. Jennings, Mr. Woodhouse—these characters live in a world of objects (ribbons, gruel, baize curtains, hats) more than in the world of ideas, and Austen implicitly condemns them for it. Austen herself is stingy with particularizing details in the novels. Emma is handsome and Mr. Knightley is tall, but that is about as much physical description as we are generally vouchsafed. This refusal to particularize was a stricture of literary practice for Austen, for when her niece Anna showed Austen some of her fledgling efforts as a novelist, Austen's praise was leavened

---

[38]   Not all of her abusers of language come from the lower or aspiring classes, but most do. Babb claims that the linguistic sins of figures such as Lucy Steele, Isabella Thorpe, and Mrs. Elton "betray their improper social aspirations—they are anxious to rise more rapidly than the natural [*sic*] processes of society permit, and without the justification of exceptional merit, out of the class to which by birth and education they belong" (158). Page also concurs that while "a 'low' expression tends to be symptomatic of unsatisfactory moral or ethical standards," Austen is "well aware that . . . vulgarity and foolishness are not the monopoly of a single class" (148); Lady Catherine de Bourgh of *Pride and Prejudice* and Lady Denham of *Sanditon* provide relevant examples. Marilyn Butler is right to add to this roster of classless clods General Tilney of *Northanger Abbey*: "General Tilney, the richest character in the novel and a man whose ancestors acquired their present home at the Reformation, is also the novel's greatest vulgarian" ("Purple Turban" 486).

[39]   Norman Page argues that "[i]n her private writings, as the Letters repeatedly demonstrate, Jane Austen was quite capable of finding a source of lively interest in the pattern of a new gown. In the novels, on the other hand, there is a carefully-guarded frontier between the serious use of abstract language by the narrator and those characters who command respect, and the foolish or absurd or suspiciously frivolous use of the concrete" (59).

by her criticism of Anna's propensity to put in too many details.[40] Where details emerge, such as the mud on Elizabeth's petticoat or locked gate at Sotherton, they do so because they are freighted with cultural and moral meaning.[41] Unlike Dickens' world in which objects take on hallucinatory anthropomorphic qualities, the accrual of value to objects in Austen's works is always related intimately to the creation of character. Lady Bertram's sofa and pug tell a moral tale, and they would not have been included otherwise.[42] Austen's sense of novelistic decorum in part also explains this bias against details, because we know she imagined her heroines so particularly that she could recognize them at a painting exhibition, as she does in 1813 when she recognized a portrait as being of Jane, now Mrs. Bingley: "Mrs. Bingley's is exactly herself, size, shaped face, features & sweetness; there was never a greater likeness" (*L* 212; Weinsheimer 132). But the importance given to generalizations—those abstractions that express the solidity of the universe and its values—explains more fully her propensity to leave the details of the physical environment unreported.

Austen's twentieth-century critics, particularly those who have focused on her use of language, have joined in noting her predilection for employing abstractions— words she consistently capitalized in her manuscripts. The consensus on this count runs from Mary Lascelles (*Jane Austen and Her Art*, 1939) through C. S. Lewis ("A Note on Jane Austen," 1954), and up to Howard Babb (*The Novels of Jane Austen: The Fabric of Dialogue*, 1962), David Lodge ("The Vocabulary of *Mansfield Park*," 1966), K. C. Phillipps (*Jane Austen's English*, 1970), Norman Page (*The Language of Jane Austen*, 1972), Stuart Tave (*Some Words of Jane Austen*, 1973), and Jocelyn Harris (*Jane Austen's Art of Memory*, 1989). In their several ways, these critics explore the connection between Austen's reliance on abstractions and her inheritance of eighteenth-century values, both religious and secular. Lascelles' metaphor is particularly apt, and historically laden: "To us Jane Austen appears like one who inherits a prosperous and well-ordered estate—the heritage of a prose style in which neither generalization nor abstraction need

---

[40]   The exact terms of this correction are as follows: "You describe a sweet place, but your descriptions are often more minute than will be liked. You give too many particulars of right hand & left" (*L* 275).

[41]   See Armstrong on the power of objects in Austen's world. She notes that a novel such as "*Emma* . . . demonstrates that there is indeed no such thing as an object that doesn't convey emotion along with sensation" (18).

[42]   Nancy Armstrong argues that Austen's treatment of objects connects moral values to class values, a point that seems largely true: "Those conversant in the language of objects sometimes called 'taste' can distinguish good object relations from bad in another person on the basis of whether they display moderation, taste, concern for others, and a reluctance to deceive" (18). Thus, for instance, when we learn that Henry Crawford's chain is too large to fit through the amber cross Fanny most values as an ornament, something is suggested of the pretentiousness of Henry's values. The more properly judging Edmund has given Fanny a plainer chain, and the cross fits in it more readily. Thus Edmund, more a gentleman, has greater taste, and his level of taste befits his higher moral standing.

signify vagueness, because there was close enough agreement as to the scope and significance of such terms" (107). This inherited, prosperous, and well-ordered estate is the neo-classical legacy of natural law and its corollary ideas, a worldview in which language represents God-given truths and in which values are presumed to remain constant.[43] As C. S. Lewis noted, "The great abstract nouns of the classical English moralists are unblushingly and uncompromisingly used . . . These are the concepts by which Jane Austen grasps the world. In her we still breathe the air of the Rambler and Idler. All is hard, clear, definable" (363). It is not simply that Austen relies on abstractions; rather, it is the exactitude of her diction that most shows her alignment with neo-classical values: "The firmness and precision of the words used and used again are now a token of the clear and unambiguous standards by which human behavior is assessed. . . . [T]he moral basis of the author's judgments, conveyed in her language, finds modes of expression which leave us in no doubt as to her standpoint" (Page 48).[44]

---

[43]   An important strand in Austen criticism has interpreted Austen's abstractions as tarnished by monetary and economic concerns. Dorothy van Ghent and Mark Schorer in particular have argued that Austen's style—and her abstractions—are based on a language of commerce and property. Certainly, words like "principle," "interest," "property," and "credit" have financial implications, and Austen at times makes full ironic use of those echoes of the marketplace, as in the famous first sentence of *Pride and Prejudice*, in which the "surrounding families" presume that "a single man in possession of a good fortune" is the "rightful property of some one or other of their daughters" (3). Van Ghent argues that these economic abstractions are central to the shape of Austen's mind: "the general directions of reference taken by Jane Austen's language . . . are clearly materialistic. They reflect a culture whose institutions are solidly defined by materialistic interests—property and banking and trade and the law that keeps order in these matters—institutions which determine, in turn, the character of family relations, the amenities of community life, and the whole complex economy of the emotions . . . . Somehow, using this language of acquisitiveness and calculation and materialism, a language common to the most admirable characters as well as to the basest characters in the book, the spiritually creative persons will have to form their destinies" (373). In many cases, however, both Schorer and Van Ghent seem to over-value the financial connotations of these dead metaphors, or, perhaps, to assume that if an economic meaning is available, it occludes or overrides the moral sense. Rather, as Crabb's *English Synonymes* (1816) makes plain, Austen's cultural logos was replete with abstractions in which the moral sense was primary but in which secondary economic connotations had arisen as a consequence of a robustly capitalist scene.

[44]   David Lodge concurs in this interpretation: "It is hard to think of another major novelist whose diction provides, to a comparable extent, a key to the qualities held to be desirable and, ultimately, to the moral attitudes behind the novels" (55). Page further notes that it is not just that the novels are "written in language of conscious precision and exceptional subtlety: the early novels in particular are to a striking extent about language, in that the use and abuse of words is a frequently recurring theme" (12–3). See also Harris, 24–5, who lists the dozens of abstractions about "human understanding" that Austen deploys in *Northanger Abbey* (Harris' larger point is to trace the after-effects in the novel of Locke's *Essay on Human Understanding*), concluding, "[b]esides these brilliant charges and counter-charges of reason and nonsense, the Napoleonic wars must pale" (25).

If author and reader are in general accord about what words mean, the judgment of characters can be enacted on firm ground, partially through the authority of the narrator, and partly through the evidence of a given character's language. Perhaps no element of Austen's art has been more widely explored than the way in which she allows characters to define themselves through language, often through its misuse. The better characters align themselves with the narrator's values. Thus, they use words precisely—that is, ethically—or are taught to do so, as when Catherine Morland learns the pitfalls of the word "nice" from Henry Tilney. The faulty characters do not merely expose themselves as such through the "vulgarisms" deplored by language mavens of the late eighteenth century. They may also wrestle with words, descending at times into gibberish, as Sir Edward Denham's rhapsodies in *Sanditon* demonstrate ("all the usual Phrases . . . descriptive of the undescribable" [*MW* 396]). Or, characters may show that they are incapable of finding the right word, as when Henry Crawford admires Fanny's virtues without being able to name them adequately ("he was too little accustomed to serious reflection to know them by their proper name" [294]) or when his sister Mary grapples to find a word in between "love" and "compliments" to describe her relation with Edmund (had her religious principles been stronger, she and Edmund would have been engaged and "love" would have been exactly the right term [287]).

The late-eighteenth-century fascination with synonyms encouraged this interest in precise discrimination among abstractions. There were many popular publications on the subject; the title of Mrs. Piozzi's *British Synonymy; or an Attempt at Regulating the Choice of Words in Familiar Conversations* (1794) reflects the supervisory role such books were meant to fill.[45] Readers in Austen's day were used to discerning minor differences in meaning between synonymous words; moreover, this widespread practice was bound to ideas of moral value (without knowing the exact word one cannot make the exact moral judgment) and to ideas of social value (using the exact words shows propriety and elegance; using words inexactly shows plebeian vulgarity). We see the same interest in "the best chosen language" in many of the authors Jane Austen most relished: Cowper, Richardson, Johnson, Burney, Goldsmith, and Edgeworth. Repeatedly, such authors rely on generalizations and abstractions that are presumed to have substantial and precise meanings.[46] Unlike the paper notes or the coins debased by

---

[45] Others included John Trusler's *The Difference between Words Esteemed Synonymous in the English Language; and the Proper Choice of them Determined* (1766); James Leslie's *Dictionary of the Synonymous Words and Technical Terms in the English Language* (1806); G. H. Poppleton's *Dictionnaire de Synonymes Anglais* (1812); William Taylor's *English Synonyms Discriminated* (1813); and George Crabb's *English Synonymes* (1816) (this Crabb was not the poet of the same name, otherwise spelled). See Page, pp. 78–9.

[46] See Page, 78ff. He notes that "fine discrimination was, evidently, not a private monopoly of Jane Austen's but part of the linguistic climate in which she grew up" (78) and further that "[m]any of these usages . . . belong to Jane Austen's milieu and to a common stock of vocabulary available to all: [this] diction was not the monopoly of any individual writer, but a significant element in the language ready to be drawn on whether the composition in question were an ode, a sermon or a letter to a friend" (81).

lead or tin of the Georgian age, the currency of words for conservative thinkers and writers in the late eighteenth century is presumed sound; their exact value is known and understood. For this reason, Edgeworth can begin *Belinda* (1801) with four attributes that tell us the most important characteristics of her heroine: "handsome, graceful, sprightly, and highly accomplished" (Edgeworth 7; Page 83). The linguistic worldview upon which such usage rests is Austen's as well, as we see in her introduction of Emma to the reader as "handsome, clever, and rich" (5).[47] The moral measure of characters can be known, assessed, even assayed with quasi-scientific precision through the medium of words. As Crabb claimed in the preface to his *English Synonymes* (1816),

> [s]hould any object to the introduction of morality in a *work of science*, I beg them to consider, that a writer, whose business it was to mark the nice shades of distinction between words closely allied, could not do justice to his subject without entering into all the relations of society, and showing, from the acknowledged sense of many moral and religious terms, what has been the general sense of mankind on many of the most important questions which have agitated the world. (italics mine; vi)

Crabb's preface was penned in the year 1815, the year Austen was finishing *Emma*. His orientation towards the problem of language is plainly derived from natural law—we can know what words mean, though the act of such discrimination requires care, and the meaning of words derives from general, tradition-ruled considerations of moral economy. Our understanding of Austen's words can be much enhanced by attention to his and other synonym books. For instance, chapter nine of the second volume of *Emma* begins thus: "Emma did not regret her condescension in going to the Coles" (249). Crabb groups "condescension" with "complaisance" and "deference" as a means of settling the minor differences of tone and shade among them. "Condescension," he notes, "marks the act of condescending from one's own height to yield to the satisfaction of others, rather than rigorously to exact one's rights"; he then adds an elucidating quotation from Addison. Austen must have relished the precision of the term regarding Emma's attitude, for, as we learn from Crabb,

---

[47]   Babb argues that "this stylistic habit is basic in Jane Austen's work [in which] terms pervade the introduction of each character, where they assess him against a scale of absolutes" (10). Here, for example, is the introduction of Mary in *Persuasion*: "Though better endowed than the elder sister [Elizabeth], Mary had not Anne's understanding or temper. While well, and happy, and properly attended to, she had great good humour and excellent spirits; but any indisposition sunk her completely; she had no resources for solitude; and inheriting a considerable share of the Elliot self-importance, was very prone to add to every other distress that of fancying herself neglected and ill-used" (35). Austen presumes her reader knows the precise difference between, say, "understanding" and "temper" or "neglect" and "ill-use."

All these qualities spring from a refinement of humanity; but *complaisance* has most of genuine kindness in its nature; *deference* most of respectful submission; condescension most of easy indulgence. . . . *Condescension* is not without its alloy; it is accompanied with the painful sentiment of witnessing inferiority, and the no less painful apprehension of not maintaining its own dignity. (200)

It is almost impossible for a contemporary reader to take Crabb's last dictum unironically, that is, as casting aspersions against those who practice condescension; however, it was certainly not meant to be understood in that way. Crabb—and by extension the world of his readers—takes for granted a world of social ranks, in which superiority and inferiority are natural states. Contemporary readers tend to understand the term "condescension" in Austen's sentence almost entirely as ironic, because a fully democratic age cannot understand "condescension" as anything but negative. This attitude Crabb deplores, for he still holds to the idea that ranks in society are unproblematic reflections of God's plan: "it is the common characteristick of ignorant and low persons when placed in a state of elevation, to think themselves degraded by any act of condescension" (*sic*; 200).

The reflexive conservatism of this understanding, both about language and about the ordering of the social world, is notable not only because the self-assurance with which it is pronounced but also because of the fact that this certainty about language and a rational, stable Christian universe will largely disappear within 50 years.[48] We are blocked in many ways from fully knowing the meanings of Austen's novels that were available to her original audience. In part, this is simply because human culture has changed so much, and we do not recognize the names her age employed for many articles of clothing, vehicles, dishes of food, and household items (what, after all, is a ragout or a curricle, the modern reader asks?). It is also because some words we do recognize now have other meanings and connotations, as the discussion of "condescension" has demonstrated (the even more significant shift in the meaning of the word "candor" and its implications will be discussed in detail in Chapter 4). But most importantly, we no longer possess that eighteenth-century certitude, the confidence that natural law guarantees the trans-historical validity of language, particularly of those terms that describe the generalities of human behavior.[49] Readers tend to give less attention to Austen's unironic moral

---

[48]   The radical social changes from the agrarian world Austen took for granted to the urban industrialism of the Victorian mid-century were not, curiously, accompanied by radical aesthetic shifts in the form of the novel, a subject discussed in detail by Frei. He notes, for instance, that the English novel was much more likely than its French or German cousin to present social structures as "given and eternally fixed" (147); the marvel is the coherence of the art form despite the extraordinary social changes of the period (147ff).

[49]   David Lodge has famously articulated the process of reading for contemporary readers, especially in *Mansfield Park*, a novel he argues "schools" them in the older mode of judgment Austen employs. He asks: "how have we been persuaded to endorse a system of values with which we have no real sympathy at all?" (94). In answer, he suggests "that Jane Austen succeeds . . . in schooling her readers in a vocabulary of discrimination

reflections and aphorisms; we instead relish and disproportionately attend to her ironies, because they suit our modern debunking and skeptical temper.[50] This modern mode of reading necessarily shapes Austen's novels to conform to modern ideological commitments and inevitably hampers our ability to understand the novels in close accord with her original meanings.

## Social Rank

Austen's use of "condescension" in *Emma* is highly complex, as is treatment of social hierarchies more generally. For Austen is well aware of the problems with rank society, problems *Emma* exposes in detail. We are not to take Emma's "condescension" at face value, that is, as the morally appropriate response of a "higher" person in the face of a "lower," as Crabb would encourage us to do. Nor is it simply that the social-climbing and newly rich Coles represent a tricky social situation. Rather, Emma is herself far too given to assuming her own superiority, that is, her moral and intellectual superiority as opposed to her social superiority. And this distinction between social rank and intrinsic moral and intellectual merit forms the heart of Austen's treatment of the language of rank, and her most salient critique of her neoclassical inheritance. Austen both adheres to presumptions about social rank found in natural law *and* subjects them to a thorough and

---

which embraces the finest shades of social and moral value, and which asserts the prime importance, in the presented world of the novel, of exercising the faculty of judgment. . . . The subtle and untiring employment of this vocabulary, the exact fitting of value terms to events, the display of scrupulous and consistent discrimination, have a rhetorical effect which we cannot long resist. We pick up the habit of evaluation, and resign, for the duration of the novel at least, the luxury of neutrality" (99). Lodge is aware that the modern reader cannot read Austen's abstractions as "naturally" as her first readers did: "The actual values with which Jane Austen is concerned may have lost some of their cogency with the passing of time . . . but she puts every generation of readers to school, and in learning her own subtle and exact vocabulary of discrimination and evaluation, we submit to the authority of her vision, and recognize its relevance to our own world of secularized spirituality" (113).

[50]  See both Donovan and Babb on the pervasiveness of aphorism in Austen's style. Donovan notes that her prose is dominated by "generalized reflections about life, often aphoristic in form, nearly always moral in tendencies" as well as by "moralizing passages which, without any attempt to achieve aphoristic concision or point, content themselves with the expression of traditional or even commonplace wisdom as it relates to characters or situations" (115). Babb argues that her reliance on aphorisms, "almost maxims," "apparently brings to bear universal wisdom, so fundamental that we can all assume ourselves ready to call on it at any moment. And the form itself becomes a kind of guarantee because it automatically resurrects the sense of a trustworthy public community of views—even if the generalization really expresses a private opinion. So to generalize is to dramatize the unity of author and audience" (15). This implied unity between the values of audience and author is exactly what has become increasingly difficult to maintain in the face of contemporary values far removed from neoclassical values derived from Christian articulations of natural law.

consequential exposure. Repeatedly, we find her using the language of spatial hierarchy to describe differences in station: people "rise" or "fall," are "superior" or "inferior," "high" or "low," "well-bred" or "ill-bred." In many cases, these usages are not freighted with irony, because Austen still to some very basic degree takes as "natural" the Great Chain of Being and the idea that everyone has a God-given rank in society. After all, social cohesion seemed (self-evidently) to rely on the general acceptance of one's place, and differential status was an unquestioned given of her social world. Social rank was displayed in every conceivable social dimension, "by every outward sign"; with every form of dress, manner, speech, every bite of food and every shift in a chair or yawn or bow, people in Regency society manifested their social standing (Perkin 24–5).

Mainstream Anglican rhetoric fully endorsed this world of rank distinctions, because the world of rank revealed the natural hierarchies found in the universe more broadly. As Bishop Bagot sermonized in 1788, the evidence was overwhelming that God had placed man in society "with all the various distributions of rank, wealth, power, and all the exterior circumstances of life" (Soloway 22). The Christian doctrine of humility also helped reinforce the ideal of accepting one's place in the social hierarchy, as did constant invectives against the sin of pride (for a young woman, the issue was often one of vanity, of dressing and bedecking oneself beyond one's station, a misdeed noted, for instance, by Fordyce in those *Sermons for Young Women*, which Lydia and Kitty yawned through in *Pride and Prejudice*).[51] Further, the strictures against pride implied that trying to move beyond one's social station was in some sense an act of rebellion against nature and the system of the universe. As Pope noted, "order is heaven's first law"; to leave one's place in society was to invert the laws of order (that Pope was himself a social climber we might charitably put aside). Moreover, according to the conservative Anglican position, political thinkers who hypothesized about a "state of nature" existing before ranks or political systems began were employing themselves perversely. As Bishop Burgess claimed in the revolutionary year of 1789, there was no need to debate about "whether there was a savage state of nature" for "God only created people in society, only in nature were there savage beasts" (Soloway 24). Likewise, the Bishop of Norwich, George Horne, saw no evidence of a state of nature, especially one in which all humans began as equal: "from the beginning, some were born subject to others; and the power of the father, by whatever name it be called, must have been supreme at the first, when there was none superior to it" ("Origin of Civil Government" 177–8).[52] Anglican orthodoxy was sure that Scripture and

---

[51]  As Fordyce notes, "Is not a constant pursuit of trivial ornament the indubitable proof of a trivial mind? . . . Is the spending whole hours every morning at the toilet, a likely method of marking the rest of the day down for wisdom? . . . If to sparkle here a few years be the supreme ambition, Hereafter will be hardly thought of" (I. 50).

[52]  Such eighteenth-century assertions of the "naturalness" of human rank of course defended the status quo from revolutionary and leveling ideas, ideas that had circulated in England at least since Wat Tyler's rebellion (1381), in which the serfs marching on London with pitchforks chanted, "When Adam delved / And Eve span / Who was then the gentleman?"

history supported these patriarchal explanations of human origin: "Scripture and history . . . both were far more reliable than self-generating abstractions drawn from corrupt man's overweening pride in his reason" (Soloway 25).

In general, Austen seems to be in accord with these Anglican positions, seeing the divisions between poor and rich as "natural" and God-given, in fact, as providential. Her presumptions in this regard have been noted by Marxist critics such as Arnold Kettle who argue that her works demonstrate little interest in changing the class structure; her attitude to the poor is essentially one of *noblesse oblige*. Kettle proclaimed that "the one important criticism of Jane Austen . . . is that her vision is limited by her unquestioning acceptance of class society" (98), and he questioned her place in any literary pantheon because, in the face of class divisions, she could not even "notice the *existence* of the problem" (99).[53] Another important Marxist critic, Raymond Williams, agreed about Austen: "Where only one class is seen, no classes are seen" (117). Unsurprisingly, she had little to say, either in the novels or the letters, about the troubles of the working poor, unlike contemporaries such as Cobbett or Clare or even Wordsworth (Butler, "Politics" 202). The visit to the hovel in *Emma* represents Austen's most sustained treatment of the problem of the poor, and here she plainly endorses feudal obligations of charity and compassion: "The distresses of the poor were as sure of relief from her personal attention and kindness, her counsel and her patience, as from her purse" (93). Emma, Austen claims, understands the poor, but this understanding does not involve wanting to raise their station or re-create them as members of the middle-class. That sort of ambition, Austen notes, is unrealistic—or, rather, in her term, "romantic": "[Emma] understood their ways, could allow for their ignorance and their temptations, had no romantic expectations of extraordinary virtue from those, for whom education had done so little; entered into their troubles with ready sympathy, and always gave her assistance with as much intelligence as good-will" (93). This conception of the poor follows from feudal notions of rank or standing; the (later) Marxist idea of class, in which each social stratum stands in perpetual conflict with the others, had little place in the socio-political presumptions of the Anglican gentry. Austen seems unable to imagine a world without the poor.[54] For

---

[53]    The contemporary assumption that the question of "class" rather than "rank" dominates Austen's novels leads to misreadings of two sorts. Mark Parker has argued that "*Emma* can generate two readings of class: a progressive one, which emphasizes the insidious workings of class in Emma's disposal of Harriet; and a reactionary one, which sees and accepts this working as part of the price of social stability" (358). Both contemporary readings are anachronistic in light of neoclassical ideas about social hierarchy; it was not "reactionary" in Austen's day to believe in the morality of holding to one's God-given social position, nor would Austen have seen Emma's gentry rank (or her own) as naturally antagonistic to those "beneath." The idea that the classes exist in perpetual competition had arisen by the early 1800s, but only in embryonic form in radical milieus, as in Godwin's circle; Marx's full articulation of class warfare was yet to come.

[54]    Austen's attitude towards laborers is revealed in a (very) minor work of 1807, a piece of doggerel written as part of a family competition as to who could write the most clever poem based entirely on rhymes for "rose." The form of the competition itself implies

Austen and other conservative Christians of her day, a world without the poor is impossible—and not even desirable—for the world without poverty occurs only in the world to come, in the re-made "new heaven and new earth" promised for Christ's second coming (*Revelation* 21.1). Anglican sermons could of course cite the ultimate authority, Christ, who said "the poor ye shall always have with you" (*Matthew* 26:11).

Austen's own novels, however, reveal a world in which social order is becoming dramatically more fluid. Major landowners such as Darcy and Mr. Knightley do not seem affected, but we see other large estates at risk because of improvidence (for example, Mansfield Park and Kellynch). Estates can also leave the control of the immediate family, the threat to the Bennets in *Pride and Prejudice* and the actual happenstance for Mrs. Dashwood and her daughters in *Sense and Sensibility*. Marriages raise or lower the fortunes of young women: Fanny Price's mother marries far down, while her aunt catches a baronet; Jane Fairfax and Miss Taylor (Mrs. Weston) are saved from being governesses by marrying wealthy men (further, neither Frank Churchill nor Mr. Weston were born into wealth himself). Former members of the merchant class are transformed into members of the gentry: Sir William Lucas in *Pride and Prejudice* now has a knighthood, while the Coles in *Emma* can throw lavish parties. And the navy stands alone as an engine for rapid advancement for the able and ambitious, just as it did for Austen's two brothers, Charles and Frank (both ultimately admirals in His Majesty's Navy).

---

a parodic stance towards the aristocratic love poetry of the past (which featured "rose" and its rhymes to a risible extent), and certainly Austen's entry takes full burlesque advantage of the ironic distance between the usual poetic tropes related to "rose" and her own subject, a virtuous laborer going to church:

Happy the lab'rer in his Sunday clothes!
In light-drab coat, smart waistcoat, well-darn'd hose,
And hat upon his head, to church he goes;
As oft, with conscious pride, he downward throws
A glance upon the ample cabbage rose
That, stuck in button-hole, regales his nose,
He envies not the gayest London beaux.
In church he takes his seat among the rows,
Pays to the place the reverence he owes,
Likes best the prayers whose meaning least he knows,
Lists to the sermon in a softening doze,
And rouses joyous at the welcome close. (*LM* 243–4)

The laborer is superior to the smart set in London, and has no envy of their fashionable lot. Though clownish (his cabbage rose is a large and comic boutonniere) and ignorant about the substance of his worship (he "likes best the prayers whose meaning least he knows" and sleeps through the sermon), his simple faithfulness is worthy of praise. The poem most seems to admire the laborer for his willingness to play his role in village society without complaint and to be satisfied with his clothes, his rank, his ornaments, his mode of worship, and his place in the world. Austen evidently sees no conflict between her admiration of this pious laborer and her presumption of her own superiority.

In the face of the social flux Austen witnessed, and wrote about, it would have been impossible for natural law's presumptions about social hierarchy to remain unquestioned. Austen's depictions—based on what she knew—seem also to have been significantly re-aligned by Anglican evangelical discourses about the poor, as well as by Austen's own assessment that the holders of aristocratic privilege in many cases (say, the Prince Regent in historical fact, or Sir Walter as fictional examples) lacked the moral and spiritual qualifications for their positions. Evangelical championing of the "lower" classes was a widespread and highly public endeavor. From the closing decades of the eighteenth century and on through the whole of the nineteenth century, evangelicals defined their Christian mission as one of aiding every sort of member of "low estate" in the Great Chain: beggars, laborers and their children, "drunkards," orphans, lunatics, immigrants, slaves, gypsies, prostitutes, and "heathens" abroad. Evangelicals like Hannah More and William Wilberforce founded innumerable societies for the welfare of those on the bottom rungs; innumerable efforts of reform were promulgated.[55] Inevitably, this focus on the "low" interfered with hierarchical models of society, especially ones heavily inflected by the claims of the Great Chain. As Bynum argues, "those men and women engaged in attempts to improve the lot of various groups of human beings would not likely be drawn towards a model of nature in which these same groups inevitably and of necessity created a continuity between man and brute" (12). A more egalitarian Christianity followed, in which "the capacity to lead a spiritual life was judged as more important than the trappings of nobility" (Hall C. 59).[56]

---

[55] Ford K. Brown lists the nearly 100 of these organizations founded between 1780 and 1810, including The Society for the Abolition of the Slave Trade (1787), The Asylum for the Support and Encouragement of the Deaf and Dumb Children of the Poor (1792), The African Education Society (1807), and The Society for the Suppression of Juvenile Vagrancy (1808) (329ff).

[56] Bynum argues that "the evangelical endeavour was grounded on a consciousness—partly humanistic and partly religious—of a brotherhood of all men founded on the blood relationship devolving from a common ancestry" (12). Hall points to a passage from a 1790 poem by Cowper, "that favorite Christian poet of the middle classes," as evidence of this transition from thinking derived from the Great Chain to more egalitarian and democratic models of Christian society:

My boast is not that I deduce my birth
From loins enthron'd or rulers of the earth
But higher far my proud pretensions rise
The son of parents pass'd into the skies.
(*Poems* [1798] 322; qtd. in Hall 59)

But Cowper also asserted the "naturalness" of social hierarchy as well, as evidenced here in his famous long poem *The Task:*

Some must be great. Great offices will have
Great talents. And God gives to every man
The virtue, temper, understanding, taste,
That lifts him into life and lets him fall
Just in the niche he was ordain'd to fill.
(177; Book IV, ll. 788)

To the degree that Austen critiqued the presumption that those higher in status belonged there through divine prerogative, she seems to have done so in part because she felt the democratic influence of evangelicals and in part because the moral paralysis of the upper classes and the problem of her own merit relative to those more privileged than she made the issue of God-given place highly relevant to her. It is notable that her three prayers—which bear strong marks of evangelical self-searching—speak of "fellow-creatures," in five separate mentions.[57] "Fellow-creatures" is a term that focuses on the shared human subordination before God. For their part, her novels seem to progress towards an ameliorated view of natural law: God places people in their spheres; the talented and the good are sometimes called to move upward, sometimes stricken with ill fortune they must bear with Christian fortitude. Providence becomes a test of moral and spiritual worth, a test Sir Walter fails, for instance, by not having "principle or sense enough to maintain himself in the situation in which Providence had placed him" (*P* 248).

Austen's suspicion of "natural" social hierarchies is expressed most often when she allows the language of gradation to emerge from those characters whose social climbing, general buffoonery, or unearned sense of merit automatically makes their rhetoric of rank suspect. The word "superior," for instance, occurs in *Emma* some 30 times, often in the speeches of worthies such as Mrs. Elton (Phillipps 59), while in *Pride and Prejudice* the effusions of Sir William Lucas ("'I am fond of superior society'" [*PP* 28]) also render the term ironic. We find the vocabulary of the Great Chain in Mrs. Elton's boasting about the family she proposes Jane Fairfax should go to as a governess, the Bragges: "'Delightful, charming, superior, first circles, spheres, lines, ranks, every thing'" (*E* 359).[58] This mangling of social order seems even more convoluted than the epicycles of pre-Copernican cosmology. It is left to Mr. Elton, affronted by the idea of his marrying Harriet, to proclaim the edict of natural law: "'Every body has their level'" (*E* 132). From Lady Catherine de Bourgh comes a full-throated defense of aristocratic merit; in arguing against Elizabeth's claims, she speaks of her family's "'noble line,'" and its "'respectable, honorable, and ancient, though untitled families'" (*PP* 356). Most crassly, she employs the language of defilement: "'are the shades of Pemberley to be thus polluted?'" (396). Since Lady Catherine's worth—moral, intellectual, or spiritual—is negligible, her

---

[57] See a fuller discussion of the prayers in Chapter 2. Her clearest statement on the subject of Evangelicals is not exactly clear, but shows she had at least some important sympathies with the evangelical movement: "I am by no means convinced that we ought not all to be Evangelicals" (*L* 280).

[58] The name of this family, the Bragges, encapsulates the practices of the social-climbing Mrs. Elton and her circle. Incidentally, Sir William in *Pride and Prejudice* also uses the term "first circles." Speaking to Darcy at the Netherfield ball, Sir William gushes, "'I have been most highly gratified indeed, my dear Sir. Such very superior dancing is not often seen. It is evident that you belong to the first circles. Allow me to say, however, that your fair partner does not disgrace you'" (*PP* 92). Exactly how much Elizabeth or her family (her circle) represents a "disgrace" is of course a key consideration for Darcy here and later in the novel.

claims on account of blood seem particularly weak. Sir Walter's adherence to the idea of rank is ridiculed from the first page of *Persuasion*. The narrator's mimicry of his inner musings notes his self-affirming view of his family's status among the "limited remnant of the earliest patents" in contrast to "almost endless creations of the last century," titles whose novelty undermines their social elevation (*P* 3).[59] Like Lady Catherine, Sir Walter speaks with fluency about social rank as natural. The navy is bad, he declares, because it brings "'persons of obscure birth into undue distinction, and raising men to honours which their fathers and grandfathers never dreamt of'" (21). Mr. Shepherd obsequiously opines about Sir Walter's situation, noting that "'consequence has its tax'" (19), and Lady Russell employs the expected metaphor of spatial hierarchy to explain why Sir Walter must go to Bath because "[i]t would be too much to expect [him] to descend into a small house in his own neighborhood" (16). Sir Walter's perspective about family privilege also emerges in free indirect speech when Mr. Elliot's breach with the rest of the family is explained early in the novel. The worst of Mr. Elliot's crimes, we learn, is that he had spoken contemptuously "of the very blood he belonged to" (*P* 9).

At points Austen's mockery of snobs and her related attack on the presumption that natural law endorses social hierarchies become extremely pointed. Echoing the 1748 strictures of Lord Chesterfield against those "low in rank, low in parts, low in manner and low in merit" (322), Sir Walter inveighs against Anne's intent to visit Mrs. Smith: "'Upon my word, Miss Anne Elliot, you have the most extraordinary taste! Every thing that revolts other people, low company, paltry rooms, foul air, disgusting associations are inviting to you'" (170–71). The contrast between Sir Walter's idea of "low" and the Christian imperative of aiding the unfortunate is rendered all the more striking by the "nothingness" of Sir Walter's vacuous relations, the Viscountess and her daughter. A comic version of a similar moment occurs in *Pride and Prejudice*, when an uproar in the Collins household leads Elizabeth to exclaim, "'And is this all? . . . I expected at least that the pigs were got into the garden, and here it is nothing by Lady Catherine and her daughter!'" (179) Elizabeth's debunking of those above her is strengthened by the foolishness of Sir William, who stands in the doorway "in earnest contemplation of the greatness before him . . . constantly bowing whenever Miss De Bourgh looked that way" (180).

---

[59]    Austen implies that the Baronetage that so absorbs Sir Walter is a kind of a rival Bible, a blasphemous substitute for the real one. From Sir Walter's perspective we learn that it is "the book of books" (*P* 7). It substitutes in this way for Elizabeth as well, for when we learn of her earlier hopes to marry Mr. Elliot, we are told that "[t]here was not a baronet from A to Z, whom her feelings could have so willingly acknowledged as an equal" (9). This invocation of alpha and omega (A to Z) only reinforces the sense that the Baronetage has supplanted the "book of books" Elizabeth and Sir Walter should have been reading, for Christ identifies himself as the alpha and omega (*Revelation* 1:8), the first and the last, and the Christian Bible was understood to be structured by that narrative of alpha and omega, of Christ's beginning (before the creation of the world) to Christ's reign (at the end of the world and creation of the new).

Not every attack on a snob is meant to hold, however. For instance, Elizabeth assails Darcy's presumed snobbery when Mrs. Gardiner hopes that Mr. Bingley might meet Jane in London: "'My dear aunt, how could you think of it? Mr. Darcy may perhaps have *heard* of such a place as Gracechurch Street, but he would hardly think a month's ablution enough to cleanse him from its impurities, were he once to enter it; and depend upon it, Mr. Bingley never stirs without him'" (161). However, as events prove, Darcy is *not* a snob about Elizabeth's aunt or uncle. Further, Elizabeth's own error is shown by the potent confusion of tropes she employs, as she imagines ablution, a religious ritual by which one is cleansed of sins, as a remedy for visiting "Gracechurch." As she will later ruefully note, she had no reason to believe Darcy lacking in religious principles, but her metaphors seemed to suggest he did, confusing spiritual impurity with social contamination.[60] Conversely, Elizabeth defends Wickham against Miss Bingley, whose warnings about Wickham conclude thus: "'but really considering his descent, one could not expect much better'" (94). Elizabeth ignores the charges of immorality Miss Bingley has put forward, and focuses only on her snobbery: "'His guilt and his descent appear by your account to be the same,' said Elizabeth angrily; 'for I have heard you accuse him of nothing worse than of being the son of Mr. Darcy's steward, and of *that,* I can assure you, he informed me himself'" (106).

Perhaps more importantly, Austen sometimes clearly endorses social rank and consequence. For instance, when Mr. Collins presumes to introduce himself to Mr. Darcy, Elizabeth urges him not to: "it was not in the least necessary there should be any notice on either side, and that if it were, it must belong to Mr. Darcy, to superior in consequence, to begin the acquaintance." It is Mr. Collins who makes the Evangelical and democratic argument, an argument Austen implies is foolish (at least in this circumstance): "'permit me to say that there must be a wide difference between the established forms of ceremony amongst the laity, and those which regulate the clergy; for give me leave to observe that I consider the clerical office as equal in point of dignity with the highest rank in the kingdom" (109). Later, while viewing the "noble" hills of Pemberley, "crowned with wood," Elizabeth muses on the virtues and appropriateness of feudal dispensations when a wise and good man happens to hold the superior position: "As a brother, a landlord, a master, she considered how many people's happiness were in his guardianship! How much of pleasure or pain it was in his power to bestow! How much of good or evil must be done by him!" (277). This view of feudal obligations properly fulfilled has Austen's approval, for we find a similar approval of Mr. Knightley's feudal care of

---

60   Austen makes an intriguing choice in Gracechurch Street as the address for the Gardiners. Not only is the street named for a famous church, and that church named for the especial gift of forgiveness and providence given by God, but Gracechurch Street also was built over the ancient site of Londinium, where the basilica and forum had once stood. Austen may also have known that William Penn was arrested in Gracechurch Street in 1670, for giving a speech at the Quaker meeting place there situated. One anachronistic note of interest is that Estella and Pip meet at the Swan with Two Necks inn in Gracechurch Street in *Great Expectations*.

those within his reach in *Emma*. Elizabeth herself takes the considerations of rank seriously, to at least some important degree, for when Lady Catherine challenges her birth and pedigree, Elizabeth makes a counter-claim for her own merits based on being a "'gentleman's daughter'" (she is partly silenced by Lady Catherine's response: "'But who was your mother?'" [395]).[61]

*Emma* too ultimately endorses "natural" social hierarchies, and shows that Emma has been wrong to try to create them on her own. With Austen's presumed endorsement, for instance, Mr. Knightley argues that rank matters, when he claims that Harriet "'is the natural daughter of nobody knows whom, with probably no settled provision at all, and certainly no respectable relations'" (64). While highly distasteful to our modern sensibilities, Emma's conclusion about Harriet once she finds out that Harriet is a tradesman's daughter follows from natural law:

> Such was the blood of gentility which Emma had formerly been so ready to vouch for! –It was as likely to be as untainted, perhaps, as the blood of many a gentleman: but what a connexion had she been preparing for Mr. Knightley –or for the Churchills—or even for Mr. Elton! --The stain of illegitimacy, unbleached by nobility or wealth, would have been a stain indeed. (526)

This language of "stain" and contamination strikes modern readers as reprehensible, but because her original audience took the considerations of natural law seriously, this perspective would have been unexceptionable to most. For contemporary audiences in particular, it is hard enough to understand and sympathize with the ideas of social hierarchy presumed by Austen's world, to sympathize, for instance, with the "natural" boundaries that are re-installed between Emma and Harriet at the end of the novel ("The intimacy between [Harriet] and Emma must sink;

---

[61] Austen commonly deploys spatial metaphors as a register of social value, but her underlying attitudes are sometimes difficult to discern. Physical height can represent status, as when Emma's portrait of Harriet depicts her as too tall, for Emma is trying not only to make Harriet more attractive but also to raise her social rank (see Chan). Given the many parallels between *Emma* and *A Midsummer Night's Dream* (and the one direct allusion, when Emma quotes "'The course of true love never did run smooth'" only to note that "'a Hartfield edition of Shakespeare would have a long note on that passage'"), one might imagine that in the debate over how tall Harriet is, Austen was remembering Hermia's complaint about her romantic rival Helena: "She hath urged her height" (*E* 80; *MND* III. ii. 291). A similar moment when height becomes confused with social power occurs in *Pride and Prejudice* when Darcy's stuffy Aristotelian inquiry about the hypothetical question of bending to a friend's request ("'will it not be advisable . . . to arrange with rather more precision the degree of importance which is to appertain to this request, as well as the degree of intimacy subsisting between the parties?'") is met by Bingley's joking invocation of height: "'By all means . . . let us hear all the particulars, not forgetting their comparative height and size; for that will have more weight in the argument, Miss Bennet, than you may be aware of. I assure you that if Darcy were not such a great tall fellow, in comparison with myself, I should not pay him half so much deference'" (55). Elizabeth notes that Darcy seems "rather offended" (55).

their friendship must change into a calmer sort of goodwill; and, fortunately, what ought to be, and must be, seemed already beginning, and in the most gradual, natural manner" [526–7]). It is harder still to see social hierarchies endorsed and championed by the dominant theological discourse of her day, and to see democratic impulses by the same measure as potentially sinful, staining, and disruptive.

Only in *Persuasion* does Austen seem to discard entirely her previous and partial endorsement of social hierarchies, promoting instead the idea of meritocracy. Captain Wentworth has merit: vigorous achievement on the seas and intelligence and sensitivity on the home front. Anne's merit is "elegance of mind"; she knows she is the superior (intellectually and morally) of Henrietta or Louisa Musgrove even as she dismisses her claim to superiority on the grounds of being a baronet's daughter (Fott 26). Evangelical merit is displayed too, in the typological pilgrimage of Mrs. Smith, who has been the recipient of the "choicest gift of Heaven": "elasticity of mind" and the "disposition to be comforted" (167). As Alistair Duckworth has shown in detail in his *The Improvement of the Estate*, *Persuasion* replaces the values of the estate with the values of the navy, where individual merit allows anyone to rise to stations higher even than that of profligate baronets. The reversal of value between Sir Walter and Captain Wentworth is completed by the end of the novel; Sir Walter has lost the place Providence gave him while "Captain Wentworth, with five-and-twenty thousand pounds, and as high in his profession as merit and activity could place him, was no longer nobody" (270).[62] In fact, Austen explicitly inverts the usual language of rank when she describes Anne's final "inferiority," which emerges from one point only: "having no relations to bestow on [Wentworth] which a man of sense could value" (273). The Great Chain has been loosened in this novel, but natural law still holds—at least the law that one reaps as one sows, for Elizabeth and Sir Walter are left in the purgatory their snobbery created for them: "They had their great cousins, to be sure, to resort to for comfort; but they must long feel that to flatter and follow others, without being flattered and followed in turn, is but a state of half enjoyment" (273).

## History

The theological worldview Austen inherited from eighteenth-century Anglicanism helped create her understanding of time and history. Her attitude towards history has been the subject of substantial critical debate, focusing on her putative

---

[62]    Perhaps nothing demonstrates Sir Walter's movement out of the Great Chain than his testimony about standing in the streets of Bath, counting women whose looks fail to suit his standards: "once as he had stood in a shop in Bond-street, he had counted eighty-seven women go by, one after another, without there being a tolerable face among them" (*P* 153). In a democratic, deracinated urban space, the aristocrat totals up strangers from every class. The number 87 is a prime, comically not representative of anything beyond itself. Nothing could more plausibly dethrone Sir Walter from his presumptions of hierarchical claims than this burlesque.

refusal to pay attention to history or to contemporary events (a vein of criticism successfully countered in the last few decades), her proto-feminism and her claims for women's importance in history, and her place in the account of the emerging form of the novel relative to the more established genre of history.[63] Devoney Looser, for example, has persuasively argued that Austen seems to feel that the histories most worth knowing are probabilistic narratives grounded in ordinary experience; that is, her own novels: Austen's "history-as-fiction" takes "certain elements from schoolroom history and historical fiction" and makes "romance probable."[64] Looser adds, "Novels teach what history cannot—how to (and how not to) function in the present" (57). Certainly, Austen's view of history was shaped by her response to schoolroom history, most importantly, Goldsmith's *The History of England from the Earliest Times to the Death of George II* (1771), which she parodied in her own *The History of England*, written when she was 16. Austen's contribution, a burlesque that presents a comically bigoted preference for the Stuarts and that exults in its lack of dates or other specific historical data, ridicules the practice of history. By foregrounding her own biases so broadly, Austen implies that other historians have equal, if better hidden, biases, such as Goldsmith's own preference for Whigs. In particular, Austen's satire asks if triumphalist Whiggism is not in fact blinded by its own victory into disregarding the strengths and virtues of those it has defeated.[65]

However, while Austen was interested enough in the literary practice of history to write her own debunking version as well as to proffer a naïve and readily rebutted condemnation of history through her heroine in *Northanger Abbey* ("the

---

[63]   Of the many figures arguing that Austen had a substantial interest in history, or at least in contemporary and recent events as she knew them, some of the most salient include Amis, Wiesenfarth ("History and Myth"), Butler (*Jane Austen*), Duckworth, Kirkham, and Greene ("Myth"). See also Warren Roberts' *Jane Austen and the French Revolution* regarding her many connections to the French Revolution and the Napoleonic wars that followed. Looser's work surveys these critics and related feminist treatments, refuting first Gilbert and Gubar's 1978 *Madwoman in the Attic*, which proposes that "Austen realize[s] that history and politics . . . have been entirely beyond the reach of women's experience" (134; qtd. in Looser 55). For more recent and equally persuasive treatments of Austen and history, see Macdonagh, Kent, Looser, and Galperin's *The Historical Austen*; Galperin's later "'Describing What Never Happened: Jane Austen and the History of Missed Opportunities'" provides a reading of the alternative histories of Austen's plots relative to the narrator's own historiography.

[64]   That Austen had no interest whatsoever in writing "romantic history" is evidenced by the comic episode of James Stanier Clarke, the librarian at Carlton House for the Prince Regent, later George IV, who tried to interest Austen in writing a novel vaguely based on his own experiences as a worldly clergyman, and, failing that, a "historical romance illustrative of the History of the august House of Cobourg." She was polite in her refusal, but her "Plan for a Novel" shows exactly how risible she found his suggestions.

[65]   As Christopher Kent argues, Austen "brashly inverts the Whig view of history, the convention within which most history [of her age was] presented. By this convention the present determines what past developments deserve emphasis" ("Learning History" 64).

quarrels of popes and kings, with wars or pestilences, in every page; the men all so good for nothing, and hardly any women at all—it is very tiresome" [110]), her own view of history and the past was also broadly shaped by Christian precepts. For the Christian, history has a specific narrative: the world was created, the Fall occurred, Christ redeemed the creation from the consequences of the Fall with His death and resurrection, and Christ will come again at the end of the world to create a "new heaven and a new earth." Thus, Christian history is teleological, and the history of any one individual can be understood typologically as a small re-enactment of this salvation history (one is born, falls into sin, is redeemed, dies, and waits in heaven for the new creation).[66] History is not progressive in this view, nor does human nature change—both of these presumptions, incidentally, are reinforced by the doctrines of natural law.[67] History, therefore, is useful primarily to proffer moral examples about how to live a good or bad life; thus Caesar's faults and Mary Stuart's virtues (or Caesar's virtues and Mary Stuart's faults) are directly applicable to present-day humanity, while the specific cultural contexts that alter how people behaved are by definition of limited interest. In practice, this means that the particularities of the past (beyond the particularities important to the Christian arc of salvation, such as the details of the Gospel narratives) are not that important—what matters is human character in the face of perennial moral and spiritual challenges. Purely secular history will be relatively unenlightening, as it is in *Mansfield Park* for the Bertram girls who are proud they have learned the Roman emperors "as low as Severus" (Severus, who ruled from 193–211 A.D., was a military dictator and an oppressor of the early Christian Church; the fact that the Bertram girls' education in Roman history began with this figure, and not with the earlier republic or later, with Constantine and Christianized empire, constitutes an oblique criticism of their tutelage). [68]

Thus, sacred history overrides secular history, and the past becomes a field in which human beings reveal their universal propensities, both good and bad.[69]

---

[66] As Giffin argues, "Austen's novels are about reordering the disordered personality, family, community, and church. In Georgian England these things were still understood to be related to each other in an organic way. In Austen's vision of society, every person and every institution lives under the sign of the fall and is in need of salvation" (6).

[67] Austen seems remarkably unimpressed by the idea of progress, an idea strictly at odds with Christian ideas of history. The progress of progress, as it were, is in full bore in *Sanditon*, where Austen mocks the commercialization and pretense of this new form of public space. Galperin notes regarding Austen's view of history that "Austen's writing . . . reveals her radically skeptical . . . refusal to regard history as a template for the future. For Austen the historical has 'really happened,' with the pencil marks to prove it" (364).

[68] Knowing the "chronology of kings" and "a great deal of the Heathen Mythology" (21) is also of little service in Maria and Julia's education, for as Sir Thomas reflects bitterly at the novel's close, "They had been instructed theoretically in their religion, but never required to bring it into daily practice" (536).

[69] See Korshin, 390ff, for a discussion of the relation between sacred history, typology, and secular history.

One of Austen's most interesting off-hand comments about history comes from an 1814 letter to her niece Anna critiquing Anna's draft of a novel. She objects to the phrase "vortex of Dissipation," explaining "I do not object to the Thing, but I cannot bear the expression; --It is such thorough novel slang—and so old, that I dare say Adam met with it in the first novel he opened" (*L* 277). Of course, Austen was aware that novels have a particular origin in history (she is, after all, making a joke), and yet her a-historicity here suggests her view of the past more generally.[70] Adam and the world of the novel are not alien to each other, because the novel deals with human behavior, and Adam was a human being. In part, this way of thinking follows from the Christian knowledge that history was contained and relatively knowable. After all, the world was only about 6,000 years old—a vast stretch of time, to be sure, but nothing like the almost unimaginable scope of millions of years we now know constituted the earth's past.[71] This way of perceiving history was reinforced by the many sermons Austen heard or read, for Georgian divines often discussed Biblical characters on probabilistic grounds extrapolated from everyday experience. The presumption was that present-day believers could not only identify with the problems of Job or St. Thomas, but also that Job and St. Thomas were bound to reason more or less as pew-sitters did in the here-and-now. Sherlock, Austen's favorite writer of sermons, provides a relevant example. He is discussing the *Book of Job*, and arguing for its historicity by comparing Job's situation to both classical and contemporary experience. In a movement common to eighteenth-century Anglican argument, he argues for the probability of the account being true based on its improbability; that is, we must assume the truth of the account because it is impossible to believe that any poet or fiction-monger would write such improbabilities:

> For supposing the Book to be a mere *poetical Fiction*, upon what Ground of Probability does the Author furnish *Job* with such exalted Sentiments of Religion, and, at the same Time suppose them to be such *Secrets* to all his Friends? Is there any such Instance in any Author? *Cicero*, in his Dialogues,

---

[70]    Dickens will later make a similar anachronistic joke, but by his day, the issues of the "historical" as opposed to the Christian past had become so vexed that his joke is almost unintelligible in its narrative and temporal complexity. In his 1865 *Dr. Marigold's Prescriptions*, Dickens describes the great span of an elderly couple's marriage, noting the wedding happened "so long ago that upon my word and honour it took place in Noah's Ark, before the Unicorn could get in to forbid the banns by blowing a tune upon his horn" (the Unicorn seems not to have survived the Flood). Austen can invoke a novel-reading Adam without anxiety, but Noah's Ark will become for Dickens and his Victorian contemporaries a site of extraordinary cultural and narrative turmoil. See my "When the Megalosaurus Disembarked from the Ark: Dickens, *Genesis*, and Early Paleontology."

[71]    In Austen's day, most Anglicans still accepted the seventeenth-century calculations of Bishop Ussher (Archbishop of Armagh) who placed the creation of the world at nightfall on the night preceding October 23, 4004 B.C. Thus when Austen wrote to her niece Anna about Adam's novel-reading habits, she would have been presuming that 5,818 years had passed in the interim.

introduces *Philosophers*, of different Opinions, but we find them all *acquainted* equally with the *common Notions* of their *own* Times; and it wou'd be absurd in Any Author, to suppose the Contrary, without very evident Reason; and there can be no such Reason but the *Evidence* of *History*. . . . This Circumstance is natural, and agreeable to the Times, supposing the History to be true; but 'tis unnatural, and without Probability, which is the very *Life* of *poetical Fiction*, supposing the Book to be a mere Fable or Parable. (276–7)

Job and his friends can be compared to first-century A.D. Romans and to British citizens of the eighteenth century without difficulty. In a similar vein, in *Northanger Abbey* Elinor Tilney defends history by noting the similarity between the historian's evidence and ordinary experience: "'In the principle facts [the historians] have sources of intelligence in former histories and records, which may be as much depended on, I conclude, as any thing that does not actually pass under one's own observations'" (*NA* 110). This view that one person's observations recorded hundreds or even thousands of years ago may serve about as well as that of someone now living would certainly worry the practitioners of modern historiography, but if the nature of humankind is constant, as the Christian view of history implies, then Elinor (and, presumably, Austen) are on firm ground.[72]

The one feature of this universalized past that distinguishes itself for Austen is church history, particularly the English Reformation, the break between the Roman Catholic Church and the Church of England. In particular, Austen views the Catholic pre-Reformation past in England, symbolized by abbeys and other monastic ruins, as a permanent but essentially non-historical foundation of religious principle and faith. The adult Austen was not a crypto-Catholic of any sort, but her *History of England* shows a juvenile enthusiasm for this Catholicism of the past. She says that she is "partial to the roman catholic religion" (27), and downplays Mary I's execution of Protestants: "Many were the people who fell Martyrs to the protestant religion during her reign; I suppose not fewer than a dozen" (19). Transforming Guy Fawkes' attempted mass assassination into a breach of manners, she gives only a mild rebuke to the Catholic Gunpowder Plot: "I am necessitated to say that in this reign [of James I], the roman Catholics of England did not behave like Gentlemen to the protestants. Their Behaviour indeed to the Royal Family & both Houses of Parliament might justly be considered by

---

[72]   Yet another example of the late-eighteenth century's presumption that the values and ideas of the past have currency in the present comes from the frontispiece for Hannah More's 1777 *Essays on Various Subjects, Principally Designed for Young Ladies*, which quotes Pericles' *Oration to the Athenian Women*: "AS for you, I shall advise you in a few words: aspire only to those virtues that are PECULIAR TO YOUR SEX; follow your natural modesty, and think it your greatest commendation not to be talked of one way or the other." More evidently thought it perfectly reasonable to apply the moral strictures of Athenian society to contemporary women; Pericles' words have pride of place in the book as epitaph.

them as very uncivil" (27–8).[73] The heart of her support of Catholicism is in the service of a fanatical and romantic devotion (satirized by Austen even as it is expressed) to the cause of Mary, Queen of Scots, a "bewitching Princess" in this account (21).[74] She castigates Mary's Protestant critics: "could you Reader have beleived it possible that some hardened & zealous Protestants have even abused her for that steadfastness in the Catholic Religion which reflected on her so much credit? But this is a striking proof of their narrow souls & prejudiced Judgements who accuse her" (*sic*; 22–3). She also has harsh words for Henry VIII's destruction of the monasteries:[75]

> The Crimes & Cruelties of this Prince, were too numerous to be mentioned . . . & nothing can be said in his vindication, but that his abolishing Religious Houses & leaving them to the ruinous depredations of time has been of the infinite use to the landscape of England in general, which probably was a principal motive for his doing it, since otherwise why should a Man who was of no Religion himself be at so much trouble to abolish one which has for ages been established in the Kingdom. (13–4)

First, by playfully suggesting that the main reason Henry dissolved the monasteries was because he wanted to leave picturesque ruins for tourists in Austen's day, Austen is deploying the logic of Whig history (that is, the past is only prelude to the present) with a vengeance. But she is also showing respect for the long-

---

[73]    Incidentally, Austen would have heard annual thanksgivings in church for Guy Fawkes' failure, as a collect for this purpose was included the 1662 *Book of Common Prayer* (Jenkins 39).

[74]    The *History* is organized to highlight Tudor crimes and to promote the Stuart cause. It begins with the first Tudor king, Henry IV, who ascends to the throne "having prevailed on his cousin & predecessor Richard the 2nd to resign it to him, & to retire for the rest of his Life to Pomfret Castle, where he happened to be murdered" (3). It ends with the execution of Charles I, "vindicate[ed] from the Reproach of arbitrary & tyrannical Government" by a simple and self-affirming argument: "he was a STUART" (34). Austen's thoroughgoing partisanship for the Stuarts and against Cromwell is also fully shown in her marginalia in her own copy of Goldsmith's *The History of England*, in which she vents against Cromwell (e.g., "Detestable Monster!") and praises the royalists (e.g., Falkland, killed at Chalgrave Field, "The last was indeed a great & noble Man") (*J* 323, 320).

[75]    When we read in *Mansfield Park* about Henry Crawford's performance of the parts of Shakespeare's *Henry VIII*, each rendered with vigor ("The King, the Queen, Buckingham, Wolsey, Cromwell – all were given in turn" [389]), Austen's view of that monarch should be remembered. Certainly, the play is as germane in its own way to the novel as is *Lovers' Vows*, concerning as it does a battle between church authority on the one hand and secular desires on the other, as well as one man's abandonment of one woman in his rush to take up with another.

established character of Catholicism.[76] Further, that Catholicism stands for the establishment and authority of religion more generally.

The idea that this earlier British church represents a foundation for religion is expressed clearly in a late passage in *Sense and Sensibility*, which features one of the most marked and sustained use of religious symbolism in all Austen's novels. As Anne Richards has demonstrated in detail, the scene in which Marianne shows Elinor the spot where she first met Willoughby and in which she sets out her plans for moral and spiritual recovery is rife with religious meaning. The two sisters are on High Church Down, and Marianne notes "'that projecting mound—there I fell; and there I first saw Willoughby'" (390). Marianne's Fall is even more pregnant with spiritual meaning than is Louisa's in *Persuasion* (or the carriage accident and fall that begins *Sanditon*). She details her plan for repentance, her need for "'atonement to my God, and to you all'" (391) and then speaks of her plans for the spring, that time of new birth:

---

[76] A very full and excellent account of how Austen may have felt about the dissolution of the monasteries as such and England's Catholic past, at least as evidenced by *Northanger Abbey*, is rendered by Moore. Austen was not sufficiently ardent, however, about earlier Catholicism as to want to know much precisely about it. Writing in 1813 to Cassandra, who was visiting the Bigg-Withers at Manydown, she gives the news that she has been "applied to for information as to the Oath taken in former times of Bell Book & Candle—but have none to give." Her reluctance seems mostly to follow from a dislike of long scholarly reading (note the four adjectives in a row she deploys against quartos—"enormous great stupid thick") and less from a lack of interest in the Church: "Perhaps you may be able to learn something of its Origin & Meaning at Manydown. –Ladies who read those enormous great stupid thick Quarto Volumes, which one always sees in the Breakfast parlour there, must be acquainted with everything in the World. –I detest a Quarto. --Capt. Pasley's Book is too good for their Society. They will not understand a Man who condenses his Thoughts into an Octavo" (*L* 206). The phrase "bell, book, and candle" refers to the most extreme act of excommunication performed in the Catholic Church, the rite of anathema, a rite not much practiced since the Middle Ages. Captain Pasley's book, first published in 1810, was the seminal *An Essay on the Military Policy and Institutions of the British Empire*; much experienced in battles around the world, Pasley argued for a significantly enlarged military to govern Britain's expanding colonial possessions. If Austen enjoyed Pasley, as this passage suggests, there is no question that she knew a good deal about geopolitical realities of the early nineteenth century. Similarly, in *Mansfield Park* she seems to approve of Fanny's reading about Lord Macartney's embassy to the Chinese courts in 1793–1794 with all its tale of martial danger and geopolitical maneuvering, though once Edmund has disturbed Fanny with the news that he intends to act in *Lovers' Vows*, there is "no reading, no China, no composure" for her (183; for Macartney, see Staunton). The most famous incident in Macartney's history is his refusal to "kow-tow" (that is, make a full prostrate bow) before the Chinese emperor. Austen may be making an oblique reference to this act of courageous resistance, for Fanny will also resist kow-towing to the authority of everyone, including Edmund, who wishes her to act in *Lovers' Vows*.

'When the weather is settled . . . we will take long walks together every day. We will walk to the farm at the edge of the down, and see how the children go on; we will walk to Sir John's new plantation and Barton Cross, and the Abbeyland; and we will often go to the ruins of the Priory, and try to trace its foundations as far as we are told they once reached. I know we shall be happy.' (388)

The edge of the down is the edge of the High Church; the "new plantations" recall the final lines of Milton's *Lycidas* ("At last he rose, and twitched his mantle blue: / Tomorrow to fresh woods, and pastures new"), and the goals of Barton Cross and the Abbeyland are explicitly within the mode of Christian pilgrimage.[77] Further, she relies on the history of the church to find the ruins of the priory—she is bent on tracing the foundations of the English religious past "as far as we are told they once reached." Austen was a devoted Anglican, but the Catholic past of England stands as a marker for religious fidelity and stability. It is perhaps in this same spirit of reverence for an idealized, more thoroughly Christian past that *Mansfield Park*'s Fanny wears her amber cross—amber, after all, preserves the past and symbolizes it at the same time (Harris 220).

Austen's endorsement of the value of the Catholic past thus is not in conflict with her primary interest in history as a providential path for increased "true" faith, i.e., Protestantism. In 1813, Austen expressed this sense of historical trajectory leading to the dominance of Protestantism in Europe. Writing to her brother Frank, about to undertake a naval appointment to Sweden, she says, "Gustavus-Vasa, & Charles 12th, & Christiana, & Linneus —do their Ghosts rise up before You? –I have a great respect for former Sweden. So zealous as it was for Protestanism!" (*sic*; *L* 214–5). Gustavus Vasa (1496–1560) introduced Protestantism to Sweden; Charles XII (1682–1718) made Sweden the European center of Protestantism in the aftermath of the Thirty Years War. Christina (1633–1689) is perhaps a curious figure for Austen to include, as she abdicated her throne in 1654 so she could practice Catholicism (she is one of only four women to be buried in St. Peter's Basilica). But popular histories about Christina often argued that her abdication furthered the Protestant cause, in that by doing so she brought her Protestant cousin, Charles XI, to the throne. Linnaeus (1707–1778), the famous naturalist, helped reinforce the Great Chain of Being and hierarchical views of nature with his *Systema Naturae* (1735), a work that places all plants and animals into kingdoms, classes, genera, and species. The cover of the first edition showed Adam giving names to all the animals in Eden, and Linnaeus liked to think of himself as a second Adam, reportedly using as a personal motto "God creates, Linnaeus disposes." Thus all the figures Austen invokes can be understood broadly as participating in Sweden's

---

[77]   Austen rarely uses again such allegorical language. In *Persuasion*, there is a Monkford, the town where Wentworth's brother the curate lives, but the name carries no particular resonance. Somewhat more important may be the name of Edmund's parish in *Mansfield Park*, Thornton Lacey. John Lacy was a prominent religious enthusiast of the seventeenth century, a firebrand of the sort deplored by Austen's contemporary Anglican divines, while the name "Thornton," like "Thornfield" in Brontë's *Jane Eyre,* implies a site of painful religious test.

history as a country "zealous" for Protestantism. For Austen, the most important history is Christian history. Thinking of the dangers of another possible war with the United States, she wrote in 1814 to Martha Lloyd: "If we *are* to be ruined, it cannot be helped—but I place my hope of better things on a claim to the protection of Heaven, as a Religious Nation, a Nation in spite of much Evil improving in Religion, which I cannot believe the Americans to possess" (*L* 273–4). Thus, she reads history primarily as the story of God's Providence and of the rise and fall of religious and irreligious nations; this is the narrative pattern of the Old Testament, and Austen assumes it applies to Great Britain as well.

## Nature

Austen's view of the created world is no less Christian than is her view of time and history. Of course, her views on nature, particularly landscapes, grounds, and gardens, also reflected the aesthetics of the late eighteenth and early nineteenth century, including ideas about "improvement," the picturesque, and the sublime; her novels and letters reflect her continuing engagement and debate with what, for instance, was "true" improvement and what was dictated by pretense and fads. But these contemporary issues overlaid Austen's deeper commitment to the view of nature proposed by natural law, in which nature's plenty, variety, and ingenuity display proofs of God's goodness and reason. In particular, the argument from design would have been unexceptionable in her Anglican world—a truism, in fact, even for most naturalists of her day. For instance, Thomas Bewick, whose *History of British Birds* was a bestseller in 1797 and reprinted often in the next several decades, prefaces his work by noting that it is to demonstrate the "Great Truths of Creation" and that "[i]n no part of the animal creation are the wisdom, the goodness, and the bounty of Providence displayed in a more lively manner than in the structure, formation, and various endowments of the feathered tribe" (vii). Austen's readers will be helped by a lively remembrance about the difference between the ideas dominant in her world and the scientific materialism that was ultimately to dominate the nineteenth century. In fact, the presumption that nature shows forth God's design persisted in the popular imagination and among popular natural historians long past Austen's death, having a robust presence despite the publication of Lyell's *Principles of Geology* (1830–1833) or Darwin's *On the Origin of Species* (1859). Women naturalists and Anglican clergymen wrote most of the early- and mid-nineteenth-century works of popular science, and as Bernard Lightman notes, these two groups "formed a formidable group whose common agenda could frustrate the goals of [the] scientific naturalists" (163).[78]

---

[78] See in particular chapter two of Lightman's *Victorian Populizers of Science* (2007), "Anglican Theologies of Nature in a Post-Darwinian Era." In fact, as contemporary debates demonstrate, scientific naturalism has never entirely silenced the argument from design or its underlying orthodox commitments in the popular imagination, despite its thorough victory in the scientific and educational communities.

Because Austen's worldview about nature is so removed from our own, our critical conclusions about her relation to nature in the fiction can be oddly disconnected from her values. For the most part, Austen did not describe nature unless it helped her delineate character and plot. Where there is no moral to be drawn, Austen is often content to characterize nature in flat and general terms, such as the "very large" park or "beautiful woods" at Pemberley (Van Ghent 369). There are only a few expressive or poetic appreciations of nature in Austen's works. One might cite her brief description of Beechen Cliff in *Northanger Abbey*; the praise for the grounds at Donwell Abbey in *Emma*; Fanny's effusions for the stars or the evergreen in *Mansfield Park* (discussed below); the lyrical delight expressed about Lyme in *Persuasion*; and the brief but vigorous description of the sea in *Sanditon*, "dancing and sparkling in Sunshine & Freshness" (*LM* 161). The passage in *Persuasion* is perhaps most important, partly because of its length and elaboration and partly as it seems to refer to Austen's own prior visits to Lyme (the narrator speaks with the authority of a practiced tourist):

> [A] very strange stranger it must be, who does not see charms in the immediate environs of Lyme, to make him wish to know it better. The scenes in its neighbourhood, Charmouth, with its high grounds and extensive sweeps of country, and still more its sweet retired bay, backed by dark cliffs, where fragments of low rock among the sands make it the happiest spot for watching the flow of the tide, for sitting in unwearied contemplation; --the woody varieties of the cheerful village of Up Lyme, and, above all, Pinny, with its green chasms between romantic rocks, where the scattered forest trees and orchards of luxuriant growth declare that many a generation must have passed away since the first partial falling of the cliff prepared the ground for such a state . . . these places must be visited, and visited again, to make the worth of Lyme understood. (102–3)

None of *Persuasion*'s characters visit these places, but Austen has, and thus we are authorized to imagine her watching the tide in Charmouth bay or musing on the generations—back to Adam—at Pinny.[79]

In general, however, Austen's landscapes, following the eighteenth-century tradition, are populated with "welcome signs of human habitation" (Sutherland 112). Thus, when Elizabeth Bennet asks, "'what are men to rocks and mountains'" (174), Austen expects us to criticize her attitude, expressing as it does a desire for Romantic isolation as well as Elizabeth's disappointment about Wickham's inadequacy as a suitor. Further, Austen's landscapes have meaning to the degree that her characters move within them and are characterized by their movements. For instance, in *Mansfield Park*, the visiting Bertrams and Crawfords are stopped in their transgressive wanderings at Sotherton by a locked gate at the bottom of a

---

[79]  Bharat Tandon reminds us that "un-" constructions, such as "unwearied contemplation," are a staple of Wordsworth's poetic rhetoric (236–7).

"ha-ha" that marks the boundary between the formal gardens and the wilderness.[80] This gate and the "ha-ha" are important because they represent moral boundaries. In fact the "ha-ha" is ideal for Austen's symbolic purpose, because it is a ditch that conceals the fence, so constructed that a viewer from the garden will not see the obstacle and will enjoy an uninterrupted vista, but, on coming closer, will see that the way is blocked (thus the "ha-ha" of surprise).

The fine Austen critic Joel Weinsheimer has argued that this propensity of Austen to link the depiction of nature with the depiction of character is a key weakness in Austen's art. Weinsheimer has no objection to such a symbolic use of the cultivated landscape; rather, he wishes that Austen would extend her powers into other, complementary uses of nature in her fiction: "we can nevertheless desire a novelistic world in which we are somewhat less benevolently comforted by objects that silently hymn man's self-importance" (134). Weinsheimer argues that "Jane Austen's treatment of the physical implies that mankind cannot be defined in relation to anything but itself; [she neglects] to contextualize [mankind] in a sphere of reference larger than himself" (136). But this argument can only be made by forgetting what Austen assumes, that nature—and humankind—are God's creations, and that humankind is defined in relation to God's natural law. Austen does not share the Romantic ideology that defines humankind within a sublime landscape, in which mind and imagination, hills and clouds, stand in continual refraction with each other. She is not studying humankind in a vacuum, however, even if "nature" or the universe is not the limiting horizon for her study. Weinsheimer cites Kenneth Moler, who makes a complaint corollary to his own: "self-knowledge entails not the scanning of the universe's mysteries but 'knowledge of the heart,' . . . of the particular directions in which . . . he has erred and is likely to err in the complex business of the moral life. . . . In moments of crisis Emma doesn't ask, who am I or why was I born, [but instead] examine[s] her tendency to a particular evil" (9). I contend that Emma fails to ask these questions because she is not an existential heroine who finds the universe a puzzle. Rather, she is a Christian heroine whose view of the universe follows then-Christian orthodoxy. For Austen, there are no negatives in nature; nature and the universe represent the plenitude of God's plan (Burke 19).

Her heroines, then, if right-thinking, look at nature for its aesthetic pleasure and for what it teaches about the cosmic order. A well-known conduct text of 1761, Lady Sarah Pennington's *An Unfortunate Mother's Advice to Her Absent Daughters*, sets out "pleasure and instruction" as reasons for studying the natural world: so doing is

---

[80]  Austen employs another wilderness for symbolic purposes, in *Pride and Prejudice*, when Lady Catherine de Bourgh intrudes on Longbourn late in the novel. Within the wilderness, Elizabeth is tested—and proves worthy of the test (Austen of course would have been very familiar with the story of Christ's temptations in the wilderness, told in both *Matthew* and *Luke*). As Laura Dabundo argues, she is tempted to acquiesce to Lady Catherine's will and social expectations. However, "Elizabeth is shown as a true Christian heroine, one whom her author's clerical family would certainly have venerated and esteemed" ("The Devil" 57).

... pleasing from the continual new discoveries to be made of the innumerably various beauties of nature—a most agreeable gratification of that desire of knowledge wisely implanted in the human mind—and highly instructive, as those discoveries lead to the contemplation of the great Author of nature, whose wisdom and goodness so conspicuously shine through all his works, that is impossible to reflect seriously on them without admiration and gratitude. (190; qtd. in Bradbrook 144)[81]

In *Mansfield Park,* we find Fanny Price admiring and learning from nature in two key moments, in terms wholly consonant with the views of Pennington and other orthodox Christian figures of her day. In both scenes, Fanny falls into a rhapsody, carried away by her admiration to speak fully and emotionally about her subject, in a manner strikingly at odds with her usual silence and reserve.[82]

In the first, Fanny and Edmund are at the window admiring the twilight turn to an unclouded night:

Fanny spoke her feelings. 'Here's harmony!' said she, 'Here's repose! Here's what may leave all painting and all music behind, and what poetry only can attempt to describe. Here's what may tranquillize every care, and lift the heart to rapture! When I look out on such a night as this, I feel as if there could be neither wickedness nor sorrow in the world; and there certainly would be less of both if the sublimity of Nature were more attended to, and people were carried more out of themselves by contemplating such a scene.' (132)

As Maggie Lane has noted, "when I look out at such a night as this" constitutes the only clear line of iambic pentameter in all of Austen's prose, perhaps propelled by the claim of the speech itself, that here is "what poetry only can attempt to describe" (159). Edmund and Fanny implicitly share the belief that God is the source of the harmony, repose, and beauty of the skies, and we learn that Fanny's linking of the skies with a human moral response comes from Edmund's training: "'*You* taught me to think and feel on the subject, cousin,'" she says (132; italics in original). Fanny's intense desire for harmony and goodness may have been precipitated by what she has just witnessed, a long wrangle between Edmund and Mary about his joining the priesthood. And sorrow, cares, and even the road to wickedness will re-emerge at the end of this chapter, as Edmund forsakes Fanny at the window,

---

[81]    See Bradbrook, 7–10, for the resonances between Lady Pennington's advice book and Austen's view of female education.

[82]    See Hammond for a discussion of the ways in which Fanny's adherence to "Burkean-Wordsworthian nature-worship" breaks her link with her lower middle-class origin and aligns her with the values held by the gentry—at least those members of the gentry who hold to traditional and romantic values (79). Hammond sees Fanny's admiration of feudalism (evidenced by her disappointment at the Sotherton chapel) as further evidence of her stepping out from the social position of her parents.

despite his promise to go out with her onto the lawn to view Cassiopeia, instead joining Mary and the other young people at the piano.[83]

The second rhapsody occurs near the beginning of Volume II, as Mary and Fanny sit in the Grants' shrubbery. Fanny is admiring the growth of the shrubbery from its start as a "rough hedgerow" (243), and, after marveling at the "miracle" of memory, apostrophizes the evergreen:

> 'The evergreen!—How beautiful, how welcome, how wonderful the evergreen!— When one thinks of it, how astonishing a variety of nature! –In some countries we know the tree that shed its leaf is the variety, but that does not make it less amazing, that the same soil and the same sun should nurture plants differing in the first rule and law of existence. You will think me rhapsodizing; but when I am out of doors . . . I am very apt to get into this sort of wondering strain. One cannot fix one's eyes on the commonest natural production without finding food for a rambling fancy.' (244)

Fanny's long speech bores Mary, who wittily confesses, through a reference to Voltaire's biography of the Sun King, that she "'see[s] no wonder in this shrubbery equal to seeing myself in it'" (209). The Venetian doge who had made the original comment to which Mary alludes was amazed that he was there at Versailles in the midst of all its baroque magnificence; Mary, reversing the trope, is amazed that she has been willing to forsake city pleasures for the country for "'nearly five months'" (244). Mary is incapable of reading nature to see God's design, in this case the plenitude of trees, both deciduous and evergreen, or of looking to nature to see a "rule or law of existence," as Fanny does. The evergreen is an emblem of fidelity, apt for Fanny (Mary's idea of a long adherence, is, as noted above, "five months.") Fanny is performing the reasoning required by natural law, "reflect[ing] on nature in order to arrive at a sense of what is 'good'" (Giffin 25).[84] Mary by contrast can only marvel at herself, her situation, and her desires.

---

[83]   There may be some morals to be drawn from the star Fanny wishes Edmund to see with her. Cassiopeia was a vain queen who boasted about her own beauty and that of her daughter Andromeda. The Nereids' anger at this claim led Poseidon to threaten a flood, so Andromeda was offered as sacrifice to a sea monster (she was saved by Perseus) while Cassiopeia was so placed among the stars that half the year she is upside down, to teach her a lesson about the lures of vanity. Had Edmund attended to the ancient story's moral, he might not have erred as he does in this chapter, confusing Mary's "light and graceful tread" with virtue: "'There goes good humour I am sure . . . . There goes a temper which would never give pain! How well she walks!'" (131).

[84]   Kenneth Moler notes that Fanny's speech on the evergreen closely parallels a passage in Hannah More's 1799 *Strictures on the Modern System of Education*, in which More also takes the variety of trees as evidence of God's plan. More argues that students should be "led to admire the considerate goodness of Providence in having caused the spiry fir, whose slender foliage does not obstruct the beams of the sun, to grow in the dreary regions of the north, whose shivering inhabitants could spare none of its scanty rays; while in the torrid zone, the palm-tree, the plantain, the banana, spread their umbrella leaves to break the almost intolerable fervours of a vertical sun" (Moler 115, 125; More 349).

Austen's view of nature is augmented by her eighteenth-century sense of anthropology. She knew of course of the span of humanity across the globe, and as one might expect from her day, these far reaches of human civilization for Austen stand for the most improbable, fanciful, and uncivilized realms of human experience. In her burlesque "Plan for a Novel," the hapless hero and his daughter end in Kamschatka (at the eastern verge of Asia), where he "expires in a fine burst of Literary Enthusiasm, intermingled with Invectives against Holder's of Tythes" (*LM* 228). When Austen writes a panegyric on her niece Anna, she compares Anna's imagination to Lake Ontario and her flood of wit to Niagara (*LM* 251). And when she imagines re-writing Mary Brunton's 1811 novel, *Self-Control*, she claims: "my Heroine shall not merely be wafted down an American river in a boat by herself, she shall cross the Atlantic in the same way, & never stop till she reaches Gravesent" (*sic; L* 283*)*. The other farthest reach of humankind—downward in the presumed anthropological scale—is the savage, who in *Pride and Prejudice* emerges in Darcy's cutting remark to Sir William Lucas: "'Every savage can dance'" (28).[85] Given the many eighteenth-century accounts of dancing savages, we can infer that Darcy was presumably referring to Hottentots (Lovejoy 234); they and other "uncivilized" people were often invoked in the late eighteenth-century rush to identify creatures of the gaps (what we might today understand as "missing links" from a Darwinist perspective). But these creatures of the gaps were proposed to support the Great Chain's doctrine of continuity, not to challenge it (as the naturalist Bonnet argued, "nature makes not leaps" [Lovejoy 235]). There was a place in eighteenth-century debate for the mermaid, too: did such creatures exist? Naturalists such as Robinet debated the reality of *l'homme marin*. When Harriet's guesses about the charade's solution are so wildly off, it is important to note that one of her guesses—a mermaid—in many ways describes her social position, a creature whose place in the Great Chain is problematic exactly because her origins are unknown.[86]

The Great Chain and its corollary ideas about the universe thus resonated throughout Austen's worldview and her fiction. While it is highly unlikely that contemporary readers will feel drawn to the dramatically different assumptions Austen made as she evaluated society and human behavior, it is useful to know what they were. Our views of natural world and its occupants, the past and history,

---

[85]   Darcy's disdain for the "savage" is matched by Dr. Johnson, who is repeatedly asked by Boswell and others to judge the merits of civilization versus the savage life, both in response to Rousseau and to travel reports which idealized primitive scenes. Dr. Johnson would never allow any "superiority of the savage life" (II. 71). He does, however, admit that had he been born a savage, he would never have grown to become an adult, his poor vision keeping him from the most basic of survival mechanisms, finding food: "Had I been an Indian, I must have starved, or they would have knocked me on the head, when they saw I could do nothing" (IV. 219).

[86]   Thomas Love Peacock's *Nightmare Abbey* (1818) also includes a long specious scholarly discussion of the mermaid; Peacock's satiric object is both Gothicism and pedants, especially the scholarly penchant for forcing evidence to conform to theories.

the social ladder, and the nature of language would all be very alien to Austen, and her views are in some unalterable way alien to ours. The best we can do is to remind ourselves of the nature of her different presumptions and to allow that knowledge to inform our understanding of her novels. The views of orthodox Anglicans in the late Georgian period must be re-captured through an informed exercise of the imagination. Our contemporary ideas about mermaids, evergreens, "savages," Adam, Job, servants, lords: all are apart from hers. Even her understanding of how words matter and what they mean is not consonant with ours. To read Austen is to read a missive from a different world—one familiar but strange.

# PART 2
## The Sins of the Author

# Chapter 4
# Wordplay, Candor, and Malice

Wisdom is better than Wit, & in the long run will certainly have the laugh on her side (*L* 280)

Jane Austen came from a large and clever family, where charades, word-games, impromptu theatricals, and musical performances made for an often lively household. As an adult, Austen loved to play card games such as Speculation but also enjoyed charades, acrostics, conundrums, riddles, anagrams, and other word games.[1] She loved wordplay and wit and even bad puns, and from her girlhood gave every sign of knowing how to use words with devastating satiric intent and consequence.[2] Nonetheless, Austen was also aware of the power of words to hurt, to offend, and to transgress social boundaries. After her death, her family insisted that her use of words was always harmless. Within days of her passing, her oldest brother James wrote an encomium on her virtues, which included these claims:

> Hers, Fancy quick, and clear good sense
> And wit which never gave offence:
> A Heart as warm as ever beat,
> A Temper even calm and sweet:
> Though quick and keen her mental eye
> Poor natures foibles to descry
> And seemed for ever on the watch
> Some traits of ridicule to catch.
> Yet not a word she ever pen'd
> Which hurt the feelings of a friend
> And not a line she ever wrote
> 'Which dying she would wish to blot' (*sic*; "Venta" 49).

James Austen's implied distinction is important—his sister satirized foibles, but because the foibles were presented within fiction and attached to fictional characters, no living person—no friend—could have been damaged by her wit. Six months later, her brother Henry, writing the "Biographical Notice of the Author" that prefaced the first edition of *Northanger Abbey* and *Persuasion,* also excused and commended her sharpness:

---

[1]   See Duckworth ("Spillikins") for a thorough review of Austen's own game-playing and the role of games in the novels.

[2]   For instance, she writes to Cassandra in 1800 about a pleasant evening spent with an elderly neighbor, Mr. Holder; she seems in particular to have enjoyed his "infamous puns" (*L* 56).

Though the frailties, foibles, and follies of others could not escape her immediate detection, yet even on their vices did she never trust herself to comment with unkindness. The affectation of candour is not uncommon; but she had no affectation. Faultless herself, as nearly as human nature can be, she always sought, in the faults of others, something to excuse, to forgive or forget. Where extenuation was impossible, she had a sure refuge in silence. She never uttered either a hasty, a silly, or a severe expression. ("Biographical Notice" 6)

Obviously, neither novel that this "Biographical Notice" prefaces—*Northanger Abbey* nor *Persuasion*—excuses, forgives, or forgets human faults; in fact, her witty exposure of human fault, from John Thorpe's boasts to Mrs. Clay's wiles, provides one of the chief delights of both works. Henry Austen, we conclude, must be speaking of her relations with real people, her friends and family, and informing her readers that the sharp humor of these novels did not extend to Austen's own practice in life.[3]

Certainly, the moral problem of wit dominates Austen's fiction. Heartless and self-serving wit functions as a major sin that two of her heroines, Elizabeth Bennet and Emma Woodhouse, must overcome, and it is a ruinous characteristic for Fanny Price's romantic rival, Mary Crawford. The narrator's own moral authority is also at issue in the novels, particularly at those moments when the satiric exposure of faults seems to merge with the pleasures of malice. After all, much of the keen pleasure readers take in Austen's work is created by Austen's wit. The moral problem of wit also played an important role in Austen's life, even though her brothers should be accorded some authority to give their own witness about how she behaved with those she knew. Her letters to Cassandra most freely demonstrate the connection between wit and malice—to her (probably) equally witty sister, she wrote often markedly cruel judgments. The propensity of wit to become morally unmoored, to move beyond the "descrying" of "foibles" into the pleasures of malice and self-righteousness, was an ever-present danger for Austen, and her awareness of this fault was keen.

Her three surviving prayers document this awareness most fully. Though they were composed for family worship and are not individual petitions to God, they nonetheless focus on the problem of the hurt done to other people, either knowingly or not. In the first, she prays, "Teach us to understand the sinfulness of our own Hearts, and bring to our knowledge every fault of Temper and every evil Habit in which we have indulged to the discomfort of our fellow-creatures, and

---

[3]    One of Austen's best biographers, Park Honan, has argued that Austen's novels are the means she found by which she could make a moral exercise of wit: "The effort of reconciling her faith with her fury was enough to try her, and as happy as she was in green country at Chawton she was to make amends in part through her fictional comedies in which no living being is attacked, but life itself is recreated and appraised for every reader" (255). I find persuasive this means by which the family's insistence that Austen was kind to others in practice can be reconciled with the witty exposure of fault evident everywhere in the novels.

the danger of our own Souls." Ill-temper and the habit of malicious wit, Austen knows, lead to the "discomfort" of others, and, more importantly, to the possibility threat of eternal damnation—at least if one has not acknowledged and repented one's sins. In the spirit of Evangelical self-examination, she asks, "have we . . . willingly given pain to any human Being?" The second prayer likewise notes sins against one's neighbor, especially ones of thought (presumably thoughts marred by the traditional seven deadly sins, including envy, pride, and malice): "We remember with shame and contrition, many evil Thoughts & neglected duties; & we have perhaps sinned against Thee & against our fellow-creatures in many instances of which we have no remembrance." In the third prayer, she appeals for divine aid in redirecting her inclination to make harsh judgments about others into an inclination to judge only herself harshly and to exempt others from her strict assessments: "Incline us Oh God! to think humbly of ourselves, to be severe only in the examination of our own conduct, to consider our fellow-creatures with kindness, & to judge of all they say and do with that Charity which we would desire from them ourselves" ("Prayers"). We may imagine Jane, Cassandra, their mother, and Martha Lloyd in their evening round of prayers at Chawton, bowing their heads in serious contemplation of the personal resonances these words conveyed for them all. Jane Austen herself knew all too well their application to their author.[4]

The prayers' evidence of Austen's remorse may be usefully set against the many moments in her letters that demonstrate her besetting impulse towards malice. Many, especially letters to Cassandra, reveal flashes of seeming cattiness if not heartlessness. She tells of meeting an unknown "Gentleman in a Buggy . . . in such very deep mourning that either his Mother, his Wife, or himself must be dead" (*L* 40). In the midst of news of social engagements, she gives a death notice: "Mr. Waller is dead, I see; --I cannot greive about it, nor perhaps can his Widow very much" (*L* 130). Some female neighbors drop by: "I was as civil to them as their bad breath would allow me" (*L* 61). She gives the news of another neighbor with a new wife: "Charles Powlett has been very ill, but is getting well again; --his wife is discovered to be everything that the Neighbourhood could wish her, silly & cross as well as extravagant (*L* 26). As Oliver Macdonagh has pointed out, one sees clearly in her letters how hard it was to be polite and *not* say nasty things when one is in the constant company of a few other families and households whom one sees constantly, especially if one's neighbors, such as the Digweeds at Steventon or the Middletons and Miss Benn at Chawton, have little entertaining

---

[4]  Bruce Stovel argues that the prayers represent a wholly different face of Austen: "They seem so different from her letters—chatty and observant, gossipy and often malicious—and from her novels—so worldly in tone, so seemingly silent on spiritual matters." He notes that biographers generally avoid the problem by ignoring the prayers, or dismissing them as conventional and thus inauthentic: "it is not an easy matter to reconcile the Jane Austen revealed in her prayers with the catty letter-writer and the shrewd comic novelist" (200–201).

conversation to offer (124). Repeatedly in the letters, Austen notes that people fail to amuse her, or fail to offer much beyond a satiric target. At Bath, Austen makes a new acquaintance: "Miss Langley is like any other short girl with a broad nose & wide mouth, fashionable dress, & exposed bosom" (*L* 86). Another social occasion at Bath falls short in Austen's view: "There was a monstrous deal of stupid quizzing, & common-place nonsense talked, but scarcely any Wit" (*L* 104). Most notoriously, she reports on a stillbirth: "Mrs. Hall of Sherbourn was brought to bed yesterday of a dead child, some weeks before she expected, oweing to a fright. –I suppose she happened unawares to look at her husband" (*sic*; *L* 17).[5] While E. M. Forster was being hyperbolic when he claimed to hear the "whinnying of harpies" in Austen's letters, those letters do provide ample evidence of her capacity to be callous in the service of a joke (160).

But the letters also show evidence of self-correction in the interests of charity, verbal and otherwise. We see the competing impulses of conscience and satire, for instance, when her neighbors the Webbs moved away in 1814: "The Webbs are really gone! When I saw the Waggons at the door, & thought of all the trouble they must have in moving, I began to reproach myself for not having liked them better—but since the Waggons have disappeared my Conscience has been closed again—& I am excessively glad they are gone" (*L* 278).[6] On other occasions, the moral lesson persists, as in 1798, when she paid a visit to a cottager, Betty Lovell, and had to report to Cassandra that the object of her charity had asked after Cassandra, "who called so often." Austen acknowledges the reproach, "which I am sorry to have merited, and from which I will profit" (*L* 21). We find her in 1813 reprimanding herself about some unkind words she had written about her nephews (the letter again is to Cassandra): "As I wrote of my nephews with a little bitterness in my last, I think it particularly incumbent on me to do them justice now, & I have great pleasure in saying that they were both at the Sacrament yesterday" (*L* 234). An earlier letter to Cassandra of 1808 provides another example of self-correction, for after making sundry sharp comments about "Miss Hatton's neck," Lady B., a "shameless woman" who is a "piece of impertinence," and a widower who has no "right to look higher than his daughter's Governess," she tempers her tongue: "I am forced to be abusive for want of subject, having really nothing to say" (*L* 124). Similarly, writing in 1805 about Mrs. Lloyd's final illness, Austen apologizes for her wit: "Poor woman! May her end be peaceful & easy, as the Exit we have witnessed! . . . The Nonsense I have been writing in this & in my last letter, seems

---

[5]    Carol Houlihan Flynn points out that this particularly nasty comment "is most notable . . . not so much [for] its heartless wit, but its context. It becomes in this long and rambling letter just one of many careless-seeming remarks squeezed in between reports about the uncommon largeness of Mary [her sister-in-law], about to give birth, the lying in of Dame Tilbury's daughter, and the dirtiness of Steventon's lanes" (103).

[6]    Knox-Shaw reminds the reader that Austen's dislike of the Webbs stems from her first contact with them, when she found them at home reading More's *Practical Piety* (168). Evangelical humorlessness was ever a bar to Austen's becoming a thoroughgoing Evangelical herself.

out of place at such a time; but I will not mind it, it will do you no harm, & nobody else will be attacked by it" (L 100). The reasons Austen furnishes as excuse are important: Cassandra, the letter's recipient, will not be harmed by "Nonsense," and, as the letter is private, no one else will be "attacked by it" either. Yet another moment of self-accusation admixed with self-justification occurs in 1813, when Austen meditates on the probable visit of a Miss Burdett, who seems to have been let in on the secret that Austen was the author of *Pride and Prejudice*: "I should like to see Miss Burdett very well, but . . . I am rather frightened by hearing that she wishes to be introduced to *me*. If I *am* a wild Beast, I cannot help it. It is not my own fault" (*L* 212).[7]

The letters, however, also bear witness to the charitable Austen, and the moments of charity in general balance the moments of malice, though we tend to read and remember the malicious parts more often. For instance, in 1808, she writes to Cassandra about a Southhampton neighbor in distressed circumstances: "You are very kind in mentioning old Mrs. Williams so often. Poor Creature! –I cannot help hoping that each Letter may tell of her sufferings being over. –If she wants sugar, I should like to supply her with it" (*L* 135). There is true sweetness in the desire to give, of all things, sugar to a dying woman. Likewise, she thinks with tolerance and compassion of Mrs. Stent, the poor companion of Mrs. Lloyd: "'Poor Mrs. Stent! It has been her lot to be always in the way; but we must be merciful, for perhaps in time we may come to be Mrs Stents ourselves, unequal to anything & unwelcome to everybody" (*sic*; *L* 103). Crucially, here Austen's sympathy follows from a painful exercise of the imagination, seeing herself and Cassandra as distressed spinsters of the future.

Often, the same letter will furnish evidence of both meanness and sweetness. Writing in 1801 from Bath to Cassandra, Austen tells of new acquaintances she and her mother are trying to avoid, a Mrs. and Miss Holder: "It is the fashion to think them both very detestable, but they are so civil & their gowns looks white & so very nice (which by the bye my Aunt thinks an absurd pretension in this

---

7   See Emsley ("Laughing") for a discussion of the critical history regarding the question of Austen's malice or charity; Emsley argues correctly, I believe, that Austen's malice was tempered, though not overcome, by her awareness that malice was a serious sin. Emsley also asserts that "[f]rom the publication of D. W. Harding's 1939 essay on 'Regulated Hatred: An Aspect of the Work of Jane Austen,' to the more recent books by Claudia L. Johnson (1988) and Clara Tuite (2002), critics who focus on Austen's critical, satirical perspective have tended to see it as positive rather than unkind or uncharitable, a sign that she was subversive and politically radical" ("Laughing," par. 8). For instance, in his recent biography of Austen, David Nokes quotes this same "wild Beast" passage in support of the idea that Austen rebelled against social norms. One might contend instead that Austen's invocation of a wild beast is meant to imply a wild beast caught in a trap, in a position parallel to that of Austen when visited by a stranger keen on exposing her authorship of *Pride and Prejudice*. Austen seems to be saying that her displeasure about being so cornered is a just protest against those trying to disturb her authorial privacy and anonymity.

place) that I cannot utterly abhor them, especially as Miss Holder owns that she has no taste for Music." (That Miss Holder dislikes music means that Austen will not have to hear any unwanted recitals from her.) A few sentences about house-hunting and her mother and aunt's colds follow, but next in sequence is serious news about the daughter of their doctor in Bath (presumably, the hypochondriacal aunt and mother have brought real illness to mind): "You will be sorry to hear that Marianne Mapleton's disorder has ended fatally; she was believed out of danger on Sunday, but a sudden relapse carried her off the next day. –So affectionate a family must suffer severely; & many a girl on early death has been praised into an Angel I believe, on slighter pretensions to Beauty, Sense & Merit than Marianne" (*L* 88). Austen balances the cant of the day, which praises dead young women into angels without discrimination, with Marianne's true merits; sympathy overcomes the impulse to satirize public habits.[8]

The medium of these moments of malice and repentance is important, for the exchange of letters between her and Cassandra when either was away from home was both a tedious obligation and a welcome forum in which Austen could express her private thoughts with little constraint.[9] The importance Austen's culture gave to the rule that letters were indeed *completely* private is hard perhaps for contemporary readers to grasp, but what Anne Elliot says of the impropriety of looking at a letter sent years ago from Mr. Elliot to the late Mr. Smith gives a clear sense of the proprieties, even the religious obligation, of not reading other people's letters: "[Anne] was obliged to recollect that her seeing the letter was a violation of the laws of honour, that on one ought to be judged or to be known by such testimonies, that no private correspondence could bear the eye of others" (*P* 221).[10]

---

[8]    In both the letters and the novels, Austen tends to use the word "really" to denote statements she means sincerely. For instance, in 1799 she writes of hearing of the misfortunes of a Mr. Wither while at a Steventon dinner party: "Poor man! –I mean Mr. Wither—his life is so useful, his character so respectable and worthy, that I really believe there was a good deal of sincerity in the general concern expressed on his account" (*L* 37–8). As late as *Persuasion*, we find a similar usage, as we are told of Sir Walter that "[f]or one daughter, his eldest, he would really have given up any thing, which he had not been very much tempted to do" (*P* 5).

[9]    Carol Houlihan Flynn notes, "When she chronicles her 'little matters,' Austen exploits with mundane precision the sheer tedium not only of committing oneself to practicing 'the civilities, the lesser duties of life, with gentleness and forbearance,' but of being obliged to record them in closely written letters for the inspection of others" (103). The phrase referring to "the civilities, the lesser duties of life" comes from Marianne Dashwood's resolution of virtue in *Sense and Sensibility* (247). Flynn argues—and I concur—that Austen must have felt sympathy with Marianne's aims, as well as sympathy with how difficult it can be in practice to fulfill little duties with "gentleness and forbearance."

[10]    One important exception to this understanding about privacy was the expectation that a letter from one family member to another might furnish entertainment or news to other members of the family. Thus, one would need to include in one's letters at least some quasi-public information. We are reminded of this practice when Austen asks her niece Fanny, who has been writing passionately about her doubts and hopes for marriage, to add "*something* that may do to be read or told" (*L* 287).

As we read Austen's letters, she would no doubt prefer that we remain aware that in so doing we are violating *her* privacy. Because the letters to Cassandra and other family members were meant to convey news and entertainment on a daily basis, they are a hodgepodge, giving tidings of births, weddings, and deaths, gossip and speculation about friends, family, acquaintances, and public figures, details about housekeeping, dresses and hats, market prices for food staples, reports about her social life, including travel, balls, and visits, and, in her last decade, intriguing tidbits regarding her novels and the apprentice literary work of her nieces and nephews. The letters, with their necessary investment in the quotidian, thus demonstrate her habits of thought when artistry and order are absent.[11]

The tendency to mock faults and eccentricities was central to Austen's personality, liberally expressed in the private mode of sisterly letters. Donovan is right to note that the letters show little evidence of literary discipline, little ordering of structure or content. Post-modernist approaches tend to collapse literary hierarchies and attack the idea of literary decorum, but the ideas of hierarchy and decorum were vital to Austen's own understanding of literary practice. Thus it is important to recognize the distance among the letters, with their freer wit and malice (exercised through the license of familial privacy), the novels, where wit and malice are expressed under much greater moral and artistic control, and, last, the prayers, in which wit and malice are rebuked and God's mercy and grace is asked to free Austen from the sin of wounding others with her words. However, even the letters do show signs of *moral* discipline, as Austen repeatedly tries to balance her impulsive love of witty malice with her sense of Christian obligation.

In two important moments in the letters, Austen gives a fully playful sense of how wit, "nonsense," and "laughing at . . . other people" might be corrected. In 1801, her clerical cousin, the Rev. Edward Cooper (whom she usually disliked), wrote her two "cheerful & amusing" letters. As these letters seemed to have been in stark contrast to his usual evangelical harangues, she imagines that he must punish himself for being witty: "he might be obliged to purge himself from the guilt of writing Nonsense by filling his shoes with whole pease for a week afterwards" (*L* 76). What a fantasy of rehabilitation for those erring with wit! There is much to admire here in Austen's creative sense of how to punish someone for "Nonsense," that is, the further nonsense of walking around on uncooked peas, where the discomfort is presumably to remind the errant one of the required moral chastening. Years later, in 1816, she turns the idea of correction onto herself. Explaining to James Stanier Clarke, that obtuse librarian for the Prince Regent,

---

[11]  As Robert Donovan argues,

The most striking feature of the letters . . . is not . . . that they reveal a mind wholly alien to the one which conceived the novels, but that they reveal precisely those qualities of mind which can be traced in the novels—the same habit of close observation; the same impulsive tendency to seize on whatever is ridiculous . . . even at the expense of decorum; the same conservative moral values; the same universalizing and sententious movement of thought. What is strikingly absent from the letters is the technique which controls and disciplines the substance of the novels. (125)

her reasons for not attempting a historical romance founded on the House of Saxe Cobourg, she writes, "I could not sit seriously down to write a serious Romance under any other motive than to save my Life, & if it were indispensable for me to keep it up & never relax into laughing at myself or other people, I am sure I should be hung before I had finished the first Chapter" (*L* 312). A comic death sentence looms over the writer, who cannot stop "laughing at myself or other people" even when faced with mortal threat.

We find another form of imaginary self-discipline in the two odd documents in which Austen seems to have recorded all the opinions she could locate about *Mansfield Park* and *Emma* upon their publication. Those with recorded opinions include her dearest relations (for example, her brothers and sister, her mother), other relations and close friends (and *their* friends and relations), and notable and distant figures such as Lady Gordon, the Countess Morley, or her publisher Thomas Egerton. If Austen took all the opinions in the list seriously, writing them down must have been an exercise in masochism, since for both works she records a long series of readerly reservations and objections. For instance, while *Mansfield Park* earns praise, chiefly for its realism and its depiction of character (especially that of Mrs. Norris), it is not only those far away who seem willing to say that they preferred *Pride and Prejudice*, or disliked Fanny, or had other objections—her immediate family was just as measured with its praise. The entry for "My Mother" is not atypical: "not liked it so well as P. & P. –Thought Fanny insipid. –Enjoyed Mrs. Norris" (*LM* 231). *Emma*, too, garners praise, but many of her closest family members, including her favorite niece, Fanny Knight, not only preferred *Mansfield Park* or *Pride and Prejudice* but were willing to tell Austen so themselves. Only nine of 41 respondents liked it best of her work or had no criticism whatsoever; even Cassandra liked *Mansfield Park* better. The list thus performs a kind of self-chastening, not of Austen's sense of her mastery as a novelist—she knew all too well what she had accomplished—but of pride.

I suspect, however, that with some of these entries Austen is not exactly subduing herself but is instead practicing ridicule. The means is similar to that practiced in her novels: letting fools indict themselves. Thus we know what to think of Mrs. Augusta Bramstone, who "owned that she though S & S. –and P. & P. downright nonsense, but expected to like MP. Better, & having finished the 1st vol. –flattered herself she had got through the worst" (232), or Mrs. Guiton, who felt of *Emma* that it was "too natural to be interesting" (237). Austen also again records her mother's opinion: "thought it more entertaining than M P. –but not so interesting as P. & P. –No characters in it equal to Ly Catherine & Mr. Collins" (236). Austen probably relished the fact that her sometimes annoying mother preferred the most annoying characters in her novels. Her mother's opinion is at least well informed, unlike that of the reader who disliked *Emma* because it had a Mr. Dixon in it (the reader's name was Mrs. Dickson), or Mr. Fowle, who "read only the first & last Chapters, because he had heard it was not interesting" (238). This list also testifies to Austen's attempt to balance malice with self-management; it proffers opportunities to mock and opportunities for self-chastening. We see little sign that Austen revised her literary approach based on these negative opinions. In one arena alone does she shift her ground, for she seems to have been affected by the opinion of Mr. Sherer, a clergyman whom she much admired. Mr. Sherer was displeased with the treatment of Mr. Elton on the grounds that the clergy should not be mocked; he was echoed by Mrs. Wroughton who "thought the Authoress wrong, in such times as these, to draw such Clergymen as Mr. Collins & Mr. Elton" (238). Evidently, Austen took this criticism to heart, as her next and last novel, *Persuasion,* has no major characters as clergy while those minor characters who represent the cloth (that is, Mr. Wentworth's curate brother, Charles Hayter, and Dr. Shirley) are depicted as essentially virtuous, while in *Sanditon*, there are no clergymen at all to be either mocked or praised—after all, a new seaside resort was unlikely to fit neatly into the ancient system of parishes.

## Wordplay

The realm of wordplay was an area of potential moral danger for Austen, but also a realm of innocent, even childlike pleasure. How dear is the letter Austen sent her little niece Cassandra, aged three, which begins "I hsiw uoy a yppah wen raey" and ends "Tnua Ardnassac sdnes reh tseb evol, dna os ew od lla" (translation: "I wish you a happy new year" and "Aunt Cassandra sends her best love, and so we do all") (*L* 324). A great deal of playfulness emerges in her letters to her nieces and nephews—these younger relatives seem to have lifted her spirits and engaged the best of her fancifulness. To Caroline Austen in January 1817, she teasingly proclaims that she is keeping her nephew (and Caroline's brother) Edward with her an extra day: "We have used [his family] ill by not letting him leave us before tomorrow morning, but it is a Vile World, we are all for Self & I expected no better from any of us. –But though *Better* is not to be expected, *Butter* may, at least from Mrs. Clement's Cow, for she has sold her Calf" (*L* 325). And she certainly did not disapprove of word games. She was pleased, for instance, when her newly bereaved nephews listened with somber attention to an evening service at home but were able to return to playing conundrums "the moment it was over" (*L* 151).

Her pleasure in wordplay is partly evidenced by the three charades she wrote, kept in a family volume of charades and riddles (much like the book Emma puts together with Harriet). She probably wrote many more, lost as ephemera. The tone of these three charades is light, though their matter is dark—suicide, bankruptcy, and the need for money in affairs of the heart. The first, on "hemlock," contrasts a young girl's task (to "hem") with the "lock" that "confines her to finish the piece," while "taking my whole" proves to be the young girl's release, suicide by poison (*LM* 256). Since "hemlock" speaks throughout in the first person, this nasty conclusion can be understood as proposed by the devil's advocate. The second, on "agent," contrasts "a gent," a gentleman, with the whole, "a monster, who that gentleman devours" (*LM* 256). The "agent" here could be any of the bankers, businessmen, lawyers, or insurers who managed gentlemen's affairs, often to the detriment of their unworldly clients; Austen knew personally some gentlemen who had gone bankrupt through mismanagement of business or incautious speculation, and knew many others by report.[12] The third charade is on "banknote," contrasting the river's bank by which a lover writes a billet-doux ("note") with the disappearance of the lady's "esteem and affection" if one has "none of my whole"—"think of her no more!" (*LM* 256).

Austen's love of wordplay emerges often in the proper names in her novels. It is enlightening to learn that "Marianne Dashwood" pronounced backwards becomes "would dash and marr(y)," or that Willoughby's name enacts the key question Marianne should ask were she wise: "Will 'e be?"—will he be [there]? Miss Lambe in *Sanditon* is plainly fated to serve as a sacrifice to Lady Denham's avarice, while the name of Lord St. Ives, one of the "new creations" Sir Walter deplores in *Persuasion*, reminds us of the old riddle about how many are going to St. Ives. The riddle balances anxiety about Malthusian excess (all those "kits, cats, sacks, and wives") with its solution (one) to mirror Sir Walter's anxiety about the many "new creations" who will overrun the "limited remnant" of older families.[13] Jocelyn Harris notes that other names in *Persuasion* carry meaning, such as Mr. Shepherd, whose self-serving aid to Sir Walter makes him a parody of pastoral care, and his daughter, Mrs. Clay, who molds herself to whatever sycophancy requires (201). Place names have embedded meanings as well, some obvious (e.g., Donwell Abbey) and some less so (e.g., Northanger ["north anger"] or Sanditon, or a town built on sand, as in Christ's parable in *Matthew* 7:26). The name of Longbourn House contains two meanings: Mr. Bennet has "long borne" the foolishness of his wife, while she in turn has "long borne" his children, unfortunately all daughters and no sons.

The novels embed wordplay in more complex ways as well. Austen had a fondness for *double entendre*, as when Elizabeth views Darcy's portrait at Pemberley: "As she stood before the canvas, on which he was represented, and fixed his eyes upon herself, she thought of his regard" (Phillips 71; *PP* 277). His "regard" is both his approving love and his gaze, here the portrait's. Even the most important moments of the novels can be suited with a pun, as when Mr. Knightley's jubilation at being accepted by Emma is unsuspected by Mr. Woodhouse, who asks after Mr. Knightley's health: "Could he have seen the heart, he would have cared very little for the lungs" (*E* 473; Page 47).[14] A particularly subtle bit of

---

[12]   The Harwoods, who lived at Deane House (the parish of Deane's living supplemented the Rev. George Austen's living at Steventon), were among many families ruined in this way. Mr. Harwood's speculations were discovered at his death in 1813, and the family was left with no financial support (*L* 533n).

[13]   The English version of this riddle was first published in 1730, though a similar one dates as far back as c. 1650 B.C., found on an Egyptian papyrus. If one assumes all the kits, cats, sacks, and wives, as well as the man who owns them, *and* the narrator are going to St. Ives, the answer to the riddle is 2,802 (Williams 133–5).

[14]   This lame bit of humor is the narrator's. Usually, however, if there is bad joke to be made, Austen will assign it to one of her faulty characters. For instance, Miss Bingley and Mrs. Hurst laugh immoderately over their sally at the expense of Elizabeth's relations in London—"'oh, that is capital'" (*PP* 40), while Sir Walter in *Persuasion* makes a jocular

wordplay has been unearthed by Coleen Sheehan, who found that Box Hill, the scene of Emma's disgrace, boasts the remains of one Major Labilliere, who died in 1800 and was buried upside down at its summit, because his instructions held "that the world was turned topsy-turvy, and therefore, at the end of it he should be right" ("Topsy Turvy" 214). People would picnic at the top and dance in his honor in June, the anniversary of his death (it is in June that the Highbury party makes its visit). As Sheehan notes, "in this quintessentially playful and mischievous novel about a world upside down, there could be no more perfect setting than Box Hill" (215). At the foot of the hill, which Emma's carriage reaches just as she falls into weeping at Mr. Knightley's reproach, is a village with the appropriate title of Westhumble (Sheehan 213).

*Emma*, of course, is the novel in which the moral problems inherent in wordplay are treated as a central theme. Emma's and Harriet's second joint project (the first was Emma's portrait of her protégé, where visual rather verbal miscues and mischief were key) is the "collecting and transcribing all the riddles of every sort . . . into a thin quarto of hot-pressed paper . . . and ornamented with ciphers and trophies" (74). The pursuit is flawed from its conception, as this riddle collection takes the place of the "useful reading and conversation" Emma had first planned for Harriet as part of her education. It also occasions Mr. Woodhouse's attempt to remember an eighteenth-century riddle about venereal disease ("Kitty a fair but frozen maid"), a riddle Mr. Woodhouse almost certainly never understood.[15] Last, the riddle collection inspires Mr. Elton, at Emma's invitation, to compose his charade on "courtship." Emma discerns its solution readily (unlike Harriet, who guesses "mermaid" or "shark") but she misses its meaning and its target, despite the charade's praise of the "ready wit" of the recipient. This mistake, allied with all her other misinterpretations of Mr. Elton's behavior, lead ultimately to the debacle of his Christmas Eve proposal, Harriet's disappointment and social exposure, Mr. Elton's wounded pride, and, ultimately, the disastrous addition to Highbury society of his bride, Miss Augusta Hawkins.

The capability of word-games to engender serious consequences is underscored as well in volume III, chapter five, when the main characters gather at Hartfield for an evening's entertainment. Having just made a verbal slip that threatened

---

aside to Mr. Shepherd when he notes that Admiral Croft is taking a "'a prize indeed . . . rather the greatest prize of all, let him have taken ever so many before—hey, Shepherd?'" Austen adds, "Mr. Shepherd laughed, as he knew he must, at this wit" (19).

[15] The riddle comes from David Garrick's entry into the 1771 *The New Foundling Hospital for Wit*, a compendium of verse and satire ill-fitted for the perusal of ladies. See Heydt-Stevenson, pp. 159–70, for an extended discussion of the riddle's troubling sexual violence and its possible applications to the plot and characters of *Emma*. Sheehan ("Riddles") also discusses Mr. Woodhouse's riddle at length, giving its solution as "chimneysweep" and finding less sexually explicit meanings in the verse. She also provides an answer to the first charade Emma and Harriet transcribe (beginning "My first doth affliction denote"); by linking the trickery in *Emma* to an allusory network based on *A Midsummer's Night Dream*, she gives the solution as Puck's magic flower, "love-in-idleness" (58).

to expose his secret engagement with Jane, Frank Churchill moves to cover his tracks by asking for the box of letters belonging to Emma's nephews, and he and Emma are soon composing anagrams as puzzles for each other. But Frank is also using the game for his own crafty purposes. Having put an anagram for "blunder" before Jane to solve, Frank awaits her blushing recognition. In the only moment in the novel when we shift to sharing Mr. Knightley's inner perspective, Mr. Knightley sees that blush, Frank's next offering ("Dixon"), Emma's conscious laughter, Jane's anger, and Frank's discomposure in turn, and draws a conclusion: "Disingenuousness and double-dealing seemed to meet him at every turn. These letters were but the vehicle for gallantry and trick. It was a child's play, chosen to conceal a deeper game on Frank Churchill's part" (377). The valance of the game, which switches from the innocence of children's alphabets to the calculations of an underhanded manipulator, reinforces the reader's awareness of the moral problems of wordplay in general.

This awareness comes to a fore in the last scene to feature word-games. At Box Hill, Emma has just given her disastrous rebuke to Miss Bates ("Emma could not resist"). To cover Miss Bates's dismay (who frets, "'I must make myself very disagreeable, or she would not have said such a thing to an old friend'"), Mr. Weston proffers what he means to be a socially ameliorative conundrum: "'What two letters of the alphabet are there, that express perfection?'" (403).[16] "'M. and A. –Em—ma'" is the answer, but it is an answer clearly open to dispute, given Emma's behavior. The narrator notes that Mr. Weston's sally is "a very indifferent piece of wit" and Mr. Knightley avers that "'[p]erfection should not have come quite so soon'" (404). The jealous Mrs. Elton interposes her own history with word-games, telling the assembled company that "'I had an acrostic once sent to

---

[16] Loveridge has identified one source for this conundrum, the work of moral philosopher Francis Hutcheson, *An Inquiry into the Original of our Ideas of Beauty and Virtue* (1729). Hutcheson attempts to "introduce a Mathematical Calculation into Subjects of Morality" (frontispiece) and employs a formula in which M stands for the "moment of good" and A stands for the ability to do good; thus the "Perfection of Virtue" exists "where $M = A$" (Loveridge 214–6; Hutcheson 195). Sheehan takes note of Loveridge's discovery to note that "the title of the novel itself has a double meaning: *Emma* is a riddle within a riddle" ("Riddles" 54).

Kenneth Morefield argues that the moment of Emma's wit at Miss Bates's expense sets a particular challenge to the Christian reader, for the reader has surely tired of Miss Bates almost as much as Emma has. The reader may be co-opted in satire and even sympathize with Emma's insult, because the novel creates an "allure . . . to participate in shameful jests" (204). The reader is instructed that it is our duty "to resist," that readers must "discipline their moral imaginations so that they do not find the temptation to be complicit, in whatever form it comes, to be irresistible" (204). This point about the moral test for the reader is expanded upon in Wolfson, who notes that readers are likely to have far less charity towards Miss Bates than Emma does, because she has bored the reader too: "So when Austen's narrator produces that terse, one-paragraph headline, 'Emma could not resist,' she is depending on two probabilities: our recognition that Emma has been more severely tried than we, and that we have already indulged in our own escapes and exits" (par. 6).

me upon my own name, which I was not at all pleased with'" and for once seems to occupy the higher ground morally when she states "'I really must be allowed to judge when to speak and when to hold my tongue'" (404).[17] In this scene, word-games have occasioned only disharmony, competition, and intrigue. The party breaks up; everyone has been wounded in some degree. Soon thereafter, Mr. Knightley makes plain to Emma that her wit has been an instrument of malice; she has been "insolent," "unfeeling," and has laughed at Miss Bates in the "pride of the moment" (374–5). Left by herself, Emma will acknowledge that her behavior was "brutal" and "cruel" (376), and much of the ensuing plot will follow from Emma's humiliation and attempts to make amends. Never in an English novel has one jest, one bit of wit, functioned so didactically and with such an important consequence to the plot; not until *Ulysses* will word-games carry such world-altering weight.

Because wordplay often relies on double or hidden meanings, it can sometimes cover not merely immoral purposes but actual salacious content. There is significant evidence that Austen was capable of creating bawdy jokes; there is also evidence that she came ultimately to repent using such material or at least to acknowledge the moral problems inherent in the bawdy.[18] One of Austen's earliest charades, recorded in her *The History of England* (written when she was 16), involves the favorite of James I, Robert Carr. The apparent joke of the charade is that Austen gives us the answer before she gives the clue, and then gives another clue to the answer afterwards, leaving little room for actual guesswork:

> I once heard an excellent Sharade on a Carpet, . . . and as I think it may afford my Readers some amusement to *find it out*, I shall here take the liberty of presenting it to them.

> Sharade
> My first is what my second was to King James the 1st, and you tread on my whole.
> The principle favourites of his Majesty were Car, who was afterwards created Earl of Somerset and whose name may have some share in the above-mentioned Sharade, & George Villiers afterwards Duke of Buckingham. (29–30)

However, the obvious joke hides a dirty joke, as the relation between "Car" and "pet" becomes a coded reference to the King's homosexuality, for "you tread upon my whole" puns on "hole," a reading legitimated by her earlier pun about anal sex and the King involving "penetration": "His Majesty was of that amiable disposition which inclines to Freindship, & in such points was possessed of keener

---

[17]   One inevitably wonders if Austen had worked out for herself this insulting acrostic on "Augusta," Mrs. Elton's first name.

[18]   The key critical text to treat Austen's bawdiness is Heydt-Stevenson's *Austen's Unbecoming Conjunctions: Subversive Laughter, Embodied History* (2002); regarding Heydt-Stevenson, see also notes 19, 22, 24, and 26 in this chapter.

penetration in Discovering Merit than many other people" (*sic*; 29).[19] This 16-year-old is allowing herself considerable license with forbidden material in this charade, a charade on more than one level.[20] The juvenilia are in fact replete with bawdy humor and suggestive situations; the teenage Austen was not hampered much by reticence.[21]

Her changed notions about the propriety of such jokes are evident by 1813, as she writes *Mansfield Park*. The witty Mary Crawford has taken the scene, having been forced to leave the home of her uncle, Admiral Crawford. The narrator denounces the Admiral: "[He] was a man of vicious conduct, who chose, instead of retaining his niece, to bring his mistress under his own roof" (47). Nonetheless, in chapter six, Mary introduces her uncle into the conversation at the Mansfield dining-room table, offending Edmund's sense of propriety: "Edmund was sorry to hear Miss Crawford, whom he was much disposed to admire, speak so freely of her uncle" (67). That simple mention bears no comparison, however, to the liberties Mary takes a few moments later: "'Certainly, my home at my uncle's brought me acquainted with a circle of admirals. Of *Rears*, and *Vices*, I saw enough. Now, do not be suspecting me of a pun, I entreat'" (71). Edmund's gravity at this speech conforms to the behavior recommended by conduct books; Lady Pennington, for instance, advises that if one is offended by another's speech, "show your disapprobation by a silent gravity, and by taking the first opportunity to change the subject" (199). Edmund does so, referring back to an earlier subject of conversation, the problem of getting Mary's harp delivered from London.

The long colloquy between Edmund and Fanny that begins the next chapter concerns Mary's verbal sins, especially her ribald pun (which they take care not to repeat). With a care for discrimination and restraint, the two work towards what becomes Edmund's conclusion:

---

[19]   See Heydt-Stevenson 23 and Nokes 126 for a more detailed treatment of the lewd implications of this passage.

[20]   *The History of England* is juvenile in its morality in other ways, as the main joke throughout relies on how biased the narrator is, so little interested in facts or reasons and so desirous to exercise special pleading. Austen seems to be taking malicious pleasure in her ability to judge without judgment, as her entry on Henry VI manifests:

I suppose you know all about the Wars between him & the Duke of York who was of the right side; if you do not, you had better read some other History, for I shall not be very diffuse in this, meaning by it only to vent my Spleen *against*, & shew my Hatred *to* all those people whose parties or principles do not suit with mine, & not to give information. (5)

[21]   The juvenilia show linguistic license in general to a much greater degree than one finds in the mature fiction. Page notes that the free-wheeling puns, alliteration, colloquialisms, zeugmas, and other comic devices of these writings are suppressed in the "fundamentally serious productions of later years," and suggests that Austen allowed herself the full range of linguistic play in the juvenilia exactly because these were private productions for her family (as he points out, "in later years, the letters were to retain many traces of the linguistic high spirits that could not be admitted into the fiction except upon special conditions" [14]).

'The right of a lively mind, Fanny, seizing whatever may contribute to its own amusement or that of others; perfectly allowable, when untinctured by ill humour or roughness; and there is not a shadow of either in the countenance or manner of Miss Crawford, nothing sharp, or loud, or coarse. She is perfectly feminine, except in the instances we have been speaking of. *There* she cannot be justified. I am glad you saw it all as I did.' (75–6)

Edmund's judgment has been corrupted already, for the novel's values will not endorse his conclusion that a "lively mind" is exempt from criticism as long as neither "ill humour" nor "roughness" intervenes. Austen tartly notes that as he trained Fanny's mind, she was indeed likely to follow his views, but that "he was in a line of admiration of Miss Crawford, which might lead him where Fanny could not follow'" (76). Austen makes it likely that the reader will not "follow" either, for Mary's "*Rears* and *Vices*" might well be construed as both "rough" language and as motivated by spite (since her uncle's sexual misdeeds has led to her losing her home of many years). What is notable, then, about the charade of 1791 in contrast to Mary's joke in 1813 is that though the content—crude *double entendre*—is similar, the treatment is very different. Austen does not apologize for her joke about James I, though she does cloak it. But by placing Mary's joke within the scope of Edmund's and Fanny's judgment, a judgment that takes place over several pages of conversation, and also by placing the joke implicitly within the scope of the reader's judgment, Austen admonishes the joke and the joker. She admonishes both Mary and herself.

On other occasions in the fiction that proffer possible lewd or salacious content through wordplay, one finds that assigning agency becomes problematic. Often, as with the joke about "Rears and Vices," the sally comes from the mouth of a flawed character whom we are invited to judge. This is the case when Sir John Dashwood laments Willoughby's betrayal of Marianne. Calling Willoughby "such a deceitful dog," Sir John regrets having offered Willoughby "one of Folly's puppies," thus clearly drawing a parallel between human courtship and doggy procreation (*SS* 244). Sir John's vulgarity has been established earlier, but this moment of earthiness provides further evidence. When the runaway Lydia Bennet writes to Mrs. Forster with directions that the "great slit" in her muslin dress be sewed up, the sexual meaning, that her virginity has already been lost to Wickham, is far from explicit.[22] Lydia's meaning must have been at least covert, and it takes

---

[22]    Heydt-Stevenson's *Austen's Unbecoming Conjunctions* explores this bawdy moment among many others, tying Austen's language to then-current slang (in this particular example, "muslin" could refer to a young girl and "a bit of muslin on the sly" could refer to illicit sex) (87–8). Her project is to reinstate a sense of Austen as subversive and capable of sexual rebelliousness, as well as to bring the body to the fore in our understanding of Austen's work: "An Austen liberated from predictable attributes is an artist whose comedy opens up interstices that prevailing assumptions about women (their humor, their sexuality, their married or unmarried status) have sutured" (27). Heydt-Stevenson's readings are imaginative and plausible, linked often to historical practice, including the history of slang and popular

a reader alert for bawdy content to read the inference properly. Another important moment occurs in *Mansfield Park*, when Fanny compares Portsmouth to Mansfield Park: "In a review of the two houses, as they appeared to her before the end of a week, Fanny was tempted to apply to them Dr. Johnson's celebrated judgment as to matrimony and celibacy, and say, that though Mansfield Park might have some pains, Portsmouth could have no pleasures" (454). This is a very curious application for Fanny to make, in that she is trying to avoid matrimony with Henry Crawford, who will appear at her Portsmouth doorstep two chapters later, and is hoping to return to her chaste existence at Mansfield. The sexual subtext of Johnson's sally is clear—marriage can be troublesome, but only in marriage is sexual pleasure allowed. The use of the aphorism is slanted as well, for the virginal Fanny does not exactly think it; she is only "tempted to apply" Johnson's wit to her own situation.[23]

One bawdy moment appears so subtly that it is very difficult to assign agency for its presence. In *Persuasion,* when Anne and Lady Russell promenade on the streets of Bath, Anne catches a glimpse of Wentworth, and, with anxious anticipation, awaits the moment when Lady Russell will see him too. Finally, she is sure that Lady Russell's intent gaze has fallen on the man she loves and hypothesizes what Lady Russell must be thinking:

> She could thoroughly comprehend the sort of fascination he must possess over Lady Russell's mind, the difficulty it must be for her to withdraw her eyes, the astonishment she must be feeling that eight or nine years should have passed over him, and in foreign climes and in active service too, without robbing him of one personal grace! (194–5)

The moment of comic deflation arrives with a rude joke. Lady Russell is not in fact viewing Wentworth; instead, she has been looking for a certain kind of window-curtain, the "'handsomest and best hung of any in Bath'" (195). The curtains'

---

culture. However, I believe that in Austen's mature work, the bawdiness that appears (or, rather, that lies beneath the surface) is intensely tied to moral value and even condemnation. As I argue above, Austen's dirty jokes in the mature fiction become displaced onto her faulty characters, or even onto her readers, who are judged or must judge themselves in turn. Bawdy talk and bawdy writing are wrong, according to the contemporary values of Austen's orthodox gentry, because they implicitly encourage the behavior they describe. The ultimate effect of light talk about such things as "Rears and Vices," it was understood, would be to weaken social prohibitions against illicit sexual practice (it is particularly wrong for a young unmarried woman like Mary Crawford to speak in mixed company in this way, as both her mind and the minds of her audience are at risk).

[23]   Agency is tricky to assign in another important passage in *Mansfield Park*, when we find Fanny assessing her Portsmouth home: "she might scruple to use the words, but she must and did feel that her mother was a partial, ill-judging parent, a dawdle, a slattern, who neither taught nor restrained her children" (390). Who employs these words that Fanny feels but scruples to use? Are they unsaid or unthought? The narrator certainly applies the terms to Mrs. Price with authority and conviction.

qualities, if seen in Wentworth, would confirm his physical attractions at a level of view much lower (in both senses) than Lady Russell's upraised gaze.[24] The reading of the curtains as metonymic of Wentworth's body is reinforced by the fact that Lady Russell has been looking for curtains described to her by two friends, Lady Alicia and Mrs. Frankland. "Alicia" can be etymologically understood as suggesting the "a-licit," the illicit, while Mrs. Frankland's name implies that this passage operates within the territory of the frank, the sexually candid. But who is responsible for the joke? Lady Russell is not, since had she seen Wentworth she would be unlikely to draw such a complimentary parallel, even unconsciously. Anne's own interest in Wentworth's "personal grace" allows her perhaps a brief blush at the unmeant connotations of Lady Russell's speech. But Austen herself, who wrote the passage, seems to have slipped away from its diffusive consequences.

Something similar happens early in *Mansfield Park*, when Dr. Grant speaks of the "little worth" of an apricot tree that the late Mr. Norris had planted at the rectory. Mrs. Norris rises to the tree's defense (and her husband's): "'Sir, it is a moor park, we bought it as a moor park, and it cost us—that is, it was a present from Sir Thomas, but I say the bill, and I know it cost seven shillings, and was charged as a moor park.'"[25] Dr. Grant will have none of it: "'You were imposed on, ma'am . . . these potatoes have as much the flavour of a moor park apricot, as the fruit from that tree'" (64). The conversation's subtext is the infertile (and childless) Mr. Norris, here economically linked with the apricot whose fruit cannot be eaten. Something of the same metonymic construction tells of Mr. Elton's impotence in *Emma*, for his pencil, saved as a fetish by Harriet, is really just "the end of an old pencil, --the part without any lead" (367).[26]

---

[24] Jillian Heydt-Stevenson has memorably suggested that this metonymy (well-hung curtains standing in for a well-hung man) is part of a much larger system of subversive and bawdy humor Austen incorporates in her novels. Her reading of this particular moment in *Persuasion* argues that Lady Russell's reference to the curtains covers ("curtains") the fact that she had in fact seen Wentworth, and thus she unconsciously transforms his disturbing presence into the safer and concealing curtains (193–6). Her desire to make this replacement Heydt-Stevenson sees as following from her aversion to his modest origins (194).

[25] This apricot was brought to England by Admiral Lord Anson, to his estate in Hertfordshire—Moor Park—in 1788. Alexander the Great had brought apricots to Greece from China, so they had been known to Europe for centuries and grown in abundance in Italy, but the Moor Park apricot was brought directly from China (a result of Anson's famous voyage around the world). Anson was a key hero of British naval history. Austen thus makes plain that the odious Mrs. Norris has no connections at all to the bravery of the navy, represented in this novel by Fanny's brother, William Price.

[26] Heydt-Stevenson cites this interpretation from that subversive and riveting academic, Morris Zapp, the protagonist of David Lodge's novel, *Changing Places* (Lodge 215; Heydt-Stevenson 4). Zapp's next surmise, that the moment in *Persuasion* when Wentworth removes the heavy child from Anne's shoulders represents a kind of orgasm for Anne, seems to override reasonable interpretive limits for purely comic purposes, but the connection between the leadless pencil and Mr. Elton's masculinity seems to me to be fair enough.

## Candor and Malice

Jane Austen had trouble with candor; she was not candid enough—at least in her juvenilia, in many of her letters, and (at times) in her novels.[27] If this sentence seems nonsensical, it is because the meaning of "candor" has shifted since the early nineteenth century. It now means, among other things, a willingness to tell truths, even unpleasant ones, without much regard for how the truths will be received.[28] "Let me be candid with you," we say, before saying something we know will wound. But "candor" had an almost opposite meaning in Austen's day. To be candid with others was to be generous and sympathetic, to allow for all possibilities of extenuations when it seemed another was doing wrong. Dr. Johnson's first definition of "candid" is "free from malice; not desiring to find fault."[29] Mrs. Jane West's 1806 *Letters to a Young Lady* laid out the requirements of candour:

> An adept in the practice of christian candour knows that we must invariably conform to the precept of 'thinking no evil.' Among the minute but highly important ramification of this extensive duty, we may rank all unpleasant

---

[27]   This claim I make not in defiance of Henry Austen's words in his "Biographical Notice" ("the affectation of candour is not uncommon, but she had no affectation" [6]) but in respect to Austen's practice on the page. After all, readers can be candid themselves (in the old sense) with their inferences about her behavior in real life.

[28]   Even by 1816, "candour" had begun to have some of its contemporary connotations. Crabb's *English Synonymes,* published in that year, defines "candour" as "aris[ing] from a conscious purity of intention"; it is "disinterested" and practices "no reserve." More in keeping with contemporary usage is Crabbe's assertion that "candour is a debt paid to justice from one independent being to another" (430–31). The *Oxford English Dictionary* shows the development of the word: the fourth definition, "freedom from malice, kindliness, sweetness of temper," is marked as obsolete, with its last example dating from 1806, while the fifth definition, "freedom from reserve in one's statements, openness, frankness" has examples from 1769 through 1876. The older definitions of "charity" also parallel the older definition of "candour," with the first two from the *Oxford English Dictionary* denoting "Christian love" and the third giving a description which could well be applied to a candid character such as Jane Bennet: "a disposition to judge leniently and hopefully of the character, aims, and destinies of others, to make allowances for their apparent faults and shortcomings."

[29]   In arguing that Austen's usual usage follows from this older meaning, Phillips notes Johnson's definition as well as Sheridan's Mrs. Candour in *The School for Scandal* (1777), whose name indicates that she "retails scandal under the guise of being *candid,* or charitable" (26). He also finds one "modern" usage, where the word means "telling the truth without regard to the consequences," where Mrs. Elton—and who better to inaugurate this new usage?—says, "'You know I candidly told you I should form my own opinion; . . . You may believe me. I never compliment'" (*E* 321). Norman Page finds in Dr. Johnson an employment of the word that shows plainly the difference between eighteenth-century usage and our own: "sincere, but without candour." Page points out that "the phrase is rendered nonsense by the present-day meaning" (72). See also Tave on "candor," 86–90, especially in regard to Elinor and Marianne in *Sense and Sensibility.*

constructions of the words of our associations: and, when they really will bear no other interpretation, endeavouring to show the speaker that we are desirous of understanding them in a favourable light. (43)

And William Cowper praises candor in his poem on "Charity" (primarily a work deploring slavery):

She makes excuses where she might condemn;
Reviled by those that hate her, prays for them;
Suspicion lurks not in her artless breast;
The worst suggested, she believes the best. (206)

Jane Bennet in *Pride and Prejudice* is the model of this earlier mode of candor: "her mild and steady candour always pleaded for allowances, and urged the possibility of mistake" (*PP* 157). In trying to explain why Mr. Bingley left for London, Jane urges Elizabeth to "[l]et me take it in the best light, in the light in which it may be understood" (155).[30] Elizabeth understands candour, but fails to practice it. At least she is not pretending to be candid, as are others. She tells Jane early in the novel, "'Affectation of candour is common enough;—one meets it every where. But to be candid without ostentation or design—to take the good of every body's character and make it still better, and say nothing of the bad— belongs to you alone'" (16).[31] And this claim of candor for Jane Bennet was of course echoed in Henry Austen's own words about his sister after her death: "The affectation of candour is not uncommon; but she had no affectation. Faultless herself, as nearly as human nature can be, she always sought, in the faults of others, something to excuse, to forgive or forget" ("Biographical Notice" 6). Nonetheless, our overriding impression of Jane Austen's personality seems to suggest she had more in common regarding candor with Elizabeth Bennet than Jane Bennet.

Because Austen herself found her candor sometimes wanting and because she knew her use of wit was sometimes problematic, her novels repeatedly explore the moral problem of wit. How can one be good—practicing candor, generosity, and sympathy—when one is on the alert for human failings, when one finds human foibles at every turn? Moralists of the eighteenth century endeavored to make clear distinctions between morally acceptable wit and the wit of malice, often without success. It was a commonplace among figures such as Law, Gisbourne, and Mrs. Chapone that "government of the tongue," as it was known, was a central Christian virtue. Given that presumption, eminent wits such as Johnson and Addison labored to separate wit from malice. Johnson defined wit as "the unexpected copulation

---

[30]   The moral cost of such candor is that one may sometimes be blindsided by the immoral actions of others, as Jane is by Wickham. But Elizabeth's lack of candor has not helped her be any better prepared to learn the truth about Wickham—each sister is equally surprised.

[31]   John Odmark's discussion of the virtue of candor relative to this statement from Elizabeth rightly notes that the affectation of candor is indeed a common fault in Austen's novels, and lists Wickham, Mrs. Jennings, Mrs. Norris, and Mr. Elliot as culprits (177–8). I would add Lucy Steele, Mrs. Elton, and perhaps (an interesting case) Mrs. Smith.

of ideas" and held that "an effusion of wit . . . presupposes an accumulation of knowledge" (*Rambler* no. 194; 178). His definition takes no notice of the operations of malice or of the propensity for quick ideas to be sharp ones. Addison similarly termed wit a spontaneous and instinctive "assemblage of ideas . . . [put] together with quickness and variety" (qtd. in Crabb 70). The quick and unexpected insight: this is morally acceptable wit. And yet Austen's own wit was rarely this neutral entity. It often merged into what Crabb in 1816 called "the most ill-natured kinds of wit," satire and irony (70). In Austen's novels, wit operates as a beguiling but imperfect mode of judgment. Austen knew all too well that wit is necessarily unfair; its requirements sacrifice precision for effect. She knew also that wit is incompatible with compassion and forgiveness; it occludes Christian charity. When Austen deploys wit and when she implicitly judges the wit of her characters, she does so within a broader context of moral and Christian concern—her wit is a tool of judgment, but also a confession of inadequate moral sympathy.[32]

Austen's witty protagonists all have something to learn about the morality of their snap judgments, the sort of wit that leads Elizabeth Bennet to say (incorrectly) that "'one knows exactly what to think'" (*PP* 96). Emma Woodhouse's rebuke, humiliation, and amendment have been discussed earlier. It is in *Pride and Prejudice*, however, that we find the most extended critique of wit and its darker cousin, malice.[33] Elizabeth Bennet is presented to readers as a wit, a figure

---

[32]    Robert Donovan notes Austen's irony is pervasive but not always irreverent, as irony can be in the service of morality by showing the disparity between an approved ideal of conduct and whatever violates that ideal—"struck by the hard brilliance of her irony, readers are not perhaps so inclined to notice the persistent moralizing bent of her prose" (113).

[33]    Witty characters need not be female, but Austen provides us with only one genuinely witty hero, Henry Tilney in *Northanger Abbey*. Henry's clever conversation often implies a rather sharp critique of others, as when he tells Catherine what he thinks of women's intelligence: "'Miss Morland, no one can think more highly of the understanding of women than I do. In my opinion, nature has given them so much, that they never find it necessary to use more than half'" (115). His sister must intervene, asserting that "'He is not in a serious mood. But I do assure you that he must be entirely misunderstood, if he can ever appear to say an unjust thing of any woman at all, or an unkind one of me.'" Catherine Morland, not used to cleverness or verbal play, accepts Eleanor's witness to her brother's character, and artlessly concludes that "his manner must sometimes surprise, but his meaning must always be just" (115). But the reader has reason to question the moral temper of Henry Tilney's speeches, including his ingenious and mischievous narrative about what awaits Catherine at the Abbey. He should know that his story sets an imaginative lure for his less intelligent companion (the best rational rebuttal Catherine can find for Henry's inventions is to question the probability of his merest detail: "'I am sure your housekeeper is not really Dorothy'" [162]). And Catherine, rather than Henry, will be later proved right about Captain Tilney because her sense of fair play was superior to Henry's, even though Henry had wittily prophesized that "'[t]he mess-room will drink Isabella Thorpe for a fortnight, and she will laugh with your brother over poor Tilney's passion for a month'" (156). Though Henry never explicitly apologizes for letting wit interfere with judgment, his desire to marry Catherine speaks of his acknowledgment that her goodness is worth as much, if not more, than his cleverness.

who has inherited her father's "quick parts [and] sarcastic humor" (5). Her first characterization by the narrator comes in chapter three, after Darcy has rejected her as a dancing partner: "She told the story . . . with great spirit among her friends; for she had a lively, playful disposition which delighted in any thing ridiculous" (12). In this ability to tell a story at someone else's expense with verve she shares an affinity with Mr. Bingley's sisters, who also are described early as being able to "describe an entertainment with accuracy, relate an anecdote with humour, and laugh at their acquaintance with spirit" (59). How Elizabeth is to be distinguished from these witty, malicious, and hypocritical women—or, rather, how she will learn to distinguish herself from them—creates one of the main thematic concerns of the novel.

The early sections of the novel provide many opportunities of contrasting Elizabeth's wit to Miss Bingley's. At a party given by Sir William Lucas, when Elizabeth is playful and charming about her piano playing, her arch and smiling manner leads Darcy to tell Miss Bingley "with great intrepidity" that he has been admiring Elizabeth's "pair of fine eyes." In consequence, we get a taste of Miss Bingley's wit: "'How long has she been such a favourite? –and pray when am I to wish you joy?'" (30). The chapter ends with the stream of Miss Bingley's malice: "her wit flowed long" (30). The extended narrative sequence treating Elizabeth's visit to Netherfield gives us more material to weigh. For instance, in her rush to belittle the Bennets, Miss Bingley commits an egregious pun on the London home of Elizabeth's aunt and uncle: "'Oh, that is capital!'" (40). We are told that, after this shaft, she and her sister Mrs. Hurst "indulge[ ] their mirth for some time at the expense of their dear friend's vulgar relations" (40). Austen's summary at this moment diminishes the force of Miss Bingley's satire, for we do not hear what she and her sister actually say beyond the "capital" pun. The close of chapter nine enacts the same narrative strategy, when we learn of "all [Miss Bingley's] witticisms on *fine eyes*" (50) without one of the witticisms given as such.

Elizabeth will win her competition with Miss Bingley, showing the greater wit, and, ultimately, the greater charity. From the outset, Miss Bingley's cleverness is marred by obsequiousness to Darcy, while Elizabeth feels free to say any impertinent thing. For instance, in response to Darcy's rather daring assertion that Elizabeth and Miss Bingley are promenading around the room either to share gossip or to show off their figures, Miss Bingley playfully asks, "'How shall we punish him for that remark?'" Elizabeth's reply foregrounds Miss Bingley's presumed intimacy with Darcy, an intimacy Elizabeth already suspects is one-sided: "'We can all plague and punish one another. Teaze him—laugh at him.—Intimate as you are, you must know how it is to be done.'" Miss Bingley falls into the rhetorical and emotional trap set for her, acknowledging that she is neither Darcy's equal nor his intimate: "'But upon my honour I do *not*. I do assure you that my intimacy has not yet taught me *that*. Teaze calmness of temper and presence of mind!'" (62). Elizabeth even wins exchanges when she is not present, as when Miss Bingley criticizes her behind her back as being "'one of those young ladies who seek to recommend themselves to the other sex, by undervaluing their own. . . . [I]n my opinion, it is a paltry device, a mean art.'" Darcy answers for Elizabeth: "'there is meanness in all the arts which ladies sometimes condescend to employ for captivation'" (44). Miss Bingley's jealousy ultimately deforms her wit into pure spite. At Pemberley, in the last scene in which she figures, she waits until Elizabeth has departed and then launches into categorical censure of her rival—"brown and coarse," "face too thin," "complexion [without] brilliancy," and so on. Even Elizabeth's nose figures in the catalog of abuse—it "wants character." She finally goads Darcy into saying that "'it is many months since I have considered her as one of the handsomest women of my acquaintance'" (299–300). Austen notes, "[p]ersuaded as Miss Bingley was that Darcy admired Elizabeth, this [abuse] was not the best method of recommending herself; but angry people are not always wise" (299).

Elizabeth is unaware that her own wit is sharpened in her exchanges with Miss Bingley because she is a rival to Miss Bingley for Darcy's regard; nonetheless, she has identified "teasing," "laughing," "plaguing," and "punishing" as the key activities of intimacy, the very sort of behavior avoided by those in Darcy's set out of respect for his social station and fear of his customary gravity and reserve. This is also the behavior Darcy will ultimately identify as the ground for his attraction (in the very last chapter, Elizabeth notes, with Darcy's implied approval, that "'You were disgusted with the women who were always speaking and looking, and thinking for your approbation alone. I roused, and interested you, because I was so unlike them'" [421]). However impertinent and abusive Elizabeth is in the novel's opening chapters, she also benefits from a gift of grace, a personality and temperament that soften her insults. We learn about this dispensation to Elizabeth early, when she rebukes Darcy's request to dance a reel: "'You wanted me, I know, to say "Yes," that you might have the pleasure of despising my taste; but I always delight in overthrowing those kind of schemes, and cheating a person of their premeditated contempt . . . . now despise me if you dare'"(56). This speech reeks of antagonism, but Darcy only responds, "'Indeed I do not dare.'" The narrator explains why Darcy is not offended despite Elizabeth's castigation: "there was a mixture of sweetness and archness in her manner which made it difficult for her to affront anybody; and Darcy had never been so bewitched by any woman as he was by her" (56–7).

Elizabeth's wit, then, is softened by Darcy's erotic attraction to her; it also marks her as Darcy's equal, in that she can "punish" him. As this scene continues, Darcy speaks to this key concern himself, aware, partly because of his attraction to Elizabeth, that the deployment of wit requires control lest it become morally askew: "'The wisest and the best of men, nay, the wisest and best of their actions, may be rendered ridiculous by a person whose first object in life is a joke'" (62). He implies that he may be among those "wisest and best of men" and accuses Elizabeth implicitly of being that "person whose first object in life is a joke," as she acknowledges in her response: "'Certainly . . . there are such people, but I hope I am not one of them. I hope I never ridicule what is wise or good. Follies and nonsense, whims and inconsistencies do divert me, I own, and I laugh at them whenever I can. But these, I suppose, are precisely what you are without'" (62–3).[34] She affirms that Darcy is among the "wise and good" only by sarcastic assent. This dividing line, between "the wise and good" and "follies and nonsense," will not, of course, hold firm in human affairs. On the one hand, the novel will reveal that Elizabeth is indeed given to ridiculing what is wise or good, including her "candid" sister and the virtuous if stiff Darcy. On the other hand, there is no one human being so wise and good that he or she is immune to follies or nonsense—not even the author. The scene ends with Darcy also claiming a virtue he lacks, as he explains that he has his pride under "good regulation," giving Elizabeth one last chance to mock him through hyperbole: "'I am perfectly convinced by it that Mr. Darcy has no defect. He owns it himself without disguise'" (63). By the end of the chapter, these two have identified the key conflict between them. Elizabeth again voices a sentiment whose hyperbole is entirely out of bounds for polite society: "'your defect is a propensity to hate every body.'" Darcy's reply shows he is not offended, although most men would be, for he replies with a smile, "'yours . . . is willfully to misunderstand them'" (63). The forgotten rival, Miss Bingley, stops this romantic jousting by calling for music.

Elizabeth will learn to tame her wit by learning about the disasters and wrongs her wit—allied with her biased quickness to judge—has created or supported. When she finds out about Wickham's true nature, she knows that her lack of candor is largely to blame for her mistake: "'I who have often disdained the generous candour of my sister, and gratified my vanity, in useless or blameable distrust'" (230). She is forced to acknowledge that in some senses her moral judgments have been no better than Lydia's, for when Lydia announces that Wickham had only been pursuing Miss King for her money—"'I will answer for it he never cared three straws about her. Who could about such a nasty little freckled thing?'"—Elizabeth knows that "however incapable of such coarseness of *expression* herself, the coarseness of the *sentiment* was little other than her own breast had formerly harboured and fancied liberal!'" (244). She now knows that her hope that "the wisest and best of men" were immune from her attacks was naïve, given her prejudice against Darcy: "'It is such a spur to one's genius, such an opening for wit to have a dislike of that kind. One may be continually abusive without saying any thing just; but one cannot be always laughing at a man without now and then stumbling on something witty'" (250).

Even these moral re-evaluations, however, cannot stop Elizabeth's wit completely, as she is still given in moments to witty malice. For instance, when she hears the housekeeper at Pemberley state that "'Miss Darcy is always down for the summer months,'" some spiteful imp prompts her to think, "except . . . when she goes to Ramsgate'" (274). At least this mean-spirited memory of Miss Darcy's

---

[34] Elizabeth's words are often quoted (on Austen mugs, calendars, postcards, and the like) as a kind of authorial motto. I would argue that Austen is far more aware than is her heroine that ridicule is hard to discipline, and that morally unblemished wit is extremely difficult to achieve.

almost-seduction goes unstated. "Government of the tongue" also keeps Elizabeth from saying anything witty to Darcy once he returns to her neighborhood in the last chapters. In fact, she hardly says anything to him at all, beyond a polite query after his sister, and Darcy is as grave as she. The stakes are too high, and they will not exchange witticisms until Darcy proposes, when Elizabeth can apologize for "'abusing you so abominably to your face'" and can note that they have both "'improved in civility'" (408). At the end of the chapter of the romantic resolution, Elizabeth checks her tongue, acknowledging that Darcy "had yet to learn to be laught at, and it was rather too early to begin" (412). But the final pages show that Darcy learns this lesson, and that Elizabeth learns the right form of wit—a "lively, sportive manner" with "open pleasantry" (430), the best compromise Austen can offer between wit and goodness. That we do not see any actual dialogue that would *demonstrate* how Elizabeth can laugh at Darcy without offense only strengthens our sense of how difficult it must be to marry wit to wisdom and goodness.[35]

Mary Crawford of *Mansfield Park* offers the important counter-example to Elizabeth's achievement. She cannot, ultimately, marry wit to wisdom. Blinded by Mary's attractiveness, Edmund for much of the novel attempts to claim that Mary's wit cannot have any source in ill-nature or immorality. Early on, when Mary proffers that bawdy pun on "Rears and Vices" to describe her prior home life with her uncle the Admiral, Edmund struggles to assert that her words do not represent her character: "'I do not censure her *opinions*, but there certainly *is* impropriety in making them public'" (75; italics in original). What Fanny knows but will not say to Edmund is that speech reflects mind, and that Mary's continual mockery of the church ("'a clergyman is nothing'" [107]) and her other witty endorsements of amorality ("'must always be forgiven you know, because there is no hope of a cure'" [80]) demonstrate serious moral failings. When Mary learns that Henry and Maria have run away together, she cannot find the right words to describe what has happened; to Fanny, she writes, "at any rate, . . . Henry is blameless, and in spite of a moment's *etourderie* thinks of nobody but you" (506). *Etourderie*, or "thoughtless blunder," understates the case by several magnitudes. At the climactic scene when Edmund breaks with Mary, re-imagined and re-told by Edmund to Fanny, Mary continues to err, again primarily through verbal mistakes. Her term for Maria's elopement, "folly," carries only the mildest of censures, and it is this inadequacy of language that Edmund finds particularly reprehensible:

> '. . . --but how she went on, Fanny, is not fit—is hardly fit to be repeated to you. I cannot recall all her words. I would not dwell upon them if I could. Their substance was great anger at the folly of each . . . . To hear the woman whom—no harsher name than folly given!—No reluctance, no horror, no feminine—shall I say? No modest loathings!' (525–6)

---

[35]    Similarly, when Elizabeth writes of her engagement to Darcy to her aunt, she claims to be "the happiest creature in the world" and contrasts herself to Jane: "she only smiles, I laugh" (424). This laughter must be the laughter of happiness and joy, not that occasioned by wit, jokes, or ridicule. But we see no specific examples of this kind of laughter freed from judgment or malice; it is too difficult to represent realistically because of its rarity in human experience, and Austen habitually shuns the depiction of what is not probable.

Edmund finally recognizes that Mary's flawed speech represents her flawed mind, and the "saucy, playful smile" she deploys at Edmund's departure only re-strengthens his sense of her moral corruption (531).

Since Austen corrects and judges her characters' wit, her readers inevitably wonder at Austen's own. The chief defense for her wit we saw her family put forward was that it was employed only in her fiction, where no real person could be harmed. The chief defense she herself seems to proffer *within* the novels is the claim that wit exposes the morally faulty and serves as a corrective—that Austen, if not Elizabeth, never "ridicules what is wise or good." In general, the narrator's wisdom gives her the moral authority to mock human foibles. Even read two centuries later, her novels enact precise moral judgments that still command readerly assent, even when readers would make very different moral judgments were they witness to similar circumstances in contemporary life. For instance, from the narrator's point of view, here aligned with Edmund's and Fanny's, the most damning thing Mary Crawford suggests in her last interview with Edmund is that it would be prudent for Maria to continue to live with Henry so that he would be more likely to marry her. This pragmatic view is deeply at variance with then-powerful Christian codes governing marriage and sexual fidelity, and Edmund and Fanny register total disgust at the idea. But contemporary readers might well agree with Mary, or at any rate not find her proposal so morally beyond the pale. The reading experience of *Mansfield Park* tends to create the suspension of our contemporary *mores* and their replacement by Austen's.[36]

What then happens when Austen's sure and deft moral judgment fails her? The crux most at issue for this question occurs in *Persuasion*, when the narrator attacks Mrs. Musgrove's "large fat sighings," a witty formulation that is signally lacking in charity (73). Critics have almost uniformly noted this moment as a serious ethical lapse on Austen's part, a moment that undercuts her otherwise impeccable moral authority.[37] The entire episode in fact shows a curious slippage of moral authority. The propensity to mock Mrs. Musgrove emerges in Captain Wentworth, who has just heard Mrs. Musgrove praise his care of her now-dead son: "There was a momentary expression in Captain Wentworth's face at this speech, a certain glance of his bright eye, and curl of his handsome mouth, which convinced Anne, that instead of sharing in Mrs. Musgrove's kind wishes, as to her son, he had probably

---

[36] As David Lodge has wondered, "how have we been persuaded to endorse a system of values with which we have no real sympathy at all?" (94). I endorse his answer: "I suggest that Jane Austen succeeds . . . by schooling her readers in a vocabulary of discrimination which embraces the finest shades of social and moral value, and which asserts the prime importance, in the presented world of the novel, of exercising the faculty of judgment . . . . The subtle and untiring employment of this vocabulary, the exact fitting of value terms to events, the display of scrupulous and consistent discrimination, have a rhetorical effect which we cannot long resist. We pick up the habit of evaluation, and resign, for the duration of the novel at least, the luxury of neutrality" (99).

[37] Koppel, for instance, argues that "[u]nintentionally or intentionally, Jane Austen has allowed her narrator to be outdone here by one of her characters [Anne herself]" (104). John Halperin terms it one of her "most heartless performances" (*The Life of Jane Austen* 304).

been at some pains to get rid of him" (73). By noticing Wentworth's expression and reading it as a mark of his earlier lack of perfect charity regarding "poor Richard," Anne too participates in this less-than-fully gracious moment. Anne's perception of Wentworth's sardonic inner view is immediately followed by her awareness that Wentworth has disciplined himself and his "transient . . . indulgence of self-amusement"; "in another moment he was perfectly collected and serious . . . and entered into conversation with [Mrs. Musgrove] . . . with so much sympathy and natural grace as shewed the kindest consideration for all that was real and unabsurd in the parent's feelings" (73). What follows this asymmetrical awareness of mockery turned to sympathy is the offending passage: "Captain Wentworth should be allowed some credit for the self-command with which he attended to her large fat sighings over the destiny of a son, whom alive nobody had cared for" (73). The narrative has been focalized on Anne's consciousness, however, so Anne shares some responsibility with the narrator for this unkind comment. Signally, no sooner has the narrator launched this attack than she half-apologizes for it, both on her own behalf and on Anne's:

> Personal size and mental sorrow have certainly no necessary proportions. A large bulky figure has as good a right to be in deep affliction, as the most graceful set of limbs in the world. But, fair or not fair, there are unbecoming conjunctions, which reason will patronize in vain, --which taste cannot tolerate, --which ridicule will seize. (73–4)

Austen here defends her ridicule as justified by the comic principle of incongruity, rather than by those other engines of comic effect, a malicious sense of superiority on the one hand and "psychic release" or a sense of danger averted on the other. Austen tells us that laughter follows from Mrs. Musgrove's sorrow because it is an "unbecoming conjunction" between fat and woe.[38] Incongruity is the one justification for laughter which can be morally free, but even so, Austen arrays a trio of clauses to defend her laughter, with reason, taste, and ridicule as parallel agents, all of which embody moral value. Austen cannot really successfully excuse her behavior, but the passage shows both how instinctively Austen related reason and taste to ridicule and how thoroughly she understood the shaky moral ground of all her wit.

Austen could not evade the habits of witty malice no matter how thoroughly she understood the predicaments, moral and religious, these habits created. She knew she was a habitual offender, and knew also that much of the pleasures readers gained from her novels followed from their own morally knotty enjoyment of satire. Austen could argue, as she allows Elizabeth Bennet to do, that her wit was yoked to didactic intent, that the "wise and good" were immune to her attack,

---

[38] Malicious superiority, T. G. A. Nelson argues, has its "favorite targets," "those who look as though they may prove superior, but fail to live up to their promise" (6); "psychic release" allows one to laugh at a fear that has proved groundless (7). The theory of incongruity as the cause of laughter we owe primarily to Schopenhauer, and Nelson argues that this theory "is . . . a useful weapon in the hands of those who want to rescue laughter from any necessary association with malice" (7).

and that no real person was harmed by her laughter. But whether her wit could be morally justified or not, she was not able to give it up—it was too much at the heart of her disposition and character. Three days before she died, she created one last work of art, a poem. It concerns saints and sinners, the history of the church, and present-day laxity. However, the poem was not "serious"—i.e., religious—but instead a rollicking satire. In it, Austen imagines St. Swithin, the ninth-century A.D. founder of the cathedral, rising from his grave to curse the worldly gamesters who are thronging the Winchester horse races. He curses them with rain:

> Oh, subjects rebellious, Oh Venta depraved[39]
> When once we are buried you think we are dead
> But behold me Immortal. –By vice you're enslaved
> You have sinn'd & must suffer. –Then further he said
> These races & revels & dissolute measures
> With which you're debasing a neighbouring Plain
> Let them stand—you shall meet with your curse in your pleasures
> Set off for your course, I'll pursue with my rain.
> Ye cannot but know my command in July.
> Henceforward I'll triumph in shewing my powers,
> Shift your race as you will it shall never be dry
> The curse upon Venta is July in showers. (*LM* 255)

Evidently, the Winchester races that year were a wet misery, and Austen draws upon the old wives' tale that St. Swithin controls the weather on July 15th, his saint's day, and for 40 days thereafter.[40] One wonders if she paid heed to the darker tones of her curse, in its relevance to her own nearness to death: "You have sinn'd & must suffer." Her safety must reside in her allegiance to St. Swithin and the church, rather than with the "good people" "enslav'd by vice." She has remembered him, and the Christian traditions of her country laid in place long ago, even if the sportsmen and the fashionable folk have forgotten him. She was soon to be buried in the same cathedral from which St. Swithin bounds; while her last written words were a comic curse, her last spoken words were "Pray for me Oh pray for me" (*L* 344).[41]

---

[39]   "Venta" was the Latin (Roman) name for what is now Winchester.

[40]   The applicable verse, datable back to perhaps the twelfth century, goes as follows: "St. Swithun's day if thou dost rain / For forty days it will remain / St. Swithun's day if thou be fair / For forty days will rain no more." The legend has that St. Swithin (who died in 862 A.D.) refused to be buried within his own cathedral, preferring that "the sweet rain of heaven might fall upon my grave," but in 971 A.D., after substantial additions to the cathedral, he was re-interred within, on July 15th. Forty days of rain followed this violation of the saint's wishes. Austen takes no note of the fact that St. Swithin's head was removed on this occasion and taken to the cathedral at Canterbury.

[41]   There is also a St. Swithin's in Bath, where Austen's parents were married. Her father, George Austen, is also buried in this church—yet another thread, perhaps, to Austen's musings about the link between the saint, death, burial, and resurrection.

# Chapter 5
# World-making

[T]here seems almost a general wish of decrying the capacity and undervaluing the labour of the novelist, and of slighting the performances which have only genius, wit, and taste to recommend them. (*NA* 31)

Jane Austen never includes a writer—an author—as a character in her novel. There are artist figures, such as Emma Woodhouse, but no writers—unless we admit Mr. Elton on the basis of his one mediocre charade. Nor does Austen create heroines directly based on her own personality, unlike, say, Charlotte Brontë, whose Jane Eyre and Lucy Snowe are largely autobiographical figures. Rather, the character most like Jane Austen is "Jane Austen," the quasi-god-like narrator of her novels. These considerations weigh on the question of Austen's attitude towards the morality of writing fiction, of creating worlds beyond the world provided by the Creator. The problem of fiction arises obliquely with every character who creates, imagines, fantasizes, or otherwise brings into being something that does not exist in reality. The range of Austen's "imaginists" (the term comes from *Emma*) stretches from protagonists such as Emma and Catherine Morland to heroes such as Henry Tilney and Edmund Bertram to cads such as Willoughby and Frank Churchill. It also includes legions of minor characters, whose imaginings implicitly help delineate the moral boundaries of fancy, figures such as John Thorpe, Mrs. Bennet, Miss Bates, and Sir Edward Denham. Their imaginings also help define, by contrast, the moral status of Austen's own imaginings, the very novels in which they appear. Austen's lifelong theme is the proper exercise of imagination; that she takes such a theme cannot surprise, since its development is inevitably an exercise in self-defense and self-justification for an act (writing fiction), which she knew was potentially on morally and spiritually unsteady ground.

## The Moral Problem of Novel-Writing

The moral qualms associated with artistic creation have a very long history, going back at least to Plato's attack on the poets in *The Republic*, the Judaic and Islamic prohibitions against representing the divine, the Christian unease with Gnostic ideas of sub-creation, and a more diffuse tradition within the Christian church stretching from St. Jerome to Hannah More that associates fiction with untruth, temptation, and mental and moral confusion.[1] The chorus against fiction-writing,

---

[1] One of the more interesting aspects to note about this more than millennial debate is that the main figures in the Christian tradition never to my knowledge actually refer to what Christ said about beauty and (implicitly) human creativity. This may be because he does so only once, comparing the wonders of Solomon's courtly attire with flowers: "And why take

especially novel-writing by women, swelled in the Georgian period; tracts and conduct books, sermons and essays all inveighed against the harm caused by the popular novel.[2] An early example comes from Lady Pennington's *An Unfortunate Mother's Advice to her Absent Daughters* (1761). While excepting the highly didactic and conservative works of Oliver Goldsmith from her critique, Lady Pennington warned young women that

> [n]ovels . . ., very few of them, are worth the trouble of reading . . . . Their moral parts indeed are like small diamonds amongst mountains of dirt and trash. . . . [Y]et, ridiculous as these fictitious tales generally are, they are so artfully managed as to excite an idle curiosity to see the conclusion. . . . [S]ome of them have more pernicious consequences; by drawing characters that never exist in life, by representing persons and things in a false and extravagant light, and by a series of improbable causes, bringing on impossible events, they are apt to give a romantic turn to the mind, which is often productive of great errors in judgment. (199)[3]

Pennington goes on to deplore the sometimes fatal "mistakes in conduct" to which these errors in judgment lead; she is clearly thinking of violations of the code of chastity. Writing about the same time, Mrs. Chapone argues in her conduct book, *Letters on the Improvement of the Mind* (1773), that novels "inflame the passions of youth, whilst the chief purpose of education should be to moderate and restrain them" (168; qtd. Bradbrook 24). Mrs. Chapone was also convinced that novel-reading had very specific results: "when a young woman makes it her chief amusement [it] generally renders her ridiculous in conversation, and miserably wrong-headed in her pursuits and behavior" (169). The popular novel

---

ye thought for raiment? Consider the lilies of the field, how they grow: they toil not, neither do they spin, and yet I say unto you that not even Solomon in all his glory was arrayed unto these" (*Matthew* 6:28–9). Solomon's attire, we remember, was so splendid that it had left the queen of Sheba breathless (2 *Chronicles* 9:4); Christ's one statement on beauty puts human artifice and art plainly in its place, far below the beauty of God's creation.

    [2]    For a compendium of primary documents that show this general consensus that the novel, especially the Gothic novel, was dangerous, see Taylor's *Early Opposition to the English Novel: The Popular Reaction from 1760 to 1830*.

    [3]    Pennington includes a list of approved reading for young women in her *Advice*. It recommends classical literature (Seneca, Epictetus, Cicero, Pliny, and Pope's translations of Homer); works of history, both treating antiquity and the British isles; sermons (by Fordyce, Sherlock, and, perhaps surprisingly, Sterne, though Sterne's sermons, like Swift's and—later—Charles Dodgson's, are perfectly orthodox); poetry (Milton and Dodsley's *Collection of Poems*, the latter a volume Austen owned); and only one novel: Goldsmith's *The Vicar of Wakefield* (1766). I find the greatest wonder in Pennington's commendation of Ridley's 1764 *Tales of the Genii*, a set of romances inspired by *The Arabian Nights*, the collection of ancient Persian tales first translated into French by Antoine Galland in 12 volumes between 1704 and 1717; perhaps the *Tales* were so outlandish, in both senses, that Pennington dismissed them as a possible source of young ladies' imitation and corruption.

was still a target in the last year of Austen's life, 1817, when Coleridge published his *Biographia Literaria*. Coleridge focused on the intellectual rather than moral deterioration caused by novels: "For as to the devotees of the circulating libraries, I dare not compliment their pass-time, or rather *kill-time*, with the name of reading. Call it rather a sort of beggarly day-dreaming, during which the mind of the dreamer furnishes for itself nothing but laziness, and a little mawkish sensibility" (14).[4]

Throughout Austen's day, Evangelicals, both within the Anglican camp and Dissenters without, mounted a sustained assault on novels. In the inaugural edition of the non-denominational *Evangelical Magazine* of 1793, an anonymous author railed against novels: "Novels . . . are instruments of abomination and ruin . . . . A fond attachment to them is an irrefragable evidence of a mind contaminated and totally unfit for the serious pursuits of study, or the delightful exercises and enjoyments of religion" (79). Hannah More, in the forefront of those who condemned popular fiction, wrote in 1799 that novels "become agents of voluptuousness. They excite the imagination; and the imagination thus excited, and no longer under the government of strict principle, becomes the most dangerous stimulant of the passions, promotes a too keen relish for pleasure, and . . . inventing new and pernicious modes of artificial gratification" (*Works* 86).[5]

However, More's meditations on fiction also lay the grounds for its defense, particularly in terms, as we will see, that are in keeping with the defenses Austen herself made for novels in general and her work in particular. More notes, for example, that adherence to the probabilities of life makes fiction morally acceptable, while arguing that authors who achieve this effect of "naturalness" are rare creatures: "It seems very extraordinary, that it should be the most difficult thing in the world to be natural, and that it should be harder to hit off the manners of real life, and to delineate such characters as we converse with every day, than to imagine such as do not exist" (*Essays* 207). More also insists on the importance of

---

[4]    Coleridge continues his dismissal of novels by classifying their reading among other time-wasters, such as "gaming, swinging, or swaying on a chair or gate; spitting over a bridge; smoking; snuff-taking; *tete a tete* quarrels after dinner between husband and wife; conning word by word all the advertisements of a daily newspaper in a public house on a rainy day, etc. etc. etc." (*sic*; 14).

[5]    More's criticism of fiction is undermined significantly by the fact that works such as her "Village Politics" (1793) and *Cheap Repository Tracts* (1795 and after) used fictional elements such as ballads, tales, and dialogues to inculcate "proper" moral and political perspectives (i.e., anti-Jacobin perspectives) in her working-class readership. Part of her extraordinary success with these works came, moreover, because of her ability to ventriloquize working-class voices, such as those of Jack Anvil and Tom Hood in "Village Politics." Further, More went on to write two novels herself, though in them she eschewed sensational elements and employed heavy didacticism: *Coelebs in Search of a Wife* (1809) and *Coelebs Married* (1814). See also C. Krueger on More's literary innovations within her tracts, including her "privileging simple, concrete language over the ornate or abstract; imbuing vulgar dialects with authority; and most importantly, recognizing the political implications of the diffusion of narrative authority in the novel" (15).

virtue and good sense to make fiction palatable (she seems to have been thinking of figures such as Johnson and Richardson):[6]

> When we see so many accomplished wits of the present age, as remarkable for the decorum of their lives, as for the brilliancy of their writings, we may believe, that, next to principle, it is owing to their *good sense*, which regulates and chastises their imaginations. The vast conceptions which enable a true genius to ascend the sublimest heights, may be so connected with the stronger passions, as to give it a natural tendency to fly off from the strait line of regularity; till good sense, acting on the fancy, makes it gravitate powerfully towards that virtue which is its proper centre. (*Essays* 189–90)

By "principle," of course, More meant what Austen would have meant by the term, religious principle. Religious commitments, allied with good sense, make the exercise of the imagination, either by author or reader, acceptable. Mrs. Chapone agreed about More's exception to the rule that fiction damages the reader, for while the rules of probability show that "expectations of extraordinary adventures . . . seldom happen to the sober and prudent part of mankind," when novels do delineate "excellent morality joined with the most lively pictures of the human mind," they may be held harmless (168–9). Richardson himself held that despite all the feeling inculcated by his novels, both in his characters and in his readers, his novels were designed to be "comparable with the most eternally instructive of religious texts" (Mullan 13).[7] These prescriptions for probable, reasonable, and morally exemplary fiction are all of a piece with then-current critical fashion, no matter how thoroughly the reading public ignored these strictures and showed instead its preference for sensational, improbable, and licentious romances. As

---

[6]    More continues by contrasting the often immoral and irrational works of genius to those by literary figures who combine wit with "good sense." She signals out for particular notice William Collins, an eighteenth-century poet of great talent who died of madness at age 38, in 1750: "The elegant Biographer of Collins, in his affecting apology for that unfortunate genius, remarks, 'that the gifts of imagination bring the heaviest task on the vigilance of reason; and to bear those faculties with unerring rectitude, or invariable propriety, requires a degree of firmness, and of cool attention, which does not always attend the higher gifts of the mind'" (*Essays* 187–8). More distinguishes between genius and good sense: "It is the peculiar property of genius to strike out great or beautiful things: it is the felicity of good sense not to do absurd ones. Genius breaks out in splendid sentiments and elevated ideas; good sense confines its more circumscribed, but perhaps more useful walk, within the limits of prudence and propriety" (*Essays* 183–4). Dr. Johnson himself often drew a picture of the moral problem of imagination: "imagination is a formidable and obstinate disease of the intellect; when eradicated by time its remedy is one of the hardest tasks of reason and virtue" (*Rambler* no. 89). Both Johnson and More spoke for the consensus in the Georgian period: imagination requires perpetual moral discipline.

[7]    Mullan notes that Richardson's view is "exemplified in his delighted citing of his friend Edward Young's characterization of *Clarissa* as '*The Whole Duty of a Woman*' in a letter of 1749" (13; qtd. in Carroll 141).

David Richter has noted, the many reviews of Gothic fiction in the 1790s found in such venues as *The Analytical Review*, *The Critical Review*, *The European Review*, *The British Critic*, and *The Anti-Jacobin* "differ considerably in their taste and tolerance for Gothic fiction, but all of them alike tend to discuss the novel in neoclassical or Johnsonian terms, with an emphasis on the probability, generality, and ethical probity of the narrative" (121).

Austen herself both helped condemn and defend the popular novel, both hers and the works of others.[8] The terms of her condemnation (rendered most plainly in *Northanger Abbey, Emma*, and *Sanditon*) focus, first, on the unrealistic expectations that arise when readers (including her characters) cannot discern fiction from reality and, second, on the moral unmooring that takes place when imagination is excited without proper restraint.[9] In this strain of criticism, Austen is echoing eighteenth-century anxieties about the moral valence of novels.[10] Volumes have, of course, been written on Austen's treatment of this theme. Austen's *defense* of the novel seems two-fold: novels can provide pleasurable, witty, elegant moral instruction, and they can do so while conforming to the scenes of common life and the laws of probability.[11]

---

[8] See Gary Kelly for a concise overview of Austen's achievements of realism within the politically charged field of fiction of her day, in which progressive figures such as Wollstonecraft or Charlotte Smith created plausibility by including real-life details about law and politics and conservative figures such as Edgeworth, Burney, Jane West, or More did likewise by depicting common scenes, all reacting in their several ways to the popular indictments of fiction as improbable and seductive (1505–12).

[9] While Austen depicts often the ill-effects of reading, she was also well aware that even "right" reading can only do so much. After all, in *Mansfield Park* both Crawfords have read many a sermon, including those of Blair. Margaret Doody comments that Austen seems to underline the possible insufficiency of good reading when she has Mrs. Morland search out moral pamphlets to aid her melancholy daughter at the end of *Northanger Abbey*, and when she shows in *Sanditon* that Sir Edward Denham's reading was moral enough but warped by his interpretations: "the same ill luck which made him derive only false Principles from Lessons of Morality, & incentives to Vice from the History of its Overthrow" (*MW* 404–5). As Doody notes, "Good books can't give wisdom to a fool or create a right heart in a perverse reader" ("Jane Austen's Reading" 349).

[10] Her condemnation of the improbable in fiction began, of course, when she was a teenager, in her parodies of the Gothic and romance fiction of the late eighteenth century. The admixture of the unbelievable with the unethical predominates in these fictions, as in the wonderful claim of "A Letter from a Young Lady, whose feelings being too Strong for her Judgement led her into the commission of Errors which her Heart disapproved": "I murdered my father at a very early period of my Life, I have since murdered my Mother, and I am now going to murder my Sister" (*sic; J* 222).

[11] At the same time, despite her investment in common scenes and believable events and characters, Austen did not countenance the creation of believability by basing her characters on real people. She believed it was morally wrong and indecorous to do so. James Edward Austen-Leigh defends her practice and perspective in his *Memoir*:

Austen was, it seems, particularly irritated by those who leapt to the putative high ground, those who declared novels immoral out-of-hand. For instance, in a letter of 1798 to Cassandra she wrote of her annoyance at the proprietor of the neighborhood's new circulating library:

> As an inducement to subscribe, Mrs. Martin tells us that her Collection is not to consist only of Novels, but of every kind of literature, &c &c—She might have spared this pretension to *our* family, who are great Novel-readers & not ashamed of being so; but it was necessary I suppose to the self-consequence of half her Subscribers. (*L* 26)

It seems likely, as Frank Bradbrook suggests, that the passage in *Northanger Abbey* in which Austen defends the novel as a genre was precipitated by Austen's dislike of novel-snobbery in a fellow author, Maria Edgeworth, whose advertisement for *Belinda* in 1801 begged her readership to call *Belinda* a "Moral Tale":

> The following work is offered to the public as a Moral Tale—the author not wishing to acknowledge a Novel. Were all novels like those of Madame de Crousay, Mrs. Inchbald, Miss Burney, or Dr. Moore, she would adopt the name of novel with delight. But so much folly, error, and vice are disseminated in books classed under this denomination, that it is hoped the wish to assume another title will be attributed to feelings that are laudable and not fastidious. (qtd. in Bradbrook 113)

Austen's attack on novelists who will not themselves defend the novel is famous:

> Yes, novels; -- for I will not adopt that ungenerous and impolitic custom so common with novel writers, of degrading by their contemptuous censure the very performances, to the number of which they are themselves adding. . . . Alas! if the heroine of one novel be not patronized by the heroine of another, from whom can she expect protection and regard? . . . . Let us not desert one another; we are an injured body. Although our productions have afforded more extensive and unaffected pleasure than those of any other literary corporation in the world, no species of composition has been so much decried. From pride, ignorance, or fashion, our foes are almost as many as our readers. (*NA* 30–31)

---

She did not copy individuals, but she invested her own creations with individuality of character. . . . Her own relations never recognized any individual in her characters; and I can call to mind several of her acquaintance whose peculiarities were very tempting and easy to be caricatured of whom there are no traces in her pages. She herself, when questioned on the subject by a friend, expressed a dread of what she called such an 'invasion of social proprieties.' She said that she thought it quite fair to note peculiarities and weaknesses, but that it was her desire to created, not to reproduce; 'besides,' she added, 'I am too proud of my gentlemen to admit that they were only Mr. A. or Colonel B.' (156–7)

By this report, Austen endorsed for herself the defense of irony and wit proffered by her character Elizabeth Bennet: "'Follies and nonsense, whims and inconsistencies do divert me, I own, and I laugh at them whenever I can'" (*PP* 62–3).

The terms by which she praises the novel are key: novels give their readers "extensive and unaffected pleasure" by virtue of their display of the "greatest powers of the mind," "the most thorough delineation of its varieties," "the liveliest effusions of wit and humour," all conveyed by "the best chosen language" (31).[12] Echoing More's praise of fictional wit, Austen turns the tables on the conventionally commended *Spectator;* it is both immoral and improbable, she argues. The *Spectator*'s "matter or manner" should "disgust a young person of taste," while the circumstances are "improbable" and the characters "unnatural." Worse, the "language [is] frequently so coarse as to give no very favourable idea of the age that could endure it" (31). Austen in fact had enjoyed reading the *Spectator* as a young girl, but she here cannot resist the delights of condemning then-canonical reading on the same grounds by which her own chosen genre was more usually deplored.[13]

---

[12]   *Northanger Abbey* offers a more sustained conversation about novels than any other of Austen's work, unsurprisingly given its status as half-parody of the Gothic novel and its theme of the novel's propensity to mislead unwary imaginations. Among other defenses of the novel as genre arrayed by Austen in this work is the conduct of Henry Tilney, who though a clergyman confesses without embarrassment that he is an inveterate reader of Gothic novels, having gone so far as to steal his sister's copy of *Udolpho* when she was in the middle of reading it. He also tells Catherine that his knowledge of Gothic novels is much superior to her own: "'Consider how many years I have had the start of you. I had entered on my studies at Oxford, while you were a good little girl working your sampler at home!'" (108). Henry seems to align his novel-reading with his "studies at Oxford," eliding the Oxford curriculum of Latin and Greek and replacing it with the works of Mrs. Radcliffe and her peers. The trajectory of Catherine's reading education (represented by the sampler) is also replaced, in Henry's witty formulation, by a curriculum of the Gothic. Irene Collins notes that a clergyman could read Mrs. Radcliffe's novels in Austen's day without rebuke for three reasons: because the works accord strictly to poetic justice (and natural law, in that sense); the seeming "evidence" of the supernatural is rationally explained; and the heroines pray a lot ("The Rev. Henry Tilney" 157).

[13]   James Edward Austen-Leigh noted in his *Memoir of Jane Austen* that "she was well acquainted with the old periodicals from the 'Spectator' downward" (89).

Bradbrook argues that this defense of the novel at the close of chapter 5 "is so extreme as to suggest that [Austen] is not altogether convinced by it herself, and is introducing an element of exaggeration and caricature to indicate a certain satirical and ironical reserve" (114). "Ironical reserve" may help explain what the narrator has to say after John Thorpe warns Catherine not to read Fanny Burney's *Camilla*. Thorpe claims that "'it is the horridest nonsense you can imagine; there is nothing in the world in it by an old man's playing at see-saw and learning Latin; upon my soul there is not,'" whereupon the narrator adds that "this critique, the justness of which was unfortunately lost on poor Catherine, brought them to the door of Mrs. Thorpe's lodgings" (43–4). At what level of irony can we understand Thorpe's evaluation as a just critique?

## The Probable as Ethical

I have discussed in Chapter 3 Austen's commitment to the principles of natural law in her treatment of plot, particularly the application of a moral calculus to the fates of her characters (that is, through the operations of poetic justice). But her commitment to probability is no less inflected by natural law. Here again modern readers can sometimes miss the religious significance of Austen's realism. With hindsight, we can trace, with Erich Auerbach and later theorists of mimesis, the development of realism as a literary aesthetic in the Western imagination, attending to such phenomena as the dominance of social realism in the nineteenth-century novel and the psychological realism of early modernism. Looking back through the works of authors such as Dickens, Zola, Woolf, and DeLillo, we see a complex series of negotiations enacted between representation and historical reality, mediated by a highly varied series of "realist" effects, some of which, like the dream narrative in Joyce's *Finnegan's Wake*, the montage typography of Barthelme's *Snow White*, or the recursive loops of Borges' "The Garden of Forking Paths," would have puzzled Austen no end. From the perspective of the early twenty-first century, the late-eighteenth-century presumption that "naturalness" in fiction is an uncomplicated matter seems naïve. That is, we wonder at Hannah More's wonder that "[i]t seems very extraordinary, that it should be the most difficult thing in the world to be natural." From our perspective, the views on realism in the late eighteenth-century seem under-theorized at best.

What Austen and her contemporaries had that modern readers and critics lack, however, was a sturdy belief that literary realism was inevitably tied to moral and religious principles. As the various voices of her time cited above demonstrate, there was a wide consensus that "probable" works promoted ethical and even spiritually correct behavior. Again, the dictates of natural law explain this link: God created reality, including human beings, and reality thus has a rational ontology, despite human sin and the fallen condition of nature. From this presumption a further one follows, the innate link between conforming to reality and conforming to God's law. Fantasy, fancy, romance, and the unconstrained imagination were all understood as agents of discord, making it possible for authors and readers alike to fall away from God's reason. In general, eighteenth-century empiricists and natural historians believed they were getting closer to God, not farther away, by investigating things as they were. This presumption is in deep variance with modern sensibilities, used as we are since Darwin to view nature as a proof of God's non-existence and of the random processes of the universe.

It is within this context of natural law, of the presumed seamlessness between God's reality and the moral and spiritual underpinnings of that reality, that Austen's defense of the novel as a record of the probable is best understood. We can find significant evidence of the centrality of Austen's commitment to probability everywhere in her own fiction and in her opinions about fiction of her day. The ends of her own works, of course, repeatedly invoke what one could properly expect to happen, given circumstances as they stand up to that point. In *Northanger Abbey*, she brings the issue of probability to the fore: "The means by which [Catherine's and Henry's] early marriage was effected can be the only doubt; what probable circumstance could work upon a temper like the General?" (259).[14] The final chapter of *Persuasion* begins by asking, "Who can be in doubt of what followed?" and argues that "[w]hen any two young people take it into their heads to marry, they are pretty sure by perseverance to carry their point" (270). Even the *deus ex machina* at the close of *Emma*, the pilfering of Mrs. Weston's "turkies" that makes Mr. Woodhouse long to have a strong man in the house, is proffered on the grounds of probability. The narrator argues that this incident is not as improbable as it would have been had Mr. Woodhouse changed his mind or left behind his invalidism: "In this state of suspense they were befriended, not by any sudden illumination of Mr. Woodhouse's mind, or any wonderful change of his nervous system, but by the operation of the same system in another way" (528). Austen thus offers a statement about probabilities as a kind of cover for her improbable plot turn. We are to focus on the likelihood that Mr. Woodhouse would be fearful with thieves in the neighborhood rather than on the unlikelihood that thieves would show up on schedule, as it were, just when the plot requires them.

The importance Austen placed on novelistic probability is also confirmed by the various after-plots she spun out for family members (first recorded in James Austen-Leigh's 1870 *Memoir* [158]). Admittedly, these after-plots also show Austen's fondness for fine-tuning poetic justice, but then we must remember that for Austen and other orthodox Christians of her day, poetic justice and probability were not at odds, because poetic justice will only show the operations of natural law.[15] For instance, Frank Churchill may seem in *Emma* to be a "child of fortune," as Mr. Knightley terms him (488), who is inadequately punished at the end of the novel; however, Austen's family learned that Frank's beloved wife Jane Fairfax dies after eight or nine years of marriage (W. Austen-Leigh 307). Similarly, Mr. Knightley's chivalric willingness to live at Hartfield with his difficult father-in-law is not unrewarded, for Austen's family knew that Mr. Woodhouse dies two years after the novel's close. The poetic justice of these after-plots is matched by their probability. Miss Steele of *Sense and Sensibility* never catches the doctor, but it was very unlikely that she ever would. Kitty Bennet marries a clergyman near Pemberley—what could be more likely, given her moral and mannerly improvement under the wing of her elder sister, as noted at the end of *Pride and Prejudice*? Mary Bennet can do no better than to marry one of her uncle Phillips's clerks; given her dullness, this fate too seems to conform to what

---

[14]  Admittedly, the strength of Austen's gesture is somewhat undermined by her admission a page later that marrying Eleanor off to the gentleman whose servant left behind the laundry list is in keeping with "the rules of composition [that] forbid the introduction of a character not connected with my fable" (*NA* 260).

[15]  When the dictates of natural law and poetic justice were disregarded, Austen disapproved, and disapproved strongly. Note her outburst to her niece, Caroline: "You seem to be quite my own Neice in your feelings towards Mde de Genlis. I do not think I could even now, at my sedate time of Life, read *Olimpe et Theophile* without being in a rage. It is really too bad! – Not allowing them to be happy together, when they *are* married!" (sic; *L* 310). Notice the word "allowing": Austen is clear about who controls the plots.

we would expect. That Jane Fairfax dies also seems reasonable; after all, she almost succumbs to illness within the novel itself, there is nothing in the novel to suggest that she is particularly robust, and one can readily imagine the further emotional trials to which her immature husband might subject her that might in turn lead to serious illness. That Mr. Woodhouse dies follows from his inactivity and "valetudinarian" weakness (*E* 5). Jane Bennet prospers as Mrs. Bingley, as ought to happen on both moral and realistic grounds, and as proof, a portrait that records her wifely beauty and health shows up in a London art exhibition (as Austen noted in an 1813 letter; *L* 212).

Austen's own record of the opinions held by family and friends about *Mansfield Park* and *Emma* also demonstrate how highly she rated the "natural" and plausible. The words "natural" and "unnatural" surface nine times in the comments about *Mansfield Park* alone. Admittedly, most of the opinions focus on characters, that is, which characters were the most interesting (for instance, Cassandra "delighted much in Mr. Rushworth's stupidity" [*LM* 231]). But the theme of realistic presentation emerges as a constant as well. Her brother Frank thought the people of *Mansfield Park* were "natural" while her niece Fanny "could not think it natural" that Edmund could love Mary, given Mary's lack of "Principle" (*LM* 230). "Naturalness" could be invoked by contrary opinions; for instance, her brother Edward thought it was "unnatural" for Henry Crawford to run off with Maria when he was putatively in love with Fanny, while her sister-in-law, Mrs. James Austen, demurred, thinking Henry's going off "very natural" indeed (*LM* 230, 232). It seems significant that Austen quoted at greatest length the opinions of Lady Gordon and Mrs. Pole, neither of whom knew Austen personally, for both of their opinions take the "naturalness" of *Mansfield Park* as their main theme. Mrs. Pole speaks of Austen's believable depiction of the gentry: "Everything is natural, & the situations & incidents are told in a manner which clearly evinces the Writer to *belong* to the Society whose Manners she so ably delineates" (*LM* 234). Lady Gordon makes especially high claims for Austen's realism:

> In most novels you are amused for the time with a set of Ideal People whom you never think of afterwards or whom you the least expect to meet in common life, whereas in Miss A-s works, & especially in M P. you actually *live* with them, you fancy yourself one of the family; & the scenes are so exactly descriptive, so perfectly natural, that there is scarcely an Incident or conversation, or a person that you are not inclined to imagine you have at one time or other in your Life been a witness to, born a part in, & been acquainted. (*LM* 234)[16]

---

[16]   Many years later, Virginia Woolf would echo this appreciation of Austen's "naturalness," marveling at the scope and completeness of her achievements in her particular vein of realism:

[S]he fills every inch of her canvas with observation, fashions every sentence into meaning, stuffs up every chink and cranny of the fabric until each novel is a little living world, from which you cannot break off a scene or even a sentence without bleeding it of some of its life . . . . Only those who have realized for themselves the ridiculous inadequacy of a straight stick dipped in ink when brought in contact with the rich and tumultuous

When Austen came to record the opinions of *Emma*, she focused primarily on how her readers compared *Emma* to *Pride and Prejudice* and *Mansfield Park*, and, as with her record about *Mansfield Park*, she left ample testimony about their opinions of her characters. But the issue of plausibility is still evident. One suspects she was much amused, for instance, by the brief entry she submitted for Mrs. Guiton: "thought it too natural to be interesting" (*LM* 237), and she may have balanced Mrs. Guiton's complaint by a long entry for Mrs. C. Cage that noted among other praises that "I am at Highbury all day, & I can't help feeling I have just got into a new set of acquaintance" (*LM* 238). The limits, perhaps, of probability's worth also emerge, as Austen wryly sets down the objections of one Mrs. Dickson: "liked it the less, from there being a Mr. & Mrs. Dixon in it" (*LM* 237).

Perhaps the clearest demonstration of the high value Austen placed on the probable in fiction comes in the letters she wrote to Anna Austen in September of 1814, critiquing Anna's draft novel while she was herself composing *Emma*.[17] Almost all of her criticisms focus on mimetic adequacy—how well Anna's plot, characters, and settings conform to what might likely happen in the real world of gentry England, circa 1814. Interestingly, throughout the letter, Austen veers between speaking of herself in the first person singular (e.g., "I like the scene itself") and the first person plural, a "we" that includes Cassandra; the two sisters are both operating as literary critics (e.g., "We have been very much amused . . . "; "We are not satisfied") (*L* 274–5). Anna learns from her aunts that one of her characters needs a more plausible motivation for moving to the neighborhood of a gentleman of unsteady reputation: "Remember, [Mrs. F] is very prudent; --you must not let her act inconsistently" (*L* 275). She was instructed too that "Bless my Heart" is too "familiar & inelegant" a phrase for "Sir T. H." to utter, that no

---

glow of life can appreciate to the full the wonder of her achievement, the imagination, the penetration, the insight, the courage, the sincerity which are required to bring before us one of those perfectly normal and simple incidents of average human life. (Southam II:245)

Mary Lascelles, Austen's first academic critic, also marvels at Austen's "reality effect": "How is it that a novelist who makes no pretence of writing anything but novels, lays no claim to have discovered letters, memoirs, or other documents, who even has the effrontery to mention 'the pen of the contriver,' creates this extraordinary illusion of actuality?" ("Jane Austen and the Novel" 241).

[17] When Austen speaks of other novels in her letters, she often comments on their degree of believability. She described Mary Brunton's *Self-Control* (1811) as "an excellently-meant, elegantly-written work, without anything of nature or probability in it" (readers will recognize Austen's rhetorical gesture here in which the final verdict cancels out all the praise that had preceded it). Certainly, *Self-Control* was a novel that strained credulity; at one point the heroine is abducted to Canada by a Lovelace-like villain and escapes his clutches by going over a waterfall in a canoe. Austen also criticized Laetitia-Matilda Hawkins' *Rosanne* (1814) on the grounds of likelihood. Writing to Anna Lefroy, she gave her verdict: "on lighter topics I think she falls into many absurdities; and, as to love, her heroine has very comical feelings. There are a thousand improbabilities in the story" (*L* 289). This same letter does praise *Rosanne* for its treatment of "serious," that is, religious subjects: "There are some delightful conversations and reflections on religion."

mother would let a daughter walk after heavy rains ("An anxious mother would not suffer it"), and that the heroine showed an unbelievable range of response to the hero ("She seems to have changed her Character") (*L* 275). One of the minor characters needs work, because he is too much a stock character and not enough like a real person: "Henry Mellish I am afraid will be too much in the common Novel style—a handsome, amiable, unexceptionable Young Man (such as do not much abound in real Life)" (*L* 277). The hero in particular needs something "to increase the interest for him," but Austen warns Anna to be careful not to create sensational events: "I would not seriously recommend anything Improbable, but if you could invent something spirited for him, it would have a good effect" (*L* 278). Austen herself proposes some plot movements that might create this "spirit," but critiques her own suggestions, again, by the measure of probability: "He might lend all his Money to Captain Morris—but then he would be a great fool if he did. Cannot the Morrises quarrel, & he reconcile them? –Excuse the liberty I take in these suggestions" (*L* 278).

Probability thus gives a moral imprimatur to Austen's writing of fiction. Even the more spectacular of her events could be drawn from real life, for, as she knew, spectacular things could happen: her childhood friend and mentor Mrs. Lefroy had died in a fall from a horse, her cousin's husband had been guillotined in the Terror, and her aunt had languished in prison for almost a year on a trumped-up charge of shoplifting. Thus Louisa's fall at Lyme need not be understood as an instance beyond plausible constraints. Austen argues implicitly throughout her work that what she creates could happen in the real world she knew; her further presumption holds that because what she writes is probable, it will have a greater moral and even religious effect on its readers.

## The God-like Narrator

Her moral authority, however, extends far beyond the grounds of the believability of her fictions. Rather, it follows from her role as a sub-creator, adding to the creation of God. The orthodox tradition governing human creativity held that man is to imitate God, to reflect divine attributes, to imitate Good in adding to the perfections of divine creation (Lovejoy 295).[18] While it is God's prerogative

---

[18]    Lovejoy argues that "it was not less a part of the classical tradition in aesthetics that art should imitate nature, not merely in the sense of copying natural objects or portraying faithfully the characters of men, but also in the sense of conforming to the general characteristics of nature and to the ways of working of its Author" (295). By the late eighteenth and early nineteenth century, the doctrine of the Great Chain of Being was increasingly inflected by an emphasis on God as "insatiably creative"; thus, Lovejoy notes, "Man's high calling was to add something of his own to the creation, to enrich the sum of things, and thus, in his finite fashion, consciously to collaborate in the fulfillment of the Universal Design" (296). The temporalizing of the Great Chain of Being (see Chapter 3) has wide-ranging cultural, spiritual, and intellectual effects, one of which is this justification for human creativity.

to create what has not existed (as St. Paul writes, God "calls into existence the things that do not exist" [*Romans* 4:16]), authors may claim the prerogative of sub-creating, that is, creating with what God has created, reflecting that creation's attributes. Further, God's craftiness was understood to have certain inalienable attributes, including reason, goodness, beauty, and intricacy. Austen seems to have held that the most salient of these virtues for her own work to reflect were probability, artisanal craft, and ethical suasion. The last of these is evidenced by her investment in poetic justice, her continual moralizing bent, and her satiric exposure of human fault; the craft is evident everywhere, in the polished and balanced style, in the meticulous plotting, and in the exposure of character. Most particularly, however, Austen participates in God's creative nature by generating a narrator who has seemed to a wide range of readers a pinnacle of goodness and wisdom.

There is a long tradition in Austen criticism that speaks of Austen's narrator as a god-like force. As early as 1917, Reginald Farrer spoke of her capacity to mimic God's creation, creating "ex nihilo"; Farrer also credits the "steely rigour of her judgement" and the "intense vitalization" of her characters as central to her god-like propensities (22, 24). Virginia Woolf saw Austen as a moral paragon:

> Never did any novelist make more use of an impeccable sense of human values. It is against the disc of an unerring heart, an unfailing good taste, an almost stern morality, that she shows up those deviations from kindness, truth, and sincerity which are among the most delightful things in English literature. (*Common Reader* 143)

"Impeccable" and "unerring"—Woolf's word choice implies that Austen is a novelist without moral fault—even without sin.[19] Wayne Booth followed in this tradition, famously describing the narrator, "Jane Austen," as "in short, a perfect

---

[19]   In *A Room of One's Own*, Woolf expands her argument about Austen's lofty stance:

Here was a woman about the year 1800 writing without hate, without bitterness, without fear, without protest, without preaching. . . . [W]hen people compare Shakespeare and Jane Austen, they may mean that the minds of both had consumed all impediments; and for that reason we do not know Jane Austen and we do not know Shakespeare, and for that reason Jane Austen pervades every word that she wrote, and so does Shakespeare. If Jane Austen suffered in any way from her circumstances it was in the narrowness of life that was imposed upon her. . . . But perhaps it was the nature of Jane Austen not to want what she had not. Her gift and her circumstances matched each other completely. (114)

This last idea, that Austen was immune from the ordinary hopes of humankind, we know to be untrue—her letters show the shock she underwent, for instance, in the month before her death when her family learned that Austen's uncle had not left an expected legacy to her, her mother, and her sister, directing his estate instead to his wife almost in full. But Austen's narrator knows how to present herself as beyond petty human wants, "not to want what she had not." For a comprehensive account of Woolf's attitudes towards Austen, see Emily Auerbach.

human being, within the concept of perfection established by the books she writes" (*Rhetoric* 265).[20] Gene Koppel argued that the wisdom of Austen's narrator is a precondition of her artistic achievement: "She herself must appear to be all-wise, so that her comedy has the aesthetic completeness, that almost snobbish self-sufficiency that her readers find so irresistible" (56).[21]

The seeming self-sufficiency of Austen's narrator represents a complex artistic achievement. In part, the effect is created by the very limited interjections from the narrator that imply individual or personal feeling. The narrator's cardinal virtue, economy, here restricts the personal view.[22] She is not without interjections; after all, she admits that she pities the gentleman who marries Lady Susan in the novel of that name; she implies pride in her workmanship, in her defense of novels in *Northanger Abbey* and in other moments in which she calls attention to her craft, sense of poetic justice, and neat plotting; and she makes sympathetic gestures towards her heroines at the end of each novel, especially the moment when she speaks of "my Fanny" in the final chapter of *Mansfield Park* (461). But in general, her values are expressed indirectly, in the consistently impersonal moralizing of

---

[20]  Booth's judgment relative to her perfection follows in full: "When we read [*Emma*] we accept 'Jane Austen' as representing everything we admire most. She is as generous as Knightley; in fact, she is a shade more penetrating in her judgment. She is as subtle and witty as Emma would like to think herself. Without being sentimental she is in favor of tenderness. She is able to put an adequate but not excessive value on wealth and rank. She recognizes a fool when she sees one, but unlike Emma she knows that it is both immoral within the concept of perfection established by the books she writes and foolish to be rude to fools" (265). Booth corrects himself, perhaps, decades later in *The Company We Keep* (1987) by wondering if the feminist critique mars *Emma*'s moral stature. Nonetheless, even in this re-consideration, Booth argues that the novel asks us to wonder "whether any character in this novel is perfect. You cannot answer that question without asking at the same time where your standard of perfection comes from . . . . It is derived . . . from that great woman, the implied Jane Austen, the dauntingly mature human being who underwrites every act of imagination she takes us through" (433).

[21]  This moral sure-footedness is required to create the reader's education, Robyn Warhol suggests: "[the narrator] relies on the narratee to read the story with sympathy; where the narratee's generosity may lapse, [the narrator] leads the narratee through a process of sympathetic education that closely parallels the lessons learned by the protagonists" (27). In other words, the narrator's generosity and humane bent makes the reader's moral refinement possible. Warhol is discussing Eliot's narrator in *Middlemarch*, but her account fits Austen's with equal force. The narrator's loving correction of Emma, for instance, also corrects the reader. A similar point is made by Adena Rosmarin: "Because our need to recollect and be tutored has become as great as Emma's, her guilt becomes ours, and in the page upon page of elaborately detailed remorse that follows [Mr. Knightley's correction] we are denied the luxury of distance" (230). See also Kenneth Morefield and Susan Wolfson on the reader's complicity.

[22]  See Claudia Johnson ("A Name") for a comparison of Austen's narrative and affective economies to the tradition of unbounded enthusiasm and fanhood among her readers.

her prose and equally consistent ironic depictions of error and folly, all rendered without personal animus or explicit intervention from the narrator.[23]

More central to Austen's disengaged and superior position is her employment of free indirect discourse. Here the inner thoughts of her characters may be revealed even as the narrator passes implicit judgment on those thoughts, or what a character says may be inflected by the narrator's oblique restatement. Free indirect discourse creates an arena for complex gestures of judgment and irony, for readers can never be entirely sure exactly how much of any given moment in this mode reflects the character's perspective and how much reflects the narrator's attitude.[24] Here, for instance, is Sir Thomas, noting to himself how Fanny behaves in the face of Henry's wooing: "Fanny's reception of it was so proper and modest, so calm and uninviting, that he had nothing to censure in her" (*MP* 287). What words are we to imagine were in Sir Thomas's mind? "Proper," "modest," "calm," "uninviting," perhaps, all would be natural enough terms for Sir Thomas to employ in his thoughts in reference to Fanny. But would he with equal plausibility say to himself that "he had nothing to censure in her"; that is, "I have nothing to censure in her"? The narrator has injected into this phrase her awareness of his judgmental approach and his oblivion about Fanny's disregard for Henry, for Sir Thomas plainly expects that a Fanny less controlled by decorum would have responded to Henry with greater welcome or even flirtation. What Sir Thomas thinks thus is not what he actually "thinks"; through a complex dispensation of reportage admixed with judgment, the narrator has rendered a verdict on the presumptions of Sir Thomas's authority. This moment is one of innumerable occasions in Austen's fiction in which free indirect discourse creates a free-floating space for judgment that seems impersonal and disembodied, even

---

[23] See Gary Kelly in reference to Austen's choice to eschew in her fiction dramatized first-person narration (the epistolary nature of much of the juvenilia, including *Lady Susan*, would form the exceptions). He argues that Fanny Burney and others of Austen's predecessors seem to have felt that the "first-person narration could engage readers' sympathies so powerfully that it disarmed judgment" (160).

[24] A different perspective is offered by William Galperin, who argues that Austen's movement from epistolary fiction to fiction dominated by free indirect discourse was problematic: "While plainly mindful of the significance and importance of free indirect discourse in the developing genre of the novel, Austen recognized at the time of her first novels' publication that this mode was also an especially sinister instrument of coercion . . . . Beginning with the earliest published novels, the achievement of authority we associate with Austen's realism was an ongoing problem that her continued, and continually vexed, practice of free indirect discourse has also obscured" (*Historical Austen* 10). Perhaps Galperin and I disagree less on the power of free indirect discourse and more on which moral problem dominated Austen's consciousness: for Galperin, Austen would have sensed as "sinister" the capacity of narratives to coerce readerly acceptance of then-normative social and moral behaviors; for me, the problem Austen faces is proffering human moral authority as a voice for divine authority.

god-like.[25] The pressure on the narrator, then, to make those pervasively subtle judgments from on high nonetheless seem beyond moral reproach is considerable; that Austen does so consistently is a measure of her achievement of moral, not simply narrative, authority. That this authority is achieved even as her readership with each passing generation becomes more and more removed from her moral presumptions is all the more astounding. We may not even recognize the relevance of her moral prescriptions, I would argue, but we do at least temporarily bend to her authority with each reading.[26] Only Austen herself fully knew the distance between the quasi-absolute moral authority her narrator achieved and her own inevitably human behavior, as faulty and self-interested at moments as that of her faulty and self-interested characters. However, behind that carefully constructed personal authority, Austen had a conviction that divine authority countenanced her fictions, countenanced her exercises to show how people really are and how they might become better and happier. It is important that in Austen's prayers, she asks for forgiveness only for acts of unkindness she may have committed with real people; she does not ask for forgiveness for writing novels. There is every reason to believe that when she thanks God in that third prayer for "every hour . . . of innocent enjoyment," she means to include her creation of fiction.

---

[25]    D. A. Miller argues in his brilliant *Jane Austen, or the Secret of Style* that Austen's narrator achieves an exclusiveness, a high-flying position that places her judgments beyond those of ordinary mortals and beyond ordinary desires, a position which he calls Absolute Style: "Here was a truly out-of-body voice, so stirringly free of what it abhorred as 'particularity' or 'singularity' that is seemed to come from no enunciator at all" (1). Commenting on the famous opening line of *Pride and Prejudice,* Miller notes, "no one who writes with such possession can be in want of *anything*" (34). Similarly, he notes of the role of free indirect discourse in *Emma*:

Austen's narration, though claiming authority absolutely, affirms it relationally, as an epistemological advantage over character. When free indirect style mimics Emma's thoughts and feelings, it simultaneously inflects them into keener observations of its own; for our benefit, if never for hers, it identifies, ridicules, corrects all the secret vanities and self-deceptions of which Emma, pleased as Punch, remains comically unconscious. And this is generally what being a character in Austen means: to be slapped silly by a narration whose constant battering, however satisfying—or terrifying—to readers, its recipient is kept from even noticing. (71)

Miller's sense of the moral, psychological, and ontological stature of this narrator is at extreme variance from my own, of course; ultimately, he reads Austen's style as a melancholic, even nihilist, response to Austen's own personal disappointments, especially her status as a spinster spinning conjugal narratives, in which the Style triumphs at the expense of the author's humanity.

[26]    As David Lodge has put it, in reading Austen "we submit to the authority of her vision, and recognize its relevance to our own world of secularized spirituality" (113).

## World-making

Austen's investment in the religiously proper exercise of narrative authority and creativity leads her to a corollary theme: imagination gone astray. Much has been written about this fault in reference to Austen's over-imaginative heroines, particularly Catherine Morland, Marianne Dashwood, and Emma Woodhouse.[27] Many critics have also treated the moral problems of imagination Austen treats on a larger scale through her sustained interest in "improvement"; Austen regularly demonstrates that characters desire to change physical landscapes to satisfy class fantasies (Mary's "agreeable fancies" in *Mansfield Park* to "sink the clergyman" in Edmund by making improvements to his future rectory constitute one example [289]; Mr. Rushworth's desire for greater social consequence through the demolition of his estate's elm trees makes another).[28] Critics have also had much to say about the role of *Lovers' Vows* in the same novel, a multi-chapter exploration of the loosing of imagination (and moral restraints) on a large scale. Though only a few critics have treated Austen's last and unfinished work *Sanditon*, it too presents a whole new world created by human speculation and foolishness, in which the height of creation is found in the presence of the latest fashionable commodity—blue nankin boots—in a shop window.[29]

The more extended exercises in world-making are most akin to the novelist's own pursuit, and most clearly designed to show the difference between how to write a novel properly and how to do it immorally and inartfully. In *Northanger Abbey*, Henry Tilney's extended creation of what awaits Catherine at the Abbey is one such moment; he makes an explicit and sustained parody of the Gothic that stands in implicit contrast to Austen's more dispersed parodic jabs throughout the

---

[27]    Stuart Tave some time ago (1973) gave one of the most comprehensive treatments of the moral permutations of imagination in his chapter on *Emma* in *Some Words of Jane Austen*. He also notes that Austen's work in general offers

[s]o many kinds of false freedom from limitation . . . . These false offerings hold forth a life of greater intensity and greater power, of superior vision, a higher activity of mind, feeling, body, a fulfillment of desire. They give a reality of the mind's own making and seem therefore to be dominant. They prove to be false because they are really reductions of life. They do not have more vision but see less, they do not have more power but are inadequate to life, and they do not fulfill desires because they are self-defeating. (31)

See also Halperin ("Jane Austen and Cowper"), who suggests that "almost all the major characters in *Emma* live within a reality of their own devising; the world they see is often a function of their own selfish egoism. Jane Austen's theme is ubiquitous; there are worlds and worlds in *Emma*" (202).

[28]    Alastair Duckworth's *The Improvement of the Estate* (1971) is still the best treatment of this issue.

[29]    The intrusion of fantasies of consumerism into the older fantasies of social ascension and marriage into the novel is usefully canvassed in Butler ("Purple Turban"). For a broader context, see Colin Campbell's *The Romantic Ethic and the Spirit of Modern Consumerism*, Nancy Armstrong's *How Novels Think* (especially chapter two), and McKendrick et al., *The Birth of a Consumer Society*.

text. At various points, Austen tells the reader what has *not* happened to Catherine, as when she describes Catherine's journey to Bath with the Allens: "Neither robbers not tempest befriended them, nor one lucky overturn to introduce them to the hero" (19). Henry by contrast tells Catherine what *will* happen to her, in detail. For instance, Henry prophecies that Catherine "'will discover a division in the tapestry so artfully constructed as to defy the minutest inspection, and on opening it, a door will immediately appear'" (159). His catalogue of prognostication employs the Radcliffean Gothic to advantage, but also displays, in ways that Catherine cannot yet comprehend, their intrinsic improbability.

In the novels, Austen's most extreme depiction of morally corrupt world-making appears in *Sanditon*. Above and beyond the puffery that is working to create a seaside resort out of thin air, the novel also displays that expert novel-reader, Sir Edward Denham. Sir Edward has clear views about what sorts of novels he prefers to read (he assures Charlotte that he is "'no indiscriminate novel-reader'" [*LM* 181]) and maps for Charlotte his ideal novel. This précis expresses values exactly antithetical to Austen's conception of morally and religiously sanctioned fiction:

> 'The novels which I approve are such as display human nature with grandeur—such as shew her in the sublimities of intense feeling—such as exhibit the progress of strong passion from the first germ of incipient susceptibility to the utmost energies of reason half-dethroned, --where we see the strong spark of woman's captivations elicit such fire in the soul of Man as leads him . . . to hazard all, dare all, achieve all, to obtain her.' (*LM* 182)

In other words, having read Richardson's *Clarissa* without a moral compass or much sense, Sir Edward prefers to read novels about "romantic" rape. Charlotte, who had earlier pointed out how the immorality of Robert Burns's conduct diminishes his appeal to her as a poet, is not fooled by Sir Edward's jargon and raptures: "'If I understand you aright, our taste in novels is not at all the same'" (183).[30]

Austen's other sustained parody of fictional world-making was suggested by the foolish letters from James Stanier Clarke, the Prince Regent's Librarian at Carlton House. His suggestions were both too grandiose and too narrow, as he tells Austen that her talents should be deployed in surpassing Goldsmith and La Fontaine with a portrait of "the Habits of Life and Character and enthusiasm—

---

[30]   Charlotte tells Sir Edward that "'I have read several of Burns's poems with great delight . . . but I am not poetic enough to separate a man's poetry entirely from his character; --and poor Burns's known irregularities, greatly interrupt my enjoyment of his lines. --I have difficulty in depending on the *truth* of his feelings as a lover. I have not faith in the *sincerity* of the affections of a man of his description. He felt and he wrote and he forgot'" (*LM* 175–6; italics in original). Through Charlotte, Austen is calling attention to what was widely held knowledge about Robert Burns' numerous love affairs and illegitimate children (Burns had died at 37 in 1797). The feeling behind Charlotte's dismissal of Burns—"'he felt and he wrote and he forgot'"—echoes some of Anne Elliot's belief, and perhaps Austen's, that women suffer longer after love is gone than do men.

who should pass his time between the metropolis & and Country—who should be something like Beatties Minstrel 'Silent when glad, affectionate tho' shy'" (*sic*; *L* 296). Obviously risible is Clarke's desire for a novel about himself, or at any rate a romanticized and idealized version of himself.[31] He was not deterred by Austen's polite and self-deprecatory letter demurring from the project he had outlined; his next letter tells her to "shew . . . what good would be done if Tythes were taken away entirely, and describe him burying his own mother—as I did—because the High Priest of the Parish in which she died—did not pay her remains the respect he ought to do. I have never recovered [from] the Shock" (*L* 307). This uncontrolled amalgamation of polemic and sentimental biography was grist for Austen's comic mill. Her "Plan for a Novel," written in early 1816 soon after this correspondence was exchanged, incorporates all the criticisms and suggestions she had been receiving from Clarke and from family members and friends to make for a rousingly bad plot synopsis, with footnotes that assign blame for many of its most egregious features to specific individuals. The novel will have a "striking variety of adventures," with its hero clergyman and his daughter "never above a fortnight together in one place" (*LM* 227). They end in Kamschatka (understood in Austen's day to represent the ends of the earth), where the priest expires "in a fine burst of Literary Enthusiasm, intermingled with Invectives against Holders of Tythes" (*sic*; 228–9). In this parody and in much of Austen's writing, the treatment of imagination's dangers (and stupidities) constitutes an implicit defense of her own practice. She is immune from moral censure because she is different from all the other faulty romancers; she knows she writes with moral discrimination and within the probabilities of common life.

Austen's treatment of imagination gone awry, however, does not simply arise through the major trajectories of plot and education for her protagonists but also comes to view within the chorus of hopes and fantasies of minor characters. Austen repeatedly shows a range of characters creating fantasies for the future, almost all inflected by naïve or selfish desire.[32] While these moments aid characterization,

---

[31]  In another letter of 1815, he tells Austen that he has been hiding away in a "Village" "from all bustle and turmoil—and getting Spirits for a Winter Campaign—and Strength to stand the sharp knives from which many a Shylock is wetting to cut more than a Pound of Flesh from my heart, on the appearance of James the Second" (*L* 306–7). This self-portrait sets Clarke as Shakespeare's Antonio, beset by multiple Shylocks (critics) who wish for even more flesh than Shylock had demanded. Austen cannot have been impressed but was almost certainly much amused by this hyperbole and self-aggrandizement.

[32]  Even simple lists can be instruments of fantasy. The Baronetage in *Persuasion* allows Sir Walter to insert more details about his immediate family, including writing in at the "finale" "Heir presumptive, William Walter Elliot, Esq., great grandson of the second Sir Walter" (4). Sir Walter uses the Baronetage to daydream about the past, not the future, but his daughter sees the book as a rebuke about her future, and shuns it: "Always to be presented with the date of her own birth, and see no marriage follow but that of a youngest sister, made the book an evil" (7). Anne has kept a different sort of tally, reading the navy lists regularly to track Wentworth's career; when the Musgrove girls leap to explore naval

they also reinforce Austen's theme—some forms of imagination are morally and spiritually acceptable, while others are not. These little fictions her characters create for themselves thus demonstrate the moral stakes in fictionalizing, in creating and imagining what does not exist. After all, exploding all these little wish-fulfilling fictions helps Austen create moral space for her own wish-fulfilling fictions, the kind of fiction that has the fortuneless Elizabeth Bennet marrying one of the richest men in England, and marrying him for true love. One of the silliest and most revealing of these episodes occurs early in *Pride and Prejudice*. In chapter five, the Lucas family visits the Bennets after the first ball and the discussion turns to Mr. Darcy. A "young Lucas" (this boy is never given a name) cries out his fondest hope: "'If I were as rich as Mr. Darcy . . . I would keep a pack of foxhounds, and drink a bottle of wine every day'" (22).[33] This juvenile fantasy conforms at least at some level to the hopes of many readers—a life of pleasure and indulgence supported by wealth (ultimately, Elizabeth will be allowed to be "as rich as Mr. Darcy," too). "Young Lucas" is rebuked by an unlikely Malvolio, Mrs. Bennet: "'If I were to see you at it I should take your bottle directly'" (22). Mrs. Bennet is so foolish that rather than reprimanding the moral vacancy of the fantasy, she enters into it in order to close it down, becoming an imagined actor in a scenario of juvenile correction. Austen closes the chapter with this observation: "The boy protested that she should not; she continued to declare that she would, and the argument ended only with the visit" (22). This kind of aerial castle-building leads to a nightmare of mundane repetition. Austen implies that it is stupid and immature of the boy to long for a world of idle pleasure, but even more stupid and immature

---

records to heighten their pleasurable prospects with the Captain, Anne is left to remember that her more expert reading has been a reading without a future. Austen herself played with a list of marital fantasy, when at 16 she inserted into the Steventon parish record the banns of her upcoming union to not one but three suitors of the future. Regarding the Baronetage, Tandon notes that "Austen's approximating a page of Sir Walter's book does not aspire to an accurate reproduction" (231) because the actual book mingles the original printed material ("how the paragraph originally stood from the printer's hand" [*P* 3]) and Sir Walter's annotations. We never see the text just as it is but as it has been transformed by self-interested projections both into the past and into the future.

[33]    Equally childish is Lydia's dream of her sojourn in Brighton:

In Lydia's imagination, a visit to Brighton comprised every possibility of earthly happiness. She saw with the creative eye of fancy, the streets of that gay bathing place covered with officers. She saw herself the object of attention, to tens and to scores of them at present unknown. She saw all the glories of the camp; its tents stretched forth in beauteous uniformity of lines, crowded with the young and the gay, and dazzling with scarlet; and to complete the view, she saw herself seated beneath a tent, tenderly flirting with at least six officers at once. (*PP* 232)

Whether the officers are to be there in multiples of sixes, tens, or scores (twenties), Lydia's self-admiring fantasy requires a crowd before whom her "tenderness" can be performed. Austen here perhaps intimates that when we see the newlywed Lydia, we should expect that her raptures over Wickham will last only so long and that her erotic future will include multiple if interchangeable partners.

for the adult Mrs. Bennet to take these fantasies seriously, to people them with action and consequence. The end of the chapter, mimicking as it does the end of the visit, must stand as reproach enough.

Austen loves to ridicule the human habit of making fictions entirely out of self-interest (implicitly, the reader is to learn that the happy endings achieved by her heroines have a different ethical compass). In *Sense and Sensibility*, there is a long conversation among members of the Dashwood family and Edward Ferrars about what one would do with a windfall. Young Margaret, like "young Lucas," begins with a simple statement of visionary greed: "'I wish,' said Margaret, striking out a novel thought, 'that somebody would give us all a large fortune apiece!'" This most un-novel of thoughts is followed by her elder sister, who is old enough at 17 to know better: "'Oh that they would!' cried Marianne, her eyes sparkling with animation, and her cheeks glowing with the delight of such imaginary happiness" (106). The full somatic response (for those sparkling eyes and glowing cheeks have earlier been called forward only by Willoughby) shows Marianne's spontaneous investment in this dream of plenty, one Elinor tries to bat down with a statement about reality: "'We are all unanimous in that wish, I suppose . . . in spite of the insufficiency of wealth'" (106). Edward joins in with a loving catalogue of all the cultured purchases the family would make were they to become rich: "'What magnificent orders would travel from this family to London . . . in such an event! What a happy day for booksellers, music-sellers, and print-shops!'" (106–7). Edward in fact manages to do what Elinor could not, change the topic of conversation, by reminding Marianne and Margaret of all of the higher values they hold.

That Edward is present underscores the stakes of the conversation, because only by marrying him, at this point still the heir of a large fortune, can Elinor become wealthy, while Marianne can become rich only by marrying Willoughby (he has left her for London by this point, but she has yet to learn that he has truly deserted her). This conversation also reinforces how wrong it was for Marianne and Willoughby, four chapters previously, to have toured Allenham, the estate Willoughby expects to inherit from his relative, Mrs. Smith. It is bad enough that Marianne tours the house without Mrs. Smith being present, and that Marianne has never been introduced to the owner of the house. Much worse, however, is that Marianne takes the tour in the spirit of future occupation, abetted by Willoughby's suggestions. She views the place as Mr. Collins views Longbourn, though with far less justification. She has even gone upstairs to a private sitting-room, where she has admired the view and deplored the "forlorn" furniture. There Willoughby completes her fantasy by saying that "'a couple of hundred pounds . . . would make it one of the pleasantest summer-rooms in England'" (81); he implies that he will marry her, inherit Allenham, and together they will "improve" the house. The sum Willoughby suggests for fixing up just one of Allenham's rooms, incidentally, is roughly half the amount Marianne's family has as a yearly income; we are indeed in the presence of compensatory fantasy, fantasy that is rife with danger.

Austen fills her fictions with characters creating fictions that do not and cannot come true. Some are central to her plots (Emma's plans for Harriet, Lucy Steele's plans for Edward), while some are minor exposures of folly (Mrs. Elton's plans for an *al fresco* party, complete with donkey, at Donwell Abbey, or, also in *Emma*, Frank Churchill's fantasy of decamping to Switzerland).[34] Some characters are marked by their continual exercise of inappropriate fancies. Mrs. Bennet, for example, is the most sustained and foolish imaginist in *Pride and Prejudice*. When Mr. Bennet tells her that they will have a visitor for dinner, she immediately leaps to not one but two faulty surmises. It may be Charlotte Lucas, Mrs. Bennet thinks, adding "'I hope my dinners are good enough for her'"; when told this guess is wrong, she settles on Mr. Bingley: "'Why Jane—you never dropt a word of this; you sly thing!'" (68). Like Lydia, Mrs. Bennet has fantasies about Brighton, and imagines "'a little sea-bathing would set me up for ever'" (254); all her efforts to persuade Mr. Bennet to take the family there come to nothing. Later, after Lydia's elopement but before Lydia is found, Mrs. Bennet's imagination leads her again to comical extremes, for she both presumes that Mr. Bennet will die in a duel with Mr. Wickham and that Lydia should order a full complement of wedding clothes (the two cannot both happen). This similar propensity to put her imagined cart before her imagined horse occurs when she learns of Lydia's engagement: "[H]er thoughts and her words ran wholly on those attendants of elegant nuptials, fine muslins, new carriages, and servants" (342). Her flights of fancy include planning for Lydia and Wickham's new home, though she has no reason to believe they can afford anything beyond the meanest lodgings nor that they will have any reason to settle in her neighborhood: "'Haye-Park might do . . . if the Gouldings would quit it, or the great house at Stoke, if the drawing-room were larger; but Ashworth is too far off! I could not bear to have her ten miles from me; and as for Purvis Lodge, the attics are dreadful'" (342). One might note that she rejects these homes in two cases because they are not fine enough; it is left to Mr. Bennet to explain that none of her plans will change his intention never to receive either Lydia or Wickham at Longbourn itself.

Elizabeth herself has inherited some of Mrs. Bennet's propensity to misuse the imagination. For instance, in the wake of Darcy's failed proposal, Elizabeth can't help but think of Lady Catherine's response were she to have accepted him: "she [could not] think, without a smile, of what her ladyship's indignation would have been. 'What would she have said? –how would she have behaved' were questions with which she amused herself" (*PP* 233). Elizabeth is ultimately to find out exactly how Lady Catherine will behave in the face of a presumed engagement between herself and Darcy, and she will find out that the actual moment holds

---

[34] Tave notes a particularly egregious moment of world-making in *Emma*, when the heroine paints a picture for Harriet of how Mr. Elton's family in London is receiving her portrait: "'how cheerful, how animated, how suspicious, how busy their imaginations all are!'" (59) Tave notes, "A whole secret, and nonexistent, world has been created and conferred" (209). By contrast, the real family life of the Martins (also one unmarried son, one mother, and a set of sisters) has been forgotten, even though Harriet has experienced their cheerful and supportive hearth for herself.

far more painful moral and social considerations than the easy personal triumph Elizabeth had fancied earlier. Admittedly, Elizabeth's schemes of pleasure seem nobler than her mother's. Thinking of the "tour of pleasure" her aunt and uncle propose, Elizabeth prognosticates happiness, an expectation that includes her sense that her travel will be more rational than other people's (it will certainly be more rational than chasing after the officers to Brighton): "'What are men to rocks and mountains? . . . Oh! What hours of transport we shall spend! And when we do return, it shall not be like other travelers, without being able to give one accurate idea of any thing. We will know where we have gone'" (174–5). The novel's plot will frustrate these imaginings, and Elizabeth's rejection of men for rocks will be turned on its head: there are no mountains where she is going, just Darcy and the gentle hills of his orderly estate. Pemberley's appeal creates another fantasy: "'And of this place,' thought she, 'I might have been mistress! With these rooms I might now have been familiarly acquainted! Instead of viewing them as a stranger, I might have rejoiced in them as my own, and welcomed to them as visitors my uncle and aunt'" (272). However, Elizabeth has firmer moral control over her fantasies than does her mother: "'–But no,' recollecting herself—'that could never be: my uncle and aunt would have been lost to me: I should not have been allowed to invite them.' This was a lucky recollection—it saved her from something like regret" (272). Elizabeth's better ordering of her imagination has come about gradually. Towards the end of the novel, she explains to Mrs. Gardiner in a letter that her aunt's teasing about her upcoming marriage to Darcy had been very painful to her because "You supposed more than really existed." (Mrs. Gardiner had obliquely made a prophecy: "I shall never be quite happy till I have been all round the park. A low phaeton, with a nice little pair of ponies would be the very thing" [360]). Now, however, imagination can be indulged, because it in accord with reality—it is almost certainly going to come true:

> [N]ow suppose as much as you chuse; give a loose to your fancy, indulge your imagination in every possible flight which the subject will afford, and unless you believe me actually married, you cannot greatly err. . . . Your idea of the ponies is delightful. We will go round the Park every day. (424)

Indeed the ponies are now allowable, because this fantasy is based on a very high probability (Elizabeth is now engaged).

If Elizabeth Bennet (and Emma Woodhouse) learn to use their imaginations within a proper moral compass, Stuart Tave has suggested we look to Mr. Knightley as the one character whose use of the imagination Austen endorses at every stage. He is the one figure to sense that Jane Fairfax and Frank Churchill are romantically involved (characteristically, Emma laughs at his suggestion: "'it will not do—very sorry to check you in your first essay—but indeed it will not do'" [*E* 380]). He also self-corrects, asking himself if his guesses are not merely the product of self-interest, in Cowper's lines, "'Myself creating what I saw'" (373). Mr. Knightley not only curbs his imagination, continually checking if his ideas are probable and/or grounded in evidence, but he also is very careful in positing future events. He certainly rejects Mrs. Elton's fantasy of a gypsy party at Donwell, and we learn that he has had a long discussion with Robert Martin before he proposes to Harriet, going into the young man's financial prospects and considering the possible invidious results of Harriet's illegitimacy before advising that the proposal be made. Mr. Knightley's imagination is bound by evidence, duty, and principle; it cannot be coincidental that these qualities are exactly what Jane Austen praised in Fanny Knight's fictional employment of fancy. Wondering how Fanny can be so effusively creative, Austen noted her judgment and religious commitments: "Religious Principle I fancy must explain it" (*L* 485–6). Here is Austen's most essential commitment: imagination validated by Christian precepts of duty, reason, and virtue, and happy endings endorsed by the same.

Austen also endorses one last proper employment of the imagination in a Christian context: moral chastisement.[35] At key points, her heroines must imagine a world far different from that of their hopes. Emma's misery on imagining herself left "to cheer her father with the spirits only of ruined happiness" in the chapter before Mr. Knightley proposes to her includes her full draining of the future's bitter cup:

> The child to be born at Randalls must be a tie there even dearer than herself; and Mrs. Weston's heart and time would be occupied by it. . . . Frank Churchill would return among them no more; and Miss Fairfax . . . would soon cease to belong to Highbury. . . . Mr. Knightley . . . no longer walking in at all hours, as if ever willing to change his own home for their's! . . . And if her were to be lost to them for Harriet's sake . . . if Harriet were to be the chosen, the first, the dearest, the friend, the wife to whom he looked for all the best blessings of existence; what could be increasing Emma's wretchedness but the reflection never far distant from her mind, that it had been all her own work? (*sic*; 460)[36]

---

[35]   Stuart Tave also argues that Austen sometimes shows, as in *Emma*, that what people *cannot* imagine about human nature can be harmful as well (214ff). Miss Bates can't imagine Jane could be unwell, Mr. Weston can't imagine Mrs. Churchill would be capricious with his son, and Mrs. Elton can't imagine how Mr. Knightley could forget an appointment with her husband: "Reality comes to each of these characters through such a selective vision, shaped by their own capacities and needs, that much of it is simply excluded. . . . What seems to be true is that a deficiency of imagination is the necessary correlate of an excess of imagination within a narrow range of concern" (216).

[36]   The reader should recall that the "best blessings of existence" are the very words the narrator used to describe Emma's lot in the first paragraph of the novel (3). At the same time, Emma's sense that Mr. Knightley will no longer be able to "change his own home for their's" (*sic*) casts a narrative shadow forward to the happy ending, in which Mr. Knightley has made this exchange of homes an enduring one. Importantly, Emma's consolation in her view of the future is her "resolution of her own better conduct," that the "future winter of her life" would find her "more rational, more acquainted with herself, and [would] leave her less to regret when it were gone" (461). This invocation of the ultimate end of her life, when the "future winter. . . were gone," reinforces the spiritual nature of this undertaking to live morally despite the failure of conjugal hopes—an undertaking Austen must have made for herself as well.

Similarly, at Lyme Anne Elliot, seeing the looming signs of a romantic understanding between Captain Wentworth and Louisa as well as the worth of Captain Benwick and the Hargroves, muses with sharp regret: "These too would have been my friends" (*P* 105), and even when Louisa is injured, Anne, alone at the Great House, must face the likely outcome: "A few months hence, and the room now so deserted, occupied but by her silent, pensive self, might be filled again with all that was happy and gay, all that was glowing and bright in prosperous love, all that was most unlike Anne Elliot!" (133). Incidentally, both Emma's and Anne's reflections take place in nature's chill: Anne is having her dark thoughts on a "dark November day" with "a small thick rain" (133), while Emma forces herself to see her future in the "gloom" of a "cold stormy rain" (*E* 459).

Thus, the keenest pain for both Emma and Anne is the marriages they imagine, marriages that never exist, the "prosperous love" between Wentworth and Louisa and the "best blessings of existence" Mr. Knightley finds in Harriet. Elizabeth Bennet, Catherine Morland, and Marianne Dashwood are not humiliated by such prospects (Elizabeth knows Mr. Darcy will never marry Miss Bingley, no rival for Henry Tilney ever emerges in *Northanger Abbey,* and Marianne knows that Willoughby is marrying for money). But both Elinor in *Sense and Sensibility* and Fanny in *Mansfield Park* also subdue themselves by imagining the future marriage between the man they love and his choice, in both cases highly unworthy women. Elinor has a vision of domestic life at Delaford:

> She saw [Edward and Lucy] in an instant in their parsonage-house; saw in Lucy, the active, contriving manager, uniting at once a desire of smart appearance, with the utmost frugality, and ashamed to be suspected of half her economical practices; --pursuing her own interest in every thought, courting the favour of Colonel Brandon, of Mrs. Jennings, and of every wealthy friend. (*SS* 404–5)

Elinor's fancy, however, cannot extend to Edward: "In Edward –she knew not what she saw, nor what she wished to see; happy or unhappy, --nothing pleased her; she turned away her head from every sketch of him" (405). Elinor's turned head follows from the moral quandary she faces, for if he loves Elinor, he should not be happy, and yet she cannot wish for his unhappiness. Picturing Lucy and Edward together is an act of moral chastening for Elinor; by it she practices resigning herself to a future she cannot like but must submit to with grace. Austen makes the same moral point in *Mansfield Park*, when Henry Crawford, visiting Portsmouth, tells Fanny that he looks forward to the company at Thornton Lacey (Henry assumes Edmund and Mary will marry). Fanny reprimands herself: "Fanny . . . could regret that she had not forced herself into the acknowledged comprehension of . . . his meaning, and encouraged him to say something more of his sister and Edmund. It was a subject which she must learn to speak of, and the weakness that shrunk from it would soon be quite unpardonable" (471). Elinor will practice exactly that self-control when, at the end of *Sense and Sensibility*, Edward pays his unexpected visit. She forces herself to ask, as she must, after his wife; this moral exertion leads directly to her reward, learning from Edward that Lucy has married Edward's brother instead.

We know Austen herself was a practiced hand at this sort of moral exertion, imagining what was likely but painful as a means to master vain hopes for the future.  But she also had created a working endorsement for how Christian imagination could create pleasure without taint of moral fault, how novels could be written by a good Christian. We see something of this endorsement in one of her last letters, penned five days before she abandoned *Sanditon*. Austen is writing to her favorite niece, Fanny Knight, who had been writing her aunt letters about the series of young men who were interested in marrying her, each of whom had fallen short in some important way. Austen advises Fanny to wait for true love, but the focus of the letter is a paean to Fanny's imagination. Austen compares her own imagination slightingly to Fanny's: "if I were to labour at it all the rest of my Life & live to the age of Methusalah, I could never accomplish anything so long & so perfect" (*sic; L* 332). (We should note that Austen knows she is dying, and that Methuselah's nine hundred years are not for her). Nonetheless, Fanny's triumph is described in the terms Austen endorsed for her own creative efforts:

> You are all over Imagination. –the most astonishing part of your Character is, that with so much Imagination, so much flight of Mind, such unbounded Fancies, you should have such excellent Judgement in what you do! –Religious Principle I fancy must explain it. --Well, good by & God bless you. (*L* 334)

Judgment and religious principles anchor Fanny's imagination as they anchored Austen's. Judgment and religious principles led Austen's fiction to endorse doing what was right, even when doing so was difficult; the same forces also shaped each novel to reward the exercise of virtue (each of the scenes of self-chastening for her heroines described above leads soon after to scenes of consummate reward). A re-awakened memory of these older concerns may help readers understand how and why imagination was understood to be dangerous, as well as to understand the exact terms by which Austen turned such a parlous enterprise into one in accord with her Christian obligations.

# Coda
# Austen and
# *The Importance of Being Earnest*

"In matters of grave importance, style, not sincerity, is the vital thing"
—*The Importance of Being Earnest* 301

Eighty years after the publication of *Emma* in 1815, another comic masterwork was produced, Oscar Wilde's most popular play, *The Importance of Being Earnest*. It is not to be wondered at that many of Jane Austen's devotées are also admirers of Wilde's comedy. When Austen, with exuberant false modesty, deemed her own *Pride and Prejudice* "too light & bright & sparkling," she lit upon one important reason her work has continued to be popular; in her novels, there are marks of sunny playfulness throughout, even amongst the darker themes and issues, and in each a happy ending is guaranteed (*L* 203). *The Importance of Being Earnest* (1895) seems to inherit Austen's comic spirit, and, like *Emma*, the plot brings three couples into happiness by the narrative's close; the two works, moreover, share a holiday feeling, though the cucumber sandwiches consumed in *Importance* seem to have been eaten in a blither spirit than those ultimately burdensome strawberries collected by Miss Bates, Mrs. Elton, and the others at Mr. Knightley's party at Donwell Abbey. Wilde's comedy, a triumph of wit, also has much in common with Austen's language of irony and her comic trajectories. Further, both *Emma* and *The Importance of Being Earnest* are Menandrine New Comedies; that is, they work within the conventions of romantic comedy as developed by Plautus, Terence, and, later, Shakespeare.[1] The main concern of both plots is matchmaking, and both Austen and Wilde skillfully deploy a full array of blocking devices to keep lovers from each other, until difficulties are removed through revelations of long-held secrets and the deployment of a *deus ex machina*: the turkey thieves at the end of *Emma* and the discovery that Miss Prism's handbag had once held Lady Bracknell's baby nephew in *Importance*. At the close of each work, three happy weddings are to take place.

The parallels extend further. Because each comedy concerns members of the gentry and their rules for admission to their society, each comedy includes the use of the foundling plot to create ironies about social eligibility. In *Emma*, the foundling plot concerns Harriet's unknown parentage; in *Importance*, it revolves around Jack's origin in that handbag. Each also features a secret engagement (Jane and Frank's in *Emma*; Gwendolyn and Jack's in *Importance*). Each uses

---

[1]    The conventions of New Comedy were best set out by Northrop Frye, in his 1957 *Anatomy of Criticism*, pp. 163–86. Other helpful treatments of comic convention include Nelson, esp. 19–57, Galligan, and Herbert.

that staple comic character, the killjoy, whose function is to impede romance and pleasure. In keeping with comic tradition, this figure is a member of the older generation: Mr. Woodhouse in *Emma* and Lady Bracknell in *Importance*. Both works also feature a romantically inclined clergyman, Mr. Elton in *Emma* and Dr. Chasuble in *Importance*, both of whom use a coded language of sexual attraction to express their aims. Mr. Elton has his compliments and his charade, misread by both Harriet and Emma, and Dr. Chasuble relies on *double entendres*, which require him continually to retract his apparent meaning, as when he says, "'Were I fortunate enough to be Miss Prism's pupil, I would hang upon her lips. . . . I spoke metaphorically. –My metaphor was drawn from bees'" (276). Both plots also kill off an inconvenient character we never meet, with both deaths off-stage: Mrs. Churchill's in *Emma* and Ernest's in *Importance* (admittedly, "Ernest" never actually exists, but Jack appears in full mourning dress in the honor of his demise, and we learn that Ernest died both of a sudden chill and that he "exploded"). Austen and Wilde also include two ingénues, expected by all to be best friends but in fact antagonists, Emma and Jane Fairfax on the one hand, and Gwendolen and Cecily on the other.[2] Themes common to both works include social hypocrisy, the nature of marriage, the proper upbringing of young women, the "natural" superiority of the English over the French, questions of inheritance, the nature of a true gentleman, and debates about the proper role of the church in society, of the imagination, and of writers of novels.

For all their shared treatment of plot, character, and theme, however, the worldviews behind these two works are clearly antithetical. It is not too strong to argue that Austen's Christian moral vision has been replaced by Wilde's decadent nihilism. One of the clearest registers of the seismic cultural changes that befell the nineteenth century can, I submit, be found in the foundational viewpoints of these two otherwise so similar comedies. In the happy ending of *Emma*, despite the class rigidity that offends our contemporary democratic spirit and despite the heroine's reliance on her hero which offends our contemporary feminism, we are given a vision of moral, social, and spiritual wholeness. At Wilde's happy

---

[2]    Emma's dislike for Jane Fairfax is founded on jealousy—not romantic jealousy but jealousy of Jane's many virtues, including her accomplishments and her elegance. Wilde shows his awareness of the paradigm of clashing heroines when he has Jack forecast (wrongly): "'Cecily and Gwendolen are perfectly certain to be extremely great friends. I'll bet you anything you like that half an hour after they have met, they will be calling each other sister.'" Algernon corrects Jack: "'Women only do that when they have called each other a lot of other things first'" (271). When Cecily and Gwendolen do meet, they believe each other to be romantic rivals and despite a surface adherence to proper behavior, are at war. The height of incivility comes at the tea table, as Cecily ignores Gwendolen's requests. Gwendolen rises in indignation: "'You have filled my tea with lumps of sugar, and though I asked most distinctly for bread and butter, you have given me cake. I am known for the gentleness of my disposition, and the extraordinary sweetness of my nature, but I warn you, Miss Cardew, you may go too far'" (294). As both Gwendolen and Cecily have already proved themselves tartars, Wilde shows the nastiness under both girls' vapid decorum.

ending, we are left with gaping holes in the social and moral fabric and in the cosmos. It should not surprise that Wilde's play premiered in a theatre dominated by melodramas that subverted bourgeois morality; 1893 saw the production of Pinero's *The Second Mrs. Tanqueray* and Shaw's *Mrs. Warren's Profession*, both plays about a woman's secret past. (It is worth noting that *The Importance of Being Earnest* concerns men's secret pasts, though the play's light touch encourages the audience to excuse all.) 1894 saw Shaw's *Arms and the Man*, an anti-military satire, and Maeterlinck's *The Death of Tintagiles*, a dark symbolist drama. Wilde's paradoxes and amoral aphorisms, while enormously entertaining, show how irony in service of a much darker worldview creates a very different moral message, one in which moral value, "earnestness" as such, has become radically unstable. Austen's earnestness about wit implies a stable moral ground, while Wilde, the inheritor of both Austen's comedy and of nineteenth-century social and moral upheaval, deploys unimpeded wit in the service of a looming nihilism, despite the happy endings he conjures.

As we have seen, Jane Austen takes very seriously the notions of right and wrong. She often sets as her subject the ills that befall those who practice morality operationally, that is, as it suits them. All of her cads, including Frank Churchill in *Emma*, suffer because they try to do as they please, rather than as they ought—even though, admittedly, Frank suffers less than any other of Austen's cads, primarily because he has not actually seduced anyone. Algernon and Jack in Wilde's play are like Frank Churchill, manipulative game-players. As Algernon says, "'I love scrapes. They are the only things that are never serious'" (273). But where Frank is chastened and ultimately apologizes for his immoral behavior, Algernon and Jack frolic on to the end, as Jack finds out that he was "Ernest" all along, proclaiming to Gwendolen, "'it is a terrible thing for a man to find out suddenly that all his life he has been speaking nothing but the truth. Can you forgive me?'" (313). By contrast, Austen's verdict on Frank, rendered through Mr. Knightley, is clear, and is typical of her endorsements of stable morality: "'There is one thing, Emma, which a man can always do, if he chuses, and that is, his duty; not by maneuvering and finessing, but by vigour and resolution. . . . Respect for right conduct is felt by every body'" (158–9).

Austen's deployment of this stable moral vision followed naturally from her Anglican Christianity, which was central to her identity as a person and as a writer. As Chapter 2 shows in detail, her religious commitments were profound and life-long, raised as she was in the Anglican heartland of England, with so many members of the clergy as her closest relatives. Her beliefs about death, sin, forgiveness, mercy, redemption, heaven, and the role of the church were entirely orthodox, as her three prayers written for family worship in the evening amply demonstrate. Despite her propensity not only for irony but also for malice, she believed that religious principles should guide all conduct, and that everyday exertion (the word for her almost always had a religious connotation) was the best way of doing one's duty to God and one's "fellow-creatures" (the phrase "fellow-creatures" appears five times in her prayers). She knew that particular circumstances could often affect the moral choices one made, but was equally sure that there was in every situation, no matter how delicate and perplexing, a right road of conduct, if conscientiously pursued. These foundational ideas inform all her fiction, and the didactic nature of her authorial judgment and dispensation of poetic judgment confirm them.

Wilde's play offers very different ideals. In fact, it offers no ideals at all, except its paradoxical commitment to doing without them. As Wilde himself noted, "it has its philosophy . . . that we should treat all the trivial things of life seriously, and all the serious things of life with sincere and studied triviality" (Hart-Davis 196). The most pressing concerns in the play are eating cucumber sandwiches and muffins, and marrying for money and for the most surface attractions. For instance, curly hair, the surname "Ernest," and a reputation for wickedness are all that are required to win Cecily's devotion to Algernon, and we learn that months before she actually meets him, she has written in her diary of their mutual love, his proposal, their engagement, their first lovers' quarrel, and their renewed commitment to wed (this history is, of course, all news to Algernon, who nonetheless is even more ardently interested in Cecily after she tells him what is in her diary and after she has thus been confirmed to him as a pretty but delusional egoist).[3] Those muffins and cucumber sandwiches also expose the moral rottenness of our protagonists, for any and all low deceits are deployed to gain them. For instance, in Act I, Algernon manages to eat the entire tray of cucumber sandwiches, leaving none for anyone else, and suborning his butler to lie on his behalf, who must tell Lady Bracknell: "'there were no cucumbers in the market this morning . . . not for ready money'" (261). In Act III, the heroes chomp through all the muffins after the young women have gone off in a huff; in keeping with the play's topsy-turvy values, Gwendolen watches their piggery through the window and posits, "'They have been eating muffins. That looks like repentance'" (300).[4]

The main plot follows from the idea of Bunburying. To "Bunbury" is to pretend that one has another private obligation in another place, so that one can absent oneself from one's obligations whenever one wants. Algernon has an ill friend (who doesn't exist), "Mr. Bunbury," and Algernon has a wicked younger brother, Ernest, who also doesn't exist. Such an escape valve is lauded as essential to modern life; as Algernon says, "'The man who marries without knowing Bunbury

---

[3]    A very similar moment occurs in *Emma* when we learn our heroine had been intrigued by Frank Churchill long before she met him: "There was something in the name, in the idea of Mr. Frank Churchill, which always interested her. . . . He seemed by this connection between the families, quite to belong to her" (128). Of course, Austen means the reader to see the self-serving and unrealistic elements in these musings.

[4]    When Austen uses the term "repentance," she does so with the usual weight of religious significance. For instance, Jane Fairfax breaks her engagement with Frank Churchill, and Frank relates her language, "*She felt the engagement to be a source of repentance and misery to each*" (481; italics in original). The two instances in which the term is used in *Sense and Sensibility* both refer to Willoughby's heartfelt sorrow at his behavior and at losing Marianne.

has a very tedious time of it'" (260).[5] In keeping with the amoral climate of the play, it turns out that no one is in fact much fooled by these elaborate schemes. Lady Bracknell, for instance, tells Algernon that "'I should be much obliged if you would ask Mr. Bunbury, from me, to be kind enough not to have a relapse on Saturday, for I rely on you to arrange my music for me'" (262). In fact, the play shows that no one expects goodness or even the most basic virtue from each other. The very first exchange of the play establishes its moral compass, as we find Algernon asking his butler about some missing champagne:

> ALGERNON: By the way, Lane, I see from your book that on Thursday night, when Lord Shoreman and Mr. Worthing were dining with me, eight bottles of champagne are entered as having been consumed.
>
> LANE: Yes, sir: eight bottles and a pint.
>
> ALGERNON: Why is it that at a bachelor's establishment the servants invariably drink the champagne? I ask merely for information.
>
> LANE: I attribute it to the superior quality of the wine, sir. I have often observed that in married households the champagne is rarely of a first-rate brand. (253)

Algernon assumes his butler is a thief and his butler assumes that Algernon will put up with his thievery. Wilde's characters barely rate the term "hypocrites," so forward are they with their own lack of moral values. In fact, the starkest accusation of wrongdoing comes when Cecily accuses Algernon of deception: "'I hope you have not been leading a double life, pretending to be wicked and being really good all the time. That would be hypocrisy'" (277).

The most serious concerns, on the other hand, such as marriage, death, religion, and sin are treated with witty indifference. That exchange between Lane and Algernon about the champagne is immediately followed by Algernon's exclamation: "'Good heavens! Is marriage so demoralizing as that?'" Lane replies, "'I have had very little experience of it myself up to the present. I have only been married once. That was in consequence of a misunderstanding between myself and a young person'" (253). The death of a woman's husband receives similar treatment, as Lady Bracknell tells us of "dear Lady Harbury": "'I hadn't been there since her poor husband's death. I never saw a woman so altered; she looks quite twenty years younger'" (261); Algernon pipes in that "'I hear her

---

5  Since the resurrection of Wilde's play in the 1940s (it had been off the stage since its hurried closure following Wilde's arrest in 1895), there has been speculation that "Bunburying" is a trope for homosexual behavior, and given Wilde's semi-secret practice of homosexuality even as he was married and the father of two small boys, the idea seems plausible. The fullest treatment of this hypothesis can be found in Timothy D'Arch Smith. However, both Sir Donald Sindon, who knew the original actors of *Importance*, and Sir John Gielgud, himself gay, who had played Algernon and who had a comprehensive knowledge of the play's history, strongly dispute this reading (Sindon).

hair has turned quite gold from grief'" (261). The sacrament of baptism offers a particularly broad target for comedy, since both heroes need to change their names to "Ernest" to satisfy their irredeemably shallow fiancées. In one of the most juvenile and entertaining moments of the play, Jack arranges with Dr. Chasuble for an emergency baptism. Asked if he has "'grave doubts'" about whether he has been christened before ("grave doubts" is the exact ecclesiastical term for what would be necessary to legitimate an adult baptism of this sort), Jack replies, "'I certainly intend to have'" and declares his willingness to "'trot round about five'" (281). However, he refuses to be baptized at the same time as two infant twins of the parish, proclaiming, "'Oh! I don't see much fun in being christened along with other babies. It would be childish'" (282). Likewise, the trauma of unwed motherhood, that staple of Victorian melodrama, is here given the broadest comic treatment. Believing that he is Miss Prism's lost illegitimate child, Jack bursts into a litany of clichés: "'Unmarried! I do not deny that is a serious blow. But after all, who has the right to cast a stone against one who has suffered? Cannot repentance wipe out an act of folly? Why should there be one law for man and another for woman? Mother, I forgive you!'" (311). Not one of these expressions can be taken seriously, mostly because they come in a pre-digested flood. The pieties about women's sexual transgressions come from the tradition of earnestness, and are thus there to be mocked.

This tradition of "earnestness" and its emptying out through Wilde's relentless insouciance are a key measure of the cultural shifts between Austen and Wilde. For Austen, the word "earnestness" always means moral seriousness, and she uses it at key points to lend gravity to her narrative. It is with "earnestness" that Mr. Knightley proposes (*E* 468), "earnestly" that Henry Tilney questions Catherine about her suspicions about his mother's death (*NA* 201), and with "gentle earnestness" that Fanny seconds Edmund's defense of the Church (*MP* 109). The word's meaning was tied up with the evangelical reforms of the 1790s and thereafter; "earnestness" became a hallmark of Anglican Evangelicalism in its attempts to re-infuse the Church and its practices with devotional vigor, as discussed in Chapter 1. By 1800, earnestness was firmly connected to authentic and vigorous religious practice, the emerging and powerful new commitment of the English middle class.

By the 1830s, earnestness was a broad and deep social requirement, expected of religious and non-religious people alike. It was popularized by prominent early Victorians such as Thomas Carlyle and Thomas Arnold, the famous headmaster of Rugby and Matthew Arnold's father (Houghton 218–21). "Earnestness" was a frame of mind, in which the spiritual and epochal nature of human existence was held keenly in view, and in which high moral seriousness dominated. Longfellow's 1838 poem voiced the era's preoccupations:

> Life is real! Life is earnest!
> And the grave is not its goal;
> Dust, thou art, to dust returnest,
> Was not spoken of the soul.
> ("A Psalm of Life, ll. 5–9)

Earnestness marked those who were religious, but also those, like George Eliot and Matthew Arnold, who had lost religion and embraced moral urgencies in the stead of faith. Not to be earnest for the Victorians was a grave sin, even if one was earnest only to promote correct spelling or to enact dress reform. By the time Samuel Butler wrote his withering satire on Victorian upbringing, *The Way of All Flesh*, between 1873 and 1884, the connection between earnestness and the dreariness of religious and non-religious seriousness was well-worn. His hero's christening in 1835 (thus roughly 40 years before the novel was written) is explained thus:

> Theobald [his father] had proposed to call him George after old Mr. Pontifex, but strange to say, Mr. Pontifex overruled him in favour of the name Ernest. The word 'earnest' was just beginning to come into fashion, and he thought the possession of such a name might, like his having been baptized in water from the Jordan, have a permanent effect upon the boy's character, and influence him for good during the more critical periods of his life. (106; qtd. in Houghton 218)

Butler thus precedes Wilde in his mockery of the idea that a name could confer actual value; Ernest Pontifex, Butler's anti-hero, will become a confirmed anti-bourgeois and rebellious figure.

By 1895, therefore, Wilde's treatment of the name and the cultural phenomenon it came to represent constitutes one last piling-on onto those hapless and humorless do-gooders, the generations of Wilde's parents and grandparents. As with young Ernest Pontifex, the name "Ernest" is presumed to have magical qualities. However, Wilde takes the satire a step further. The name "Ernest" does not make a man more virtuous; rather, in Wilde's farce, the name is entirely an end in itself. Gwendolen muses on its perfections:

> 'We live, as I hope you know, Mr. Worthing, in an age of ideals. The fact is constantly mentioned in the more expensive monthly magazines, and has reached the provincial pulpits, I am told and my ideal has always been to love someone of the name of Ernest. There is something in that name that inspires absolute confidence.' (263)

In Act II, Cecily will say almost the same thing to Algernon: "'There is something in that name that seems to inspire absolute confidence'" (288). Neither Gwendolen nor Cecily will consider loving or marrying a man not named Ernest, and thus the need emerges for our heroes to be christened (or re-christened, a rather shameful breach of the sacrament of baptism).

Wilde's attack on earnestness and moral responsibility sharpens in his treatment of the Church. While the plot hinges on a Christian ceremony, the play takes place in a post-Christian world. The secular dominates the play. Algernon's view is typical: "'the accounts I have heard . . . of the next world are not particularly encouraging. This world is good enough for me'" (278). The clergyman, Dr. Chasuble, really belongs to that breed of eighteenth-century clerics the Evangelicals had attacked, a breed stolidly in place before earnestness and evangelical vigor ever came to the fore, and a figure far more like those worthy divines, Mr. Collins or Dr. Grant. Though his name ("chasuble") denotes the outer garment worn by priests during the administration of communion, Dr. Chasuble is not particularly pious. He is instead a worldly man, interested more in the scholarship of arcana than in spiritual values (we learn he has four unpublished essays on the Anabaptists [308]). The titillating *double entendres* he trades with Miss Prism prepare us for his ultimate yielding to her desire that he marry her. When he tells of his favorite sermon, it becomes plain he comes from that line of eighteenth-century divines described in Chapter 1, who re-used the same sermons, ate well at table, and pandered to their patrons in the gentry:

> 'My sermon on the meaning of the manna in the wilderness can be adapted to almost any occasion, joyful, or as in the present case, distressing. I have preached it at harvest celebrations, christenings, confirmations, on days of humiliation and festal days. The last time I delivered it was in the Cathedral, as a charity sermon on behalf of the Society for the Prevention of Discontent among the Upper Orders.' (280–81)

Miss Prism, Dr. Chasuble's confederate in the education of the young, is something of a Calvinist, doctrinaire and interested in punishment. As she says of Algernon, "'I am not in favour of this modern mania for turning bad people into good people at a moment's notice. As a man sows so let him reap'" (275). Her moral judgmentalism exists only to be mocked. Miss Prism, incidentally, is trying to teach young Cecily political economics, geology, and German. It can be no accident that all three fields played a significant role in the diminishment of Christian practice and belief in the nineteenth century, through Marx and Engels (for political economy); through Lyell (for geology; it was his *Principles of Geology* of 1830–1833 that most dismantled the Creation accounts of *Genesis*); and through the German higher criticism of Biblical texts, in which scholars such as Feuerbach, Strauss, and Schleiermacher raised significant doubts about the provenance and reliability of both Old and New Testament texts. Those "grave doubts" I referenced before as legitimating a second baptism also emerge as a theme in the play, since, historically, "grave doubts" about Christianity most reversed its social power to exert moral control. In Act III, Algernon and Jack are interrogated by Gwendolen and Cecily about why they have created such a web of elaborate deceit. Both heroines are told that the deceit occurred only in the service of wooing them. Neither believes her man, but both intend to act as if they do; as Cecily says, not believing Algernon "'does not affect the wonderful beauty of his answer'" (301). This question of belief is made explicitly to parallel the problem of Christian faith in the nineteenth century, to comic effect. Speaking of her "grave doubts" that Jack is telling the truth, Gwendolen argues that "'I intend to crush them. This is not the moment for German skepticism'" (301). The joke is that skepticism is only welcome when it undermines Christian orthodoxy; it is less welcome when it hampers self-centered actors from doing as they please.

The key means by which Wilde establishes his moral vacuum is through his reliance on the witty aphorism or epigram that turns conventional morality on its head. Like Austen, Wilde deploys a battery of wit through rhetorical figures—zeugmas, puns, oxymoron, aphorisms, and paradox. His aphorisms, such as "'in married life three is company and two is none'" (260), "'It is awfully hard work doing nothing'" (271), and "'the two weak points in our age are its want of principle and its want of profile'" (305), make plain that while there may be occasional lip service to morality in this Wildean universe, no one actually abides by moral requirements or expects anyone else to. Lady Bracknell's exclamations on learning that Cecily has a fortune of 130,000 pounds are emblematic in this regard: "'Miss Cardew seems to me a most attractive young lady, now that I look at her. Few girls of the present day have any really solid qualities, any of the qualities that last, and improve with time. We live, I regret to say, in an age of surfaces'" (304).

Certainly Austen's aphorisms often include an ironic punch, as in the opening sentence of *Pride or Prejudice*, or in her assurance to the reader, on introducing Mrs. Elton, that "[h]uman nature is so well disposed towards those who are interesting situations, that a young person, who either marries or dies, is sure of being kindly spoken of" (*E* 194). However, Austen's ironies are in the service of correcting social hypocrisies, not underwriting them. For instance, when Lady Bracknell speaks against long engagements ("'They give people the opportunity of finding out each other's characters before marriage, which I think is never advisable'" [305]), she is plainly echoing the sentiments of Charlotte Lucas in *Pride and Prejudice*: "'it is better to know as little as possible of the defects of person with whom you are to pass your life'" (25). But when Elizabeth counters, "'You make me laugh Charlotte; but is it not sound. You know it is not sound, and that you would never act in this way yourself'" (25), we know Austen firmly endorses Elizabeth's point of view. It is not sound. Charlotte does indeed later make the ethically wrong but economically savvy choice to marry Mr. Collins, but we know it is wrong, even though Charlotte finds ways to be happier in her married state than one might expect. Conversely, in Wilde's world, Lady Bracknell's advice is the merest good sense, since there are no good characters ever to be found out by examination during an engagement, and, in truth, there are no deeper layers to any character at all beyond impulse, appetite, and self-aggrandizement.

Certainly, Wilde's day initiated readings of Austen herself that precluded interest in Austen's own earnestness or her investment in orthodox morality. Early Janeites, including Wilde himself, instead revered her wit and her creation of character.[6] As Claudia Johnson explains, the late nineteenth-century and early

---

6    Wilde mentions Austen two times in his letters, once when in prison he thinks of donating her works to the prison library for the "poor imprisoned fellows I live with," and once in his final years in exile, writing to his most faithful friend, Robert Ross, that "'Your letter is very maddening: nothing about yourself: no details, and you know I love middle-class tragedies and the little squabbles that build up family life in England. I have had delightful letters from you quite in the style of Jane Austen'" (Fullerton). Wilde's linking of Austen with "delight," "details," "squabbles," "family life," and "middle-class tragedies" cast a fully Janeite view on her works; "middle-class tragedies," we learn from *Importance* and from *The Picture of Dorian Gray*, denote marriages.

twentieth-century fans of Austen, worldly men themselves and, like Wilde, devoted dismantlers of Victorian earnestness and sobriety, preferred to ignore plot, especially the marriage plot, and instead dwelt on "atemporal aspects of narration, descriptive details, catchy phrases, and, especially, characterization" ("The Divine Miss Jane" 32). In particular, early Janeites enjoyed talking about Austen's characters as if they were real people, free to be imagined roaming into other Austen works rather than their own or even into a Janeite's drawing room.[7] In 1884, the year before *Importance* had its premiere, Lord Brabourne gave voice to exactly this form of appreciating Austen, writing, "I frankly confess that I could never endure Mr. Knightley . . . I always wanted Emma to marry Frank Churchill" (Lodge *Jane Austen* 59). Mr. Knightley falls short, Lord Brabourne explains, because he is too morally upright, "too respectable . . . to be a hero" (60). Moral earnestness like Mr. Knightley's is suspect, but Brabourne can so dislodge Emma from her novel and its values as to imagine her running away "with somebody possessed of an inferior intellect, but more enduring qualities" (60). Thus, by 1884 one of Austen's most important admirers (and one of her descendents) preferred to think of Emma as someone who could have no particular respect for marriage vows and who could be led entirely by considerations of pleasure. In other words, the Emma Brabourne prefers has values more in common with Wilde's Algernon and Jack than with the Emma Austen created. The late-nineteenth century flight from earnestness was indeed in full gallop.

Ultimately, however, Wilde himself knew that the backlash against moral value, however pleasurable and tempting, had to be temporary. Wilde is playing a double game with his treatment of morality in this play, as he does in his novel *The Picture of Dorian Gray*, written only a few months later. On the surface, both works explore and applaud the aesthete's commitment to pleasure, momentary sensation, and beauty; each also shows the empty heart left at the close of such commitments. For Dorian, the ending is the Faustian dénouement—death, and a lost soul. For the lovers in *The Importance of Being Earnest*, the ending's poetic justice is closest to the ending of Sartre's *No Exit*: "hell is other people." In some ways, *Importance* belongs morally to the worldview of Wilde's *Salomé*, written two years before *Importance*, a play that depicts what happens to a person whose only commitment is to beauty and self. After Salomé gains the head of John the Baptist, so that she can give the Baptist the French kiss he had refused her while alive, even the monster Herod can no longer stand her evil: "'Kill that woman,'" he instructs his guards in the final line of the play (348). We should not

---

[7]    William Galperin traces this way of reading Austen's novels as being primarily about characters who may be imagined as distinct from their texts to the 1852 essay on Austen in the *New Monthly Magazine*: "where mid-century readers depart from their earlier counterparts is in the tendency to transform a reality-effect, which earlier readers understood to be more an intervention than a transcription, into a real world shorn of all naturalizing props or techniques" ("Austen's Earliest Readers" 110). See also Tuite, "Decadent Austen Entails," on the reception and use of *Sanditon* by James, Forster, Ronald Firbank, and Ivy Compton-Burnett, for a different form of Austenian inheritance.

be surprised to learn that Wilde converted to Catholicism on his deathbed in Paris; his ultimate commitment rejected the pleasurable insincerity he both championed and mocked. Wilde's nihilism in *Importance* follows therefore in the long line of satiric exposure; it exposes the empty heart at the center of late nineteenth-century life, though it seems in itself to have no remedy in view. The moral that garnishes the end is one last joke on moral value and on religious seriousness. When Lady Bracknell admonishes Jack on the score of "'displaying signs of triviality,'" he exults in return (and this is the famous last line of the play), "'On the contrary, Aunt Augusta, I've now realized for the first time in my life the vital Importance of Being Earnest'" (313). The stage directions that follow call for a "TABLEAU," and then a "CURTAIN"—a just verdict on the characters, left forever into the frozen world of witty heartlessness.

For Austen, in *Emma*, the final tableau follows a religious ceremony, and is composed of "perfect happiness," the prediction made by those whose hearts are in the right place. Mrs. Elton has been specifically excluded from the final scene— she is a malign witness only by hearsay, sneering at reports from her husband about the wedding's lack of finery. She is firmly overruled by the narrator, whose language does not, here, admit irony, whose language is in fact, I would suggest, "earnest": "the wishes, the hopes, the confidence, the predictions of the small band of true friends who witnessed the ceremony, were fully answered in the perfect happiness of the union" (528).

# Bibliography

Abbey, Charles, and John Overton. *The English Church in the Eighteenth Century.* 2 vols. London: Longman, Green, 1878.

Addison, Joseph, and Richard Steele. *The Spectator.* Ed. Donald Bond. 5 vols. Oxford: OUP, 1965.

Allchin, A. M. "Anglican Spirituality." *The Study of Anglicanism.* Eds Stephen Sykes and John Booty. London: SPCK, 1988. 313–25.

Amis, Kingsley. "What Became of Jane Austen?" *Spectator* 199 (1957): 440.

Armstrong, Nancy. *How Novels Think: The Limits of British Individualism from 1719–1900.* NY: Columbia UP, 2005.

Aristotle. *De animalibus historia. The Complete Works of Aristotle.* Ed. Jonathan Barnes. 2 vols. Princeton: Princeton UP, 1984. 486a.

Ashton, Helen. *Parson Austen's Daughter.* London: Collins, 1949.

Auerbach, Emily. "The Geese Vs. the 'Niminy Piminy' Spinster: Virginia Woolf Defends Austen." *Persuasions On-line* 29.1 (2008). http://www.jasna.org/persuasions/on-line/vol29no1/auerbach.html.

Augustine of Hippo. *The City of God.* [c. 415]. Trans. Marcus Dods. NY: Modern Library, 1950.

Austen, Caroline. *My Aunt Jane Austen: A Memoir.* London: [Jane Austen Society], 1952.

Austen, George. 'Memorandum for the Use [of] Mr F. W. Austen on his Going to the East Indies Midshipman on Board his Majesty's Ship Perseverance Cap: Smith Decr 1788' (unpublished ms).

Austen, Henry. "Biographical Notice of the Author." *Northanger Abbey* and *Persuasion. The Works of Jane Austen.* Vol. V. Ed. R. W. Chapman. 3rd edn. Oxford: OUP, 1953, rev. 1963, 1986. 3–9.

———. *Lectures on Some Important Passages in the Book of Genesis: Delivered in the Chapel of the British Minister of Berlin, in the Year 1818.* London: printed for J. Hatchert and Son, 1820.

Austen, James. "Venta, within thy Sacred Fane." *The Poetry of Jane Austen and the Austen Family.* Ed. David Selwyn. Iowa City: U of Iowa P, 1997. 48–50.

Austen, Jane. *Emma.* Eds Richard Cronin and Dorothy McMillan. *The Cambridge Edition of the Works of Jane Austen.* Cambridge: CUP, 2005.

———. *The History of England.* [1791]. Chapel Hill: Algonquin Books, 1993.

———. *Jane Austen's Letters.* Ed. Deirdre Le Faye. 3rd edn. Oxford: OUP, 1995.

———. *Juvenilia.* Ed. Peter Sabor. *The Cambridge Edition of the Works of Jane Austen.* Cambridge: CUP, 2006.

———. *Later Manuscripts.* Eds Janet Todd and Linda Bree. *The Cambridge Edition of the Works of Jane Austen.* Cambridge: CUP, 2008.

————. *Mansfield Park*. Ed. John Wiltshire. *The Cambridge Edition of the Works of Jane Austen*. Cambridge: CUP, 2005.

————. *Minor Works. The Works of Jane Austen*. Ed. R. W. Chapman. Vol. VI. 3rd edn. Oxford: OUP, 1953, rev. 1963, 1986.

————. *Northanger Abbey*. Eds Barbara M. Benedict and Deirdre Le Faye. *The Cambridge Edition of the Works of Jane Austen*. Cambridge: CUP, 2006.

————. *The Novels of Jane Austen*. Ed. R. W. Chapman. 3rd ed. 5 vols. Oxford: OUP, 1933–69.

————. *Persuasion*. Eds Janet Todd and Antje Blank. *The Cambridge Edition of the Works of Jane Austen*. Cambridge: CUP, 2006.

————. "Prayers Composed by my ever dear Sister." Manuscripts (two quarto sheets). The Elinor Raas Heller Rare Book Room, Mills College, Oakland, California.

————. *Pride and Prejudice*. Ed. Pat Rogers. *The Cambridge Edition of the Works of Jane Austen*. Cambridge: CUP, 2006.

————. *Sense and Sensibility*. Ed. Edward Copeland. *The Cambridge Edition of the Works of Jane Austen*. Cambridge: CUP, 2006.

Austen-Leigh, James. *A Memoir of Jane Austen*. Oxford: Clarendon P, 1926.

Austen-Leigh, Mary. *Personal Aspects of Jane Austen*. NY: E. P. Dutton and Company, 1920.

Austen-Leigh, William, and Richard Arthur Austen-Leigh. *Jane Austen, Her Life and Letters: A Family Record*. London: Smith, Elder, 1913.

Babb, Howard. *Jane Austen's Novels: The Fabric of Dialogue*. Columbus: Ohio State UP, 1962.

Bailey, Richard. *Images of English: A Cultural History of the Language*. Ann Arbor: U of Michigan P, 1991.

Barrell, John. *English Literature in History: 1730–1780*. London: Hutchinson, 1983.

Best, G. F. A. *Temporal Pillars: Queen Anne's Bounty, the Ecclesiastical Commissioners, and the Church of England*. Cambridge: CUP, 1964.

Bewick, Thomas. *History of British Birds. Vol. I. Containing the History and Description of Land Birds*. Newcastle, 1797.

Bogel, Fredric. *Literature and Insubstantiality in Later Eighteenth-Century England*. Princeton: Princeton UP, 1984.

*The Book of Common Prayer, and Administration of the Sacraments, and Other Rites and Ceremonies of the Church, According to the Use of the Church of England: Together with the Psalter or Psalms of David. The Church of England*. 1662. http://www.eskimo.com/~lhowell/bcp1662/index.html. Accessed September 2007–present.

*The Book of Common Prayer, and Administration of the Sacraments, and Other Rites and Ceremonies of the Church, According to the Use of the Church of England: Together with the Psalter or Psalms of David*. [1662]. NY: Henry Holt and Co., 1992.

Booth, Wayne. *The Company We Keep: An Ethics of Fiction*. Berkeley: U of California P, 1988.

———. *The Rhetoric of Fiction*. 2nd ed. Chicago: U of Chicago P, 1983.

———. *A Rhetoric of Irony*. Chicago: U of Chicago P, 1974.

Boswell, James. *Life of Johnson*. [1791]. Ware, Hertfordshire: Wordsworth Editions, 1999.

Bourdieu, Pierre. *Distinction: A Social Critique of the Judgement of Taste*. Trans. Richard Nice. Cambridge: Harvard UP, 1984.

Bradbrook, Frank. *Jane Austen and her Predecessors*. Cambridge: CUP, 1966.

Bronson, B. H. "Personification Reconsidered." *ELH* 14 (1947): 160–73.

Brown, Colin. *Christianity and Western Thought: A History of Philosophers, Ideas and Movements*. Vol. I. Downers Grove, Ill.: InterVarsity P, 1990.

Brown, Ford K. *Fathers of the Victorians: The Age of Wilberforce*. Cambridge: CUP, 1961.

Burke, Kenneth. *The Rhetoric of Religion: Studies in Logology*. Berkeley: U of California P, 1970.

Burton, Robert. *The Anatomy of Melancholy*. 5 vols. Eds Thomas Faulkner, Nicolas Kiessling, and Rhonda L. Blair. Oxford: Clarendon P, 1994.

Butler, Joseph. "On the Nature of Virtue." [1736]. *Sermons*. NY: Robert Carter and Bros., 1858.

Butler, Marilyn. "History, Politics, and Religion." *The Jane Austen Companion*. Ed. J. David Grey. NY: Macmillan, 1986. 190–208.

———. *Jane Austen and the War of Ideas*. Oxford: Clarendon P, 1975.

———. "The Purple Turban and the Flowering Aloe Tree: Signs of Distinction in the Early-Nineteenth-Century Novel." *Modern Language Quarterly* 58.4 (1997): 475–95.

Butler, Perry. "The History of Anglicanism from the Early Eighteenth Century to the Present Day." *The Study of Anglicanism*. Eds Stephen Sykes and John Booty. London: SPCK, 1988. 28–47.

Butler, Samuel. *The Way of All Flesh*. [1903]. NY: Modern Library, 1950.

Bynum, William. "*The Great Chain of Being* after Forty Years: An Appraisal." *History of Science* 8 (1975): 1–28.

Campbell, Colin. *The Romantic Ethic and the Spirit of Modern Consumerism*. Oxford: Blackwell, 1987.

Carroll, John J. "On Annotating *Clarissa*." In *Editing Eighteenth-Century Novels: Papers on Fielding, Lesage, Richardson, Sterne, and Smollett*. Ed. G. E. Bentley. Toronto: published for the Committee for the Conference on Editorial Problems by A. M. Hakkert, 1975. 137–52.

Caruth, Cathy. *Empirical Truth and Critical Fictions: Locke, Wordsworth, Kant, Freud*. Baltimore: Johns Hopkins UP, 1991.

Chapman, R. W. "Jane Austen's Friend Mrs. Barrett." *Nineteenth-Century Fiction* 4.3 (1949): 171–4.

Chapone, [Mrs.] and Thomas Gisborne. *Letters on the Improvement of the Mind*. 1773. *Female Education in the Age of Enlightenment*. Vol. II. London: William Pickering, 1996.

Charity, A. C. *Events and Their Afterlife: The Dialectics of Christian Typology*. [1966.] Cambridge: CUP, 1987.

Chesterfield, Philip Dormer Stanhope, Earl of. *Letters Written by the Late Honorable Philip Dormer Stanhope, Earl of Chesterfield, to his Son, Philip Stanhope.* Vol. I. Dublin: printed for E. Lynch, W. Whitestone, J. Williams, W. Colles, and W. Wilson: 1774.

Clark, J. C. D. *English Society, 1688–1832: Ideology, Social Structure, and Political Practice.* [1985]. Cambridge: CUP, 2000.

Coleridge, Samuel Taylor. *Biographia Literaria. The Collected Works of Samuel Taylor Coleridge.* [1816]. Vol. VII. Eds James Engell and W. Jackson Bate. Princeton: Princeton UP, 1983.

———. *On the Constitution of the Church and State According to the Idea of Each.* [1830.] London: W. Pickering, 1837.

Collins, Irene. "Displeasing Pictures of Clergymen." *Persuasions* 18 (1996): 109–19.

———. *Jane Austen and the Clergy.* London and Rio Grande: Hambledon, 1994.

———. *Jane Austen: A Parson's Daughter.* London: Hambledon, 1998.

———. "The Rev. Henry Tilney, Rector of Woodston." *Persuasions* 20 (1998): 154–64.

Cowper, William. "Charity." *Poems by William Cowper in two volumes.* Vol. I. London: printed for J. Johnson, 1787. 185–218.

———. "Conversation." *Poems by William Cowper in two volumes.* Vol. I. London: printed for J. Johnson, 1787. 219-67.

———. "On the Receipt of my Mother's Picture Out of Norfolk." *Poems by William Cowper in two volumes.* Vol I. London: printed for J. Johnson, 1798. 317–22.

———. *The Task, a poem, in six books.* London: printed for J. Johnson, 1785.

Crabb, George. *English Synonymes.* [1816]. NY and London: Harper and Brothers, 1831.

Cuming, G. J. *A History of Anglican Liturgy.* NY: St. Martin's P, 1969.

Dabundo, Laura. "The Devil and Jane Austen: Elizabeth Bennet's Temptations in the Wilderness." *Persuasions* 21 (1999): 53–8.

Damrosch, Leopold, Jr. *God's Plot and Man's Stories: Studies in the Fictional Imagination from Milton to Fielding.* Chicago: U of Chicago P, 1986.

———. "The Redemption of the World: The Rhetoric of Jane Austen's Prayers." *Persuasions* 27 (2005): 424–51.

Daston, Lorraine and Michael Stolleis, eds. *Nature, Law, and Natural Law in Early-Modern Europe: Jurisprudence, Theology, Moral and Natural Philosophy.* London: Ashgate, 2008.

Defoe, Daniel. *Serious Reflections during the Life and Surprising Adventures of Robinson Crusoe: With his Vision of the Angelick World.* London: printed for W. Taylor, 1720.

Derham, William. *Astro-theology or, a Demonstration of the Being and Attributes of God, from a Survey of the Heavens.* [1714]. London: printed by William and John Innys, 1726.

Dillard, Annie. *Holy the Firm.* [1977]. NY: Harper, 1988.

Doody, Margaret Anne. *The Daring Muse: Augustan Poetry Reconsidered.* Cambridge: CUP, 1985.

———. "Jane Austen's Reading." *The Jane Austen Companion.* Eds J. David Grey, A. Walton Litz, and Brian Southam. London: Macmillan, 1986. 347–63.

Donovan, Robert Alan. "The Mind of Jane Austen." In *Jane Austen Today.* Ed. Joel Weinsheimer. Athens: U of Georgia P, 1975. 109–27.

Duckworth, Alistair M. *The Improvement of the Estate: A Study of Jane Austen's Novels.* Baltimore: The Johns Hopkins UP, 1971.

———. "'Spillikins, paper ships, riddles, conundrums, and cards': Games in Jane Austen's Life and Fiction." *Jane Austen: Bicentenary Essays.* Ed. John Halperin. Cambridge: CUP, 1975. 279–97.

Duffy, Joseph M., Jr. "Moral Integrity and Moral Anarchy in *Mansfield Park.*" *ELH* 23 (1956): 71–91.

Edgeworth, Maria. *Belinda.* [1801]. Ed. Kathryn Kirkpatrick. Oxford: OUP, 2008.

Elmen, Paul. "Anglican Morality." *The Study of Anglicanism.* Eds Stephen Sykes and John Booty. London: SPCK, 1988. 325–38.

Emsley, Sarah. *Jane Austen's Philosophy of the Virtues.* London: Palgrave Macmillan, 2005.

———. "Laughing at Our Neighbors: Jane Austen and the Problem of Charity." *Persuasions On-Line* 26.1 (2004). http://www.jasna.org/persuasions/on-line/vol26no1/emsley.htm. Accessed December 2, 2009.

"England's Christian Heritage." http://www.englandschristianheritage.org.uk. Accessed February 8, 2008.

Fairchild, Hoxie Neale. *Religious Trends in English Poetry.* 2 vols. NY: Columbia UP, 1939–68.

Farrer, Reginald. "Jane Austen, *ob.* July 18, 1817." *The Quarterly Review* 228, no. 452 (July 1917): 1–30.

Fergus, Jan. *Jane Austen and the Didactic Novel*: Northanger Abbey, Sense and Sensibility, *and* Pride and Prejudice. Totowa, NJ: Barnes and Noble, 1983.

Fish, Stanley. *Is There a Text in This Class? The Authority of Interpretive Communities.* Cambridge: Harvard UP, 1980.

Fleishman, Avrom. *A Reading of* Mansfield Park*: An Essay in Critical Synthesis.* Minneapolis: U of Minnesota P, 1967.

Flynn, Carol Houlihan. "The Letters." *The Cambridge Companion to Jane Austen.* Eds Edward Copeland and Juliet McMaster. Cambridge: CUP, 1997. 110–14.

Fordyce, James. *Sermons to Young Women.* [1765]. 2 vols. Dublin: Campbell and Shea, 1796.

Formigari, Lia. "Chain of Being." *The Dictionary of the History of Ideas.* http://etext.lib.virginia.edu/cgo-local/DHI/dhi.cgi?id=dv1-45. Accessed November, 2008.

Forster, E. M. "Jane Austen: Letters." *Abinger Harvest.* NY: Harcourt, Brace & World, 1964. 155–64.

Fott, David. "Prudence and Persuasion: Jane Austen on Virtue in Democratizing Eras." *Lamar Journal of the Humanities* 24.1 (1999): 17–32.

Frei, Hans W. *The Eclipse of Biblical Narrative: A Study in Eighteenth- and Nineteenth-Century Hermeneutics*. New Haven: Yale UP, 1974.

Frye, Northrop. *Anatomy of Criticism*. Princeton: Princeton UP, 1957.

———. "Towards Defining an Age of Sensibility." *Eighteenth-Century English Literature: Modern Essays in Criticism*. Ed. James L. Clifford. NY: OUP, 1959. 310–31.

Fullerton, Susannah. "Austen Citing: Oscar Wilde." Jane Austen Society of Australia. http://www.jasa.net.au/austencitings/wilde.htm. Accessed August 4, 2008.

Galligan, Edward. *The Comic Vision in Literature*. Athens: U of Georgia P, 1984.

Galperin, William. "Austen's Earliest Readers and the Rise of the Janeites." *Janeites: Austen's Disciples and Devotees*. Ed. Deidre Lynch. Princeton: Princeton UP, 2000. 87–114.

———. "'Describing What Never Happened': Jane Austen and the History of Missed Opportunities." *ELH* 73.2 (2006): 355–82.

———. *The Historical Austen*. Philadelphia: U of Pennsylvania P, 2003.

Giffin, Michael. *Jane Austen and Religion: Salvation and Society in Georgian England*. Basingstoke: Palgrave Macmillan, 2002.

Gilbert, Alan D. *Religion and Society in Industrial England: Church, Chapel and Social Change, 1740–1914*. London: Longman, 1976.

Gilpin, William. *Observations on Cumberland and Westmorland*. [1786]. Poole and NY: Woodstock Books, 1996.

Gilson, David. *A Bibliography of Jane Austen*. Oxford: Clarendon P, 1982.

Gisbourne, Thomas. *An Enquiry into the Duties of the Female Sex*. London: printed for Thomas Cadell, Jr., and William Davies, 1797.

Goethe, Johann Wolfgang von. *Elective Affinities*. Trans. Elizabeth Mayer and Louise Bogan. Chicago: Henry Regnery: 1963.

Goldsmith, Oliver. Rev. of R. Brookes' A New and Accurate System of Natural History. *The Monthly Review* 29 (1763): 283–4.

Grant, Anne. *Memoir and Correspondence of Mrs Grant of Laggan*. Ed. J. P. Grant. 3 vols. London: Longman, 1844.

Greene, Donald. *The Age of Exuberance: Backgrounds to Eighteenth-Century English Literature*. NY: Random House, 1970.

———. "Jane Austen's Monsters." *Jane Austen: Bicentenary Essays*. Ed. John Halperin. Cambridge: CUP, 1975. 262–78.

———. "The Myth of Limitation." *Jane Austen Today*. Ed. Joel Weinsheimer. Athens: U of Georgia P. 142–75.

Gregory, Jeremy. "The Eighteenth-Century Reformation: The Pastoral Task of Anglican Clergy after 1689." *The Church of England c. 1689-c. 1833: From Toleration to Tractarianism*. Eds John Walsh, Colin Haydon, and Stephen Taylor. Cambridge: CUP. 67–85.

Hall, Catherine. "The Sweet Delights of Home." *The History of Private Life*, Vol. IV. Ed. Michelle Perrot. Cambridge: The Belknap Press, 1990. 46–93.

Hall, Peter. *Sermons and Other Remains of Robert Lowth, Lord Bishop of London*. London, n.p., 1834.

Halperin, John. *The Life of Jane Austen*. Baltimore: The Johns Hopkins UP, 1984.

————. "The Worlds of *Emma*: Jane Austen and Cowper." In *Jane Austen: Bicentenary Essays*. Ed. John Halperin. Cambridge: CUP, 1975. 197–206.

Hammond, Brean. "The Political Unconscious in *Mansfield Park*." *Mansfield Park*. Ed. Nigel Wood. Buckingham: Open UP, 1993. 56–90.

Harding, D. W. "Regulated Hatred: An Aspect of the Work of Jane Austen." *Scrutiny* 8 (1940): 346–62.

Harris, Jocelyn. *Jane Austen's Art of Memory*. Cambridge: CUP, 1989.

Hart-Davis, Rupert, ed. *More Letters of Oscar Wilde*. London: J. Murray, 1985.

Hartley, David. *Observations on Man, his Frame, his Duty, and his Expectations*. Vol. II. London: printed by S. Richardson, 1749.

Harvey, Peter. *Glory, Laud, and Honour: Favourite Hymns and Their Stories*. London: SPCK Triangle, 1996.

Hatchett, Marion J. "Prayer Books." *The Study of Anglicanism*. Eds Stephen Sykes and John Booty. London: SPCK, 1988. 121–33.

Hawes, Clement. *Mania and Literary Style: The Rhetoric of Enthusiasm from the Ranters to Christopher Smart*. Cambridge: CUP, 1984.

Herbert, Christopher. "Comedy: The World of Pleasure." *Genre* 17 (1984): 401–16.

Heydt-Stevenson, Jillian. *Jane Austen's Unbecoming Conjunctions: Subversive Language, Embodied History*. NY and Basingstoke: Palgrave Macmillan, 2005.

Hill, Christopher. *The World Turned Upside Down: Radical Ideas During the English Revolution*. NY: Penguin, 1972.

Honan, Park. *Jane Austen: A Life*. London: Weidenfeld & Nicolson, 1987.

Horne, George. "The Origin of Civil Government." *Discourses on Several Subjects and Occasions*. Vol. II. Perth: R. Morison, 1794.

————. *The Providence of God Manifested in the Rise and Fall of Empires*. Oxford: Clarendon P, 1775.

Houghton, Walter. *The Victorian Frame of Mind, 1830–1870*. New Haven: Yale UP, 1957.

Hubback, John H. and Edith C. Hubback. *Jane Austen's Sailor Brothers*. London: J. Lane, 1906.

Hutcheson, Francis. *An Inquiry into the Original of our Ideas of Beauty and Virtue*. London: printed for J. Darby, 1725.

Irlam, Shaun. *Elations: The Poetics of Enthusiasm in Eighteenth-Century Britain*. Stanford: Stanford UP, 1999.

Jarvis, William. *Jane Austen and Religion*. Whitney, Oxfordshire: Stonesfield, 1996.

Jenyns, Soame. *A Free Inquiry into the Nature and Origin of Evil*. London: printed for R. and J. Dodsley, 1757.

————. *View of the Internal Evidence of the Christian Religion*. London: printed for J. Dodsley, 1776.

Johnson, Claudia L. "The Divine Miss Jane: Jane Austen, Janeites, and the Discipline of Novel Studies." *Janeites: Austen's Disciples and Devotees*. Ed. Deidre Lynch. Princeton: Princeton UP, 2000. 25–44.

————. "A Name to Conjure With." *Persuasions* 30 (2008): 15–26.

Johnson, Samuel. *A Dictionary of the English Language*. London: printed by W. Strahan, for J. and P. Knapton; T. and T. Longman; C. Hitch and L. Hawes; A. Millar; and R. and J. Dodsley, 1755–6.

————. *Lives of the English Poets*. [1779]. 3 vols. Ed. G. B. Hill. Oxford: Clarendon P, 1905.

————. *The Philosophick Mirrour, or a General View of Human Oeconomy*. Dublin: printed for M. Williamson, J. Potts, and L. Flinn, 1759.

————. *The Plan for a Dictionary of the English Language*. London: printed for J. and P. Knapton, T. Longman and T. Shewell, C. Hitch, A. Millar, and R. Dodsley, 1747.

————. *The Rambler*. Vol. VI. London: J. Payne, 1752.

Jordan, Winthrop D. *White over Black: American Attitudes toward the Negro, 1550–1812*. Chapel Hill: University of North Carolina at Chapel Hill, 1968.

Kaplan, Deborah. *Jane Austen Among Women*. Baltimore and London: The Johns Hopkins UP, 1992.

Kelly, Gary. "Religion and Politics." *The Cambridge Companion to Jane Austen*. Eds Edward Copeland and Juliet McMaster. Cambridge: CUP, 1997. 149–69.

Kent, Christopher. "Learning History with, and from, Jane Austen. *Jane Austen's Beginnings: The Juvenilia and 'Lady Susan.'* Ed. J. David Grey. Ann Arbor: U of Michigan Research P, 1989. 59–72.

————. "'Real Solemn History' and Social History." *Jane Austen in a Social Context*. Ed. David Monaghan. London: Macmillan, 1981. 86–104.

Kettle, Arnold. *An Introduction to the English Novel*. NY: Harper & Row, 1951.

Kirkham, Margaret. *Jane Austen: Feminism and Fiction*. Totowa, NJ: Barnes and Noble, 1983.

Knox, Ronald. *Enthusiasm: A Chapter in the History of Religion*. Oxford: OUP, 1950.

Knox, Vicesimus, ed. *Family Lectures*. 4 vols. London: n.p., 1791–95.

Knox-Shaw, Peter. *Jane Austen and the Enlightenment*. Cambridge: CUP, 2004.

Koelb, Clayton. *Inventions of Reading: Rhetoric and the Literary Imagination*. Ithaca: Cornell UP, 1988.

Koppel, Gene. *The Religious Dimension of Jane Austen's Novels*. Ann Arbor: U of Michigan P, 1988.

Korshin, Paul J. *Typologies in England, 1650–1820*. Princeton: Princeton UP, 1982.

Krueger, Christine L. *The Reader's Repentence: Women Preachers, Women Writers, and Nineteenth-Century Social Discourse*. Chicago: U of Chicago P, 1992.

Lambdin, Robert and Laura Lambdin. *The Companion to Jane Austen Studies*. Westport, CT: Greenwood Press, 2000.

Lane, Maggie. "Star-gazing with Fanny Price." *Persuasions* 28 (2006): 150–65.

Lascelles, Mary. *Jane Austen and Her Art*. Oxford: OUP, 1939.

————. "Jane Austen and the Novel." *Bicentenary Essays*. Ed. John Halperin. Cambridge: CUP, 1975. 235–46.

Leavis, F. R. *The Great Tradition*. London: Chatto & Windus, 1948.

Le Faye, Deirdre. *Jane Austen: A Family Record*. [1989]. Cambridge: CUP, 2004.

Legg, J. Wickham. *English Church Life from the Restoration to the Tractarian Movement*. London: Longmans, Green and Co., 1914.

Leonard, S. A. *The Doctrine of Correctness in English Usage, 1700–1800*. Madison: University of Wisconsin Studies in Language and Literature, no. 25, 1929.

Lerner, Lawrence. *The Truthtellers: Jane Austen; George Eliot; D. H. Lawrence*. London: Chatto and Windus, 1967.

Lewis, C. S. "A Note on Jane Austen." *Essays in Criticism* 4 (1954): 362–8.

———. *Studies in Words*. Cambridge: CUP, 1960.

Lightman, Bernard. *Victorian Popularizers of Science: Designing Nature for New Audiences*. Chicago: U of Chicago P, 2007.

Littlewood, Ian. *Jane Austen: Critical Assessments*. Mountfield, East Sussex: Helm Information, 1998.

Locke, John. *Essay Concerning Human Understanding*. [1690]. Ed. John Yolton. 2 vols. London: Dent, 1961.

———. *The Reasonableness of Christianity*. [1695]. Ed. George Ewing. Washington: Regnery Gateway, 1965.

Lodge, David. *Changing Places: A Tale of Two Campuses*. Harmondsworth: Penguin, 1978.

———. *Jane Austen, Emma: A Casebook*. Rev. ed. London: Macmillan, 1991.

———. "The Vocabulary of *Mansfield Park*." *Language of Fiction: Essays in Criticism and Verbal Analysis of the English Novel*. NY: Columbia UP, 1966. 94–113.

Longfellow, William Wadsworth. "A Psalm of Life." [1838]. *The Complete Poetical Works of Longfellow*. Boston: Houghton Mifflin, 1893. 38–40.

Looser, Devoney. "Reading Jane Austen and Rewriting 'Herstory.'" *Critical Essays on Jane Austen*. Ed. Laura Mooneyham White. NY: G. K. Hall, 1998. 34–66.

Lovejoy, Arthur O. *The Great Chain of Being: The Study of the History of an Idea*. [1936]. Cambridge: Harvard UP, 1978.

Loveridge, Mark. Untitled note. *Notes and Queries* 30.3 (1983): 214–16.

Lynskey, Winifred. "Goldsmith and the Chain of Being." *Journal of the History of Ideas* 6 (1945): 367–74.

Macdonagh, Oliver. *Jane Austen: Real and Imagined Worlds*. New Haven: Yale UP, 1991.

Macdonald, Michael. *Mystical Bedlam: Madness, Anxiety, and Healing in Seventeenth-Century England*. Cambridge: CUP, 1981.

Mandal, Anthony. *Jane Austen and the Popular Novel: The Determined Author*. Basingstoke: Palgrave Macmillan, 2007.

McGrade, A. S. "Reason." *The Study of Anglicanism*. Eds Stephen Sykes and John Booty. London: SPCK, 1988. 105–17.

McMaster, Juliet. "Education." *The Jane Austen Companion*. Ed. J. David Grey. NY: Macmillan, 1986. 140–42.

Mee, Jon. *Romanticism, Enthusiasm, and Regulation: Poetics and the Policing of Culture*. Oxford: OUP, 2003.

Miller, D. A. *Jane Austen, or the Secret of Style*. Princeton: Princeton UP, 2003.

Mitford, Mary Russell. *The Life of Mary Russell Mitford: Related in a Selection from her Letters to her Friends*. Ed. A. G. L'Estrange. 3 vols. London: Bentley, 1870.

Moler, Kenneth. *Jane Austen's Art of Allusion*. Lincoln: U of Nebraska P, 1968.

Moore, Roger E. "The Hidden History of *Northanger Abbey*: Jane Austen and the Dissolution of the Monasteries." *Religion and Literature* (forthcoming).

———. "Religion." *A Companion to Jane Austen*. Eds Claudia Johnson and Clara Tuite. London: Wiley-Blackwell, 2009. 314–22.

More, Hannah. *Essays on Various Subjects, Principally Designed for Young Ladies*. London: printed for J. Wilkie and T. Cadell, 1777.

———. *The Works of Hannah More. Vol. I: Strictures on the Modern System of Female Education*. [1799]. NY: Harper, 1840.

Morefield, Kenneth R. "'Emma Could Not Resist': Complicity and the Christian Reader." *Persuasions* 25 (2003): 197–204.

Morrow, John. "The National Church in Coleridge's Church and State: A Response to Allen." *Journal of the History of Ideas* 47.4 (1986): 640–52.

Mullan, John. *Sentiment and Sociability: The Language of Feeling in the Eighteenth Century*. Oxford: Clarendon P, 1990.

Murray, Lindley. *An English Grammar, Adapted to the Different Classes of Learners*. York: Wilson, Spence, and Mawman, 1795.

Nabokov, Vladimir. *Lectures on Literature*. Ed. Fredson Bowers. NY: Harcourt Brace Jovanovich, 1980.

Neil, Stephen. *Anglicanism*. [1958]. London: OUP, 1991.

Nelson, T. G. A. *Comedy: The Theory of Comedy in Literature, Drama and Cinema*. Oxford: OUP, 1990.

Nokes, David. *Jane Austen: A Life*. NY: Farrar, 1997.

Odmark, John. *An Understanding of Jane Austen's Novels: Character, Value, and Ironic Perspective*. Oxford: Basil Blackwell, 1981.

[P.] "An Essay on Reading." *The Evangelical Magazine* (August 1793): 78–80.

Page, Norman. *The Language of Jane Austen*. Oxford: Basil Blackwell, 1972.

Parker, Mark. "The End of *Emma*: Drawing the Boundaries of Class in Austen." *Journal of English and Germanic Philosophy* 91 (1992): 344–59.

Pattison, Mark. *Essays and Reviews*. London: John W. Parker, 1860.

———. "Tendencies of Religious Thought in England, 1688–1750." *Essays*. Ed. Henry Nettleship. 2 vols. Oxford: Clarendon P, 1889.

Pennington, Sarah. *An Unfortunate Mother's Advice to Her Absent Daughters*. [1761]. In *Chapone on the Improvement of the Mind and Dr. Gregory's Legacy to His Daughters. Lady Pennington's Advice to her Absent Daughters with an Additional Letter on the Management and Education of Infant Children*. London: printed for J. F. Dove, 1827.

Perkin, Harold. *The Origins of Modern English Society, 1780–1800.* [1969]. NY: Routledge, 2002.

Philips, Ambrose. "An Epistle to the Right Honourable Charles Lord Halifax, one of the Lord's Justices Appointed by His Majesty." *The Poems of Ambrose Philips.* Ed. M. G. Segar. Oxford: Basil Blackwell: 1937. 92–4.

Phillipps, K. C. *Jane Austen's English.* London: Andre Deutsh, 1970.

———. "Lucy Steele's English." *English Studies Anglo-American Supplement* (1969): lv–lxi.

Pitman, J. H. *Goldsmith's Animated Nature.* New Haven: Yale UP, 1924.

Pope, Alexander. *An Essay on Man.* London: printed and sold by Darton and Harvey, 1796.

Procter, Francis and William Howard Frere. *A New History of the Book of Common Prayer.* [1901]. London: Macmillan, 1958.

Quinlan, Maurice J. *Victorian Prelude: A History of English Manners 1700–1830.* New York: Columbia UP, 1941.

Regis, Pamela. "Vows in *Mansfield Park*: The Promises of Courtship." *Persuasions* 28 (2006): 166–75.

Richards, Anne. "The Passion of Marianne Dashwood: Christian Rhetoric in *Sense and Sensibility*." *Persuasions* 25 (2003): 141–54.

Richter, David. *The Progress of Romance: Literary Historiography and the Gothic Novel.* Columbus: U of Ohio P, 1996.

Roberts, Warren. *Jane Austen and the French Revolution.* London: Macmillan, 1979.

Rosmarin, Adena. "'Misreading' *Emma*: The Powers and Perfidies of Interpretive History." *Jane Austen, Emma: A Casebook.* Ed. David Lodge. Rev. ed. London: Macmillan, 1991. 213–41.

Rosen, David. *Power, Plain English, and the Rise of Modern Poetry.* New Haven: Yale UP, 2006.

Roston, Murray. *Prophet and Poet: The Bible and the Growth of Romanticism.* Evanston, Ill.: Northwestern UP, 1965.

Ryle, Gilbert. "Jane Austen and the Moralists." *Critical Essays on Jane Austen.* Ed. R. B. Southam. London: Routledge and Kegan Paul, 1968. 106–22.

Schorer, Mark. "Fiction and the 'Matrix of Analogy.'" *Kenyon Review* 11 (1949): 539–60.

Selwyn, David, ed. *The Poetry of Jane Austen and the Austen Family.* Iowa City: U of Iowa P, 1997.

Shaffer, Elinor S. *'Kubla Khan' and the Fall of the Jerusalem: The Mythological School in Biblical Criticism and Secular Literature 1770–1880.* London: CUP, 1975.

Sheehan, Colleen. "The Riddles of *Emma*." *Persuasions* 22 (2000): 50–61.

———. "It's a Topsy Turvy World." *Persuasions* 26 (2004): 212–6.

Sheldon, Henry. *The Modern Church, Great Britain and Ireland in the Eighteenth Century. The History of the Christian Church.* Vol. IV. London: Thomas Y. Crowell, 1895.

Sheridan, Thomas. *Lectures on the Art of Reading.* 4th edn. Dublin: Gilbert, 1790.

Sherlock, Thomas. *Several Discourses Preached at the Temple by Tho. Sherlock.* 4 vols. London: printed for Whiston, White, Owen, and Baker at Tunbridge, 1755.

———. *The Tryal of the Witnesses* (1743) and *The Use and Intent of Prophecy* (1728). [1799]. NY: Garland, 1978.

Sindon, Donald. "Letter to the Editor." The *Times* (London). February 2nd, 2001.

Smith, Olivia. *The Politics of Language, 1791–1819.* Oxford: Clarendon P, 1991.

Smith, Timothy. *Bunbury: Two Notes on Oscar Wilde.* Bicary, France: The Winged Lion, 1998.

Snell, K. D. M. and Paul S. Ell. *Rival Jerusalems: The Geography of Victorian Religion.* Cambridge: CUP, 2000.

Soloway, Richard Allan. *Prelates and People: Ecclesiastical Social Thought in England, 1783–1852.* London and Toronto: Routledge and Kegan Paul and University of Toronto P, 1969.

South, Robert. *Sermons Preached upon Several Occasions.* 7 vols. Oxford: OUP, 1823.

Southam, B. C., ed. *Jane Austen: The Critical Heritage.* 2 vols. London: Routledge, 1968.

Spacks, Patricia Meyer. *Gossip.* NY: Knopf, 1985.

———. *The Poetry of Vision: Five Eighteenth-Century Poets.* Cambridge: Harvard UP, 1967.

Staunton, George. *An Embassy from the King of England to the Emperor of China.* Philadelphia: R. Campbell, 1799.

Stephens, James. *Essays in Ecclesiastical Biography.* [1850]. 2 vols. London: Longmans, Green, Reader, and Dyer, 1872.

Stovel, Bruce. "The Sentient Target of Death': Jane Austen's Prayers." *Jane Austen's Business: Her World and Her Profession.* Eds Juliet McMaster and Bruce Stovel. Hampshire: Palgrave Macmillan, 1996. 192–205.

Sutherland, James. *A Preface to Eighteenth Century Poetry.* Oxford: Clarendon P, 1948.

Sykes, Norman. *Church and State in England in the Eighteenth Century.* [1954.] Hamden: Archon, 1962.

Sykes, Stephen and John Booty, eds. *The Study of Anglicanism.* London: SPCK/Fortress Press, 1988.

Tandon, Bharat. *Jane Austen and the Morality of Conversation.* London: Anthem, 2003.

Taylor, John Tinnan. *Early Opposition to the English Novel: Popular Reaction from 1760 to 1830.* NY: King's Crown Press, 1943.

Tave, Stuart. *Some Words of Jane Austen.* Chicago: U of Chicago P, 1973.

Todd, Janet, and Linda Bree. "Introduction." *Later Manuscripts.* Eds Janet Todd and Linda Bree. *The Cambridge Edition of the Works of Jane Austen.* Cambridge: CUP, 2008. xxxi–cxxix.

Tomalin, Claire. *Jane Austen: A Life*. NY: Knopf, 1997.

Trilling, Lionel. *Sincerity and Authenticity*. [1960]. Cambridge: Harvard UP, 2006.

Tucker, Susie I. *Enthusiasm: A Study in Semantic Change*. Cambridge: CUP, 1972.

Tuite, Claire. "Decadent Austen Entails: Forster, James, Firbank, and the 'Queer Taste' of *Sanditon* (comp. 1817, publ. 1925)." *Janeites: Austen's Disciples and Devotees*. Ed. Deidre Lynch. Princeton: Princeton UP, 2000. 115–39.

———. *Romantic Austen: Sexual Politics and the Literary Canon*. Cambridge: CUP, 2002.

Van Ghent, Dorothy. *The English Novel: Form and Function*. NY: International Thomson Publishing, 1953.

Virgin, Peter. *The Church in an Age of Negligence: Ecclesiastical Structure and Problems of Reform, 1700–1840*. Cambridge: CUP, 1989.

von Rad, Gerhard. "Typological Interpretation of the Old Testament." *Essays on Old Testament Interpretation*. Ed. Claus Westermann. Trans. James Luther Mays. London: SCM Press, 1963. 1–32.

Walsh, John, Colin Haydon, and Stephen Taylor, eds. *The Church of England c. 1689–c. 1833: From Toleration to Tractarianism*. Cambridge: CUP, 1993.

Warhol, Robyn. "Before We Go in Depth: A Narratological Approach." *Approaches to Teaching Eliot's* Middlemarch. NY: MLA, 1990. 23–9.

Wasserman, Earl. "The Inherent Values of Eighteenth-Century Personification." *PMLA* 65.4 (1950): 435–63.

———. "Nature Moralized: The Divine Analogy in the Eighteenth Century." *English Literary History* 20 (March 1953): 39–76.

———. *The Subtler Language*. Baltimore: The Johns Hopkins UP, 1959.

Watts, Isaac. "Moral Songs (no. 6)." *Horae Lyricae and Divine Songs*. Boston: Little Brown, 1854. 343.

Weil, Louis. "The Gospel in Anglicanism." *The Study of Anglicanism*. Eds Stephen Sykes and John Booty. London: SPCK, 1988. 51–76.

Weinsheimer, Joel. "Jane Austen's Anthropocentrism." In *Jane Austen Today*. Ed. Joel Weinsheimer. Athens: U of Georgia P, 1975. 128–41.

West, Jane. *Letters to a Young Lady*. Vol. III. London: Longman, Hurst, Rees, and Orme, 1806.

Whately, Richard. "Unsigned Review: *Northanger Abbey* and *Persuasion*." Originally in *Quarterly Review* 24 (January 1821): 352–76. In *Jane Austen: Critical Assessments*. Ed. Ian Littlewood. Vol. I. Mountfield: Helm Information, Ltd., 1998. 318–34.

White, Laura Mooneyham. "When the Megalosaurus Disembarked from the Ark: Dickens, *Genesis*, and Early Paleontology." International Conference on Narrative, May, 2008.

Wiesenfarth, Joseph. "Austen and Apollo." In *Jane Austen Today*. Ed. Joel Weinsheimer. Athens: U of Georgia P, 1975. 46–63.

———. "History and Myth in Jane Austen's *Persuasion*." *Literary Criterion* 11 (1974): 76–85.

Wilde, Oscar. *The Importance of Being Earnest*. [1895]. *Plays*. NY: Penguin, 1954.

———. *Salomé*. [1894]. *Plays*. NY: Penguin, 1954.

Williams, Anne. *Prophetic Strain: The Greater Lyric in the Eighteenth Century*. Chicago: U of Chicago P, 1984.

Williams, C. B. "As I Was Going to St. Ives." *Folklore* 86.2 (1975): 133–5.

Williams, Raymond. *The Country and the City*. London: Chatto and Windus, 1973.

Willis, Lesley. "Religion in Jane Austen's *Mansfield Park*." *English Studies in Canada* 23 (1987): 65–78.

Wolfson, Susan. "Boxing Emma, or the Reader's Dilemma at the Box Hill Games." *Romantic Circles*. http://www.rc.umd.edu/praxis/boxhill/wolfson/wolfson. html. Accessed February 8, 2009.

Woolf, Virginia. *The Common Reader*. NY: Harcourt Brace, 1925.

———. *A Room of One's Own*. [1929]. NY: Harcourt Brace, 1957.

Yates, Richard [Robert Southey]. *The Church in Danger: A Statement of the Cause, and of the probable Means of averting that danger, attempted, in a Letter to the Earl of Liverpool*. London: n.p., 1815.

Young, G. M. and W. D. Handcock. *English Historical Documents, Vol. XII: 1833–1874*. Gen. ed. David C. Douglas. London: Eyre and Spottiswoode, 1956.

# Index